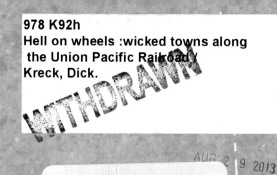

DAKOTA TERRITORY

NEBRASKA

N. Platte River

SIDNEY

CHEYENNE

JULESBURG

S. Platte River

NORTH PLATTE

OMAHA

DENVER

KANSAS

MILES FROM OMAHA

Omaha, NE, Milepost 0.0
North Platte, NE, 291
Julesburg, CO, 377.4
Sidney, NE, 413.6
Cheyenne, WY, 516.4
Sherman Summit, 552
Laramie, WY, 572.8
Benton, WY, 696
Rawlins, WY, 709.4
Green River, WY, 844.8
Bryan, WY, 858.2
Bear River City, WY, 946.0
Ogden, UT, 1032.2
Corinne, UT, 1056.6
Promontory Summit, UT, 1084.4

HELL ON WHEELS

Wicked Towns
along the
Union Pacific
Railroad

DICK KRECK

FULCRUM
GOLDEN, COLORADO

ALSO BY DICK KRECK

Colorado's Scenic Railroads

Denver in Flames

Murder at the Brown Palace

Anton Woode: The Boy Murderer

Smaldone: The Untold Story of an American Crime Family

Library of Congress Cataloging-in-Publication Data
Kreck, Dick.
 Hell on Wheels : the wicked towns along the Union Pacific Railroad / Dick Kreck.
  pages cm
 Includes bibliographical references and index.
 ISBN 978-1-55591-948-1 (alkaline paepr)
 1. West (U.S.)--History, Local. 2. Union Pacific Railroad Company--History--19th century. 3. Cities and towns--West (U.S.)--History--19th century. 4. Railroad stations--West (U.S.)--History--19th century. 5. West (U.S.)--Biography. 6. West (U.S.)--Social life and customs. 7. Frontier and pioneer life--West (U.S.) I. Title.
 F590.7.K74 2013
 978'.02--dc23
                    2013003776

Printed in the United States of America
0 9 8 7 6 5 4 3 2 1

Design: Jack Lenzo
Cover image originally published in *Historic Sketches of the Cattle Trade of the West and Southwest* by Joseph G. McCoy (Kansas City, MO: Ramsey, Millett & Hudson, 1874).

Fulcrum Publishing
4690 Table Mountain Dr., Ste. 100
Golden, CO 80403
800-992-2908 • 303-277-1623
www.fulcrumbooks.com

CONTENTS

FOREWORD

Think of it. Before railroads spanned the continent, travelers seeking to go to California or other points west had three difficult choices: They could board a ship in New York or Boston and sail for Panama, disembark there and cross the malaria-infested isthmus by a combination of boat and wagon, then once on the Pacific side, board another ship and set sail again—all in all, a 5,250-mile journey that could last more than a month. Or they could forgo the isthmus and its death-carrying mosquitoes by sailing around South America's turbulent and storm-tossed Cape Horn and head directly for San Francisco, a four-month voyage of more than thirteen thousand miles. For folks living in Ohio or Kentucky or some other interior state, add to these distances and times the trek from home to an Eastern Seaboard port, an additional journey that could take days, even weeks.

But whether headed for California or Oregon or the Pikes Peak goldfields, most westbound travelers elected to go by a third route: a two-thousand-mile, five-month wagon-train journey over the great Platte River, Oregon, and California trails. Called variously argonauts, forty-niners, Pikes Peakers, overlanders, and emigrants, these men, women, and children daily faced a host of life-threatening dangers, from crossing riverbeds full of quicksand to rattlesnakes, bad water, tainted food, flash floods, precipitous mountain roads, windstorms, gunshot accidents, and the occasional Indian attack. Ten to twenty miles a day, every day numbingly the same. Up before dawn to feed, water, and yoke or harness the animals, on the move by sunup, break at noon, back on the trail until nearly sundown, then watching over cooking fires, tending to the herds, repairing all the things that needed to be repaired, followed by a too short sleep, day after day after day, week after week. But disruptions to the routine did occur: cholera and smallpox outbreaks, busted axles, violent arguments, the thousand and one things that could happen—and did—on a long overland trek. Many were lulled to boredom by the steady creak of the wagons, the sameness of the landscape, until the crack of a broken wheel or the piercing sound of a child's scream or the loud boom of a shotgun suddenly snapped them to attention. Still, between 1842 and 1866 more than a half million people hit the trails. Not all of them made it. Diarists, many of them women, told of passing grave after grave spread along the trail, so many, in fact, that after a while they stopped counting.

Then, after the Civil War, Americans turned their eyes on the nation's newest and greatest construction project: the building of the first transcontinental railroad, a project that promised to reduce the five-month crossing to just eight days. *Eight days.* In *Hell on Wheels*, best-selling author Dick Kreck takes readers to the bridge between the wagons roads and the rails west: the hell-bent-for-leather end-of-track towns that instantly erupted when winter's cold or a shortage of supplies forced a delay in construction. Where they appeared was anybody's guess; it all depended on the progress the workers made as they gandy-danced across the prairie. But wherever they sprang up, they shared certain characteristics. They were "instant cities," populated overwhelmingly by young men, most of whom carried fistfuls of cash in their pockets and were more than willing to part with it. And the Hell on Wheels towns made spending easy. Saloons and bawdy houses—many of them prefabricated in the last Hell on Wheels town and transported over the very rails the work crews had laid—dominated the main thoroughfare. Unlike distant mining camps, which at least harbored pretensions of permanency, these prairie communities, at best a chance gathering of people, were considered only temporary stops on the way to a linkup with the Central Pacific, building eastward from Sacramento. Few inhabitants thought about founding churches or reading rooms or schools or institutions of law and order. Most were content simply to wait out the delays, eager to return to the business at hand: the laying of track across a land that school geography books labeled "the Great American Desert."

Meanwhile, the saloons and brothels beckoned.

As Kreck reveals, workers had earned a respite from the arduous work of railroading. Every mile of track laid had its challenges. The ground had to be graded level enough to receive rails; ravines and arroyos had to be spanned by bridges and trestles, and there was nothing close to an eight-hour day. From dawn to dusk, the work went on, day after day, except when interrupted by torrential downpours, those violent storms that could wash away a day's or week's progress, or when vital supplies failed to arrive.

Increasingly as they moved west, another interruption threatened to block construction: Indian attacks. American generally may have viewed the progress of the rails west with jubilation, but for the Plains tribes the coming of the railroad threatened their very existence. The "thunder wagons," as they called the smoke-billowing locomotives, frightened and scattered the bison herds on which they depended for survival. Lakota, Cheyenne, and Arapaho leaders understood from the beginning that construction must be stopped, now and forever. Otherwise, life as they knew it would end.

Dick Kreck takes time to tell this poignant story as well. How warriors swept down on construction crews, attacking the railroaders wherever and whenever they could, of how they quickly learned to bend and twist the hated tracks to derail locomotives as they chugged across the prairie.

All together, he tells the epic story of westward expansion, from the great wagon trails to the tracklayers and those Hell on Wheels towns where the West was at its wildest. It's a story wonderfully told.

David Fridtjof Halaas, former Colorado state historian
and retired library and publications director for
Pittsburgh's Smithsonian-affiliated Senator John Heinz
History Center, is historical consultant for the
Northern Cheyenne tribe and author of
*Halfbreed: The Remarkable True Story
of George Bent—Caught Between the
Worlds of the Indian and White Man*

ACKNOWLEDGMENTS

Many helping hands made this book possible. Documents, maps, photographs, diaries, and newspaper accounts are out there, but without knowledgeable guides the search can become like wandering in the wilderness.

Among those who were particularly helpful and offered service with a smile: John Bromley, Union Pacific Railroad Museum; Kenton Forrest, Colorado Railroad Museum; James Griffin, Lincoln County (Nebraska) Historical Museum; Mary McKinstry and Dallas Williams, Fort Sedgwick Historical Society; Suzi Taylor, Wyoming State Museum; the staff of the Western History and Genealogy Department, Denver Public Library; the American Heritage Center, University of Wyoming, Laramie.

Special thanks to Jim Ehernberger, who guided me through the intricacies of the Union Pacific and its many subsidiaries and provided numerous historical images; to historian Gary Roberts, whose expertise in the goings-on at Bear River City, Wyoming, were invaluable; and to my friend David F. Halaas, who checked closely my retelling of the role Native Americans played in the westward migration and wrote the foreword.

And, finally, thanks again to my patient and sharp-eyed editor, Faith Marcovecchio, who saved me many times from falling into the bottomless pit of factual, grammatical, and punctuation errors. And thanks again to crack designer Jack Lenzo. This is our third book together.

Two brilliant and detailed accounts—David Haward Bain's *Empire Express* and Maury Klein's *Union Pacific*—are the foundations upon which the bricks of this story are laid.

AUTHOR'S NOTE

For clarity and easier reading, modern-day designations of the states of Nebraska, Wyoming, Colorado, Montana, Utah, and others are used instead of the various territories that existed at the time.

The mileage posts used in the chapter titles and in the text are based on the May 10, 1869, passenger schedule of the Union Pacific, the first issued by the railroad after the joining of the tracks at Promontory Summit, Utah. Subsequent recalculations and realignments led to changes in many mileages.

I am not a fan of the use of *sic*, traditionally used to point out errors; it's interruptive and smacks of a "tsk-tsk" from a fussy English teacher. So quotes from diaries, letters, and other sources are reproduced with all their misspellings and grammatical errors to retain their feel.

Chapter One

WESTWARD HO!

The first question, of course, is why did they do it?

What magnetic power drew thousands of prairie travelers to leave their homes, friends, and families—everything familiar—for a two-thousand-mile, months-long cross-country trudge through unknown land with unknown perils? It was as far off to them as the moon. So why go? There were almost as many reasons as there were emigrants. Many were so ignorant of the territory west of the Missouri River and how long the trip might take that they had to ask directions from Indians and other travelers along the way.

Since 1840, returnees and newspaper accounts enthusiastically extolled the mild climate of Oregon and California. Travelers praised the fertile lands, available for the taking thanks to a government program that promised 160 acres or more free to each settler. The discovery of gold in California in 1848 and in Colorado a decade later set loose dances of riches in the heads of those struggling to make ends meet at home.

Failures in farming or business, they were looking for a new life or excitement. They referred to themselves as "emigrants" because they were, in fact, leaving the United States behind. They were a mixed bag ethnically—Irish, English, Scottish, Scandinavian, German, and Russian. There were few African Americans, most still mired in slavery until the end of the Civil War. Later, participation in the great migration was limited by finances; few had the resources required to put together a wagon and supplies.

Almost always, it was men who decided to pack up the family and trek across the continent in search of ... something. The financial panic of 1837 left many broke, yet they scraped together enough goods and cash to make the leap. It wasn't cheap. Guidebooks recommended carrying two hundred pounds of flour, one hundred fifty pounds of bacon, ten pounds of coffee, twenty pounds of sugar, and ten pounds of salt. In addition, there were rice, tea, beans, dried fruit, vinegar, pickles, mustard, and tallow. Cooking utensils included a kettle, frying pan, and tin plates, cups, knives, and forks. Cost for all this was about $700 in an era when the average farmworker was paid less than $1 a day. Also necessary were a rifle, powder, lead, and shot. Added up, the emigrant was looking at a bill of about $1,000, including carrying cash to pay tolls, replace broken gear en route, and get set up with foodstuffs and supplies when he and his family reached their destination.

For some, as historian George R. Stewart put it, there was "the sheer love of adventure." Making the crossing successfully was an epic achievement. "Behind that achievement lay a psychic drive, a desire, almost a passion, to keep moving—and there was only one direction: westward!"[1]

The adventurous might even go for free. In March 1846, a wealthy farmer in Springfield, Illinois, took out an advertisement in the *Sangamon Journal*:

WESTWARD HO! For Oregon and California. Who wants to go to California without costing them anything? As many as eight young men, of good character, who can drive an ox team, will be accommodated by gentlemen who will leave this vicinity about the middle of April. Come on Boys! You can have as much land as you want without costing you anything. The first suitable persons who apply will be engaged.[2]

The urge to travel outward, westward was a powerful one; "on the compass of destiny, the magnetic pull came from the West. It was a place of all-powerful attraction."[3] Americans have always been footloose. Howard Stansbury, who made the crossing in 1859, observed,

We passed also an old Dutchman, with an immense wagon, drawn by six yoke of cattle, and loaded with household furnishings. Behind, followed a covered cart containing the wife, driving herself, and a host of babies—the whole bound for the land of promise, of the distance to which, however, they seemed to have not the most remote idea. To the tail of the car was attached a large chicken-coop, full of fowls; two milch-cows followed, and next came an old mare, upon the back of which was perched a little, brown-faced, barefooted girl, not more than seven years old, while a small sucking colt brought up the rear.[4]

So off they went, despite Senator Daniel Webster, who famously and disdainfully declared in 1845,

> What do we want with this vast, worthless area? This region of savages and wild beasts, of deserts of shifting sands and whirlwinds of dust, of cactus and prairie dogs? To what use could we ever hope to put these great deserts, or those endless mountain ranges, impenetrable and covered to their very base with eternal snow? What can we ever hope to do with the western coast, a coast of three thousand miles, rock-bound, cheerless, uninviting, and not a harbor on it? What use have we for this country?[5]

The Platte River route, which cut straight across the wide Platte Valley in Nebraska and into Wyoming, was then, as now, a superhighway. Where trucks and cars today speed along Interstate 80, trappers, freighters, the Pony Express, overlanders, the telegraph, and, finally, the great Pacific Railroad in their turn saw the broad, flat prairie as a direct route to the West. The going was relatively easy. The way was clear: just follow the meandering path of the Platte River, a wide but shallow, muddy body of water whose hidden sands could be treacherous during high water; "too dirty to bathe in and too thick to drink." It wasn't a river, one emigrant complained, but moving sand. The trail's flat, hard-packed soil and gently rising terrain presented few problems. Thousands took the trail from eastern Kansas up to Nebraska, turned left, and headed toward the sunset. Their wagons left deep scars on the landscape, still visible today.

Unfortunately, too many of those who stepped off the brink of civilization at the Missouri River were unprepared for the journey and never should have embarked. First, the majority had never strayed more than fifty miles from their homes; long-distance travel was not so easy. Used to heavy farm labor, they were nevertheless physically unprepared to walk day after day for two thousand miles, oftentimes buffeted by fierce storms, beset by disease, deprived of fresh water, and subsisting on a minimal diet of bacon, beans, and biscuits.

Most of all, the earliest overlanders had little idea of where, exactly, they were going. They frequently had to rely on notes left trailside by those who preceded them. The "Bone Express," messages of warning or alternate routes often found at forks in the trail, were tacked to exposed skulls and bones of the unfortunate travelers who preceded them. Near Fort Laramie, emigrant Alonzo Delano found this message: "Look at this—Look at this! The water here is poison and we have lost six of our cattle. Do not let your cattle drink on this bottom."[6]

They were rarely alone. Despite the popular image in movies and novels, few overlanders traveled by themselves. Some, in fact, may have yearned for isolation. Wagon trains stretched for miles, sometimes as many as a hundred wagons across the dusty plains. It's estimated that in the two decades between the 1840s and 1860s a half million people made the crossing, the largest emigration in American history. On one day in 1852 so many wagons were backed up at Saint Joseph, Missouri, one of the chief jumping-off terminals, that teams rolled away twelve abreast. At the height of the emigration, in the 1850s and '60s, Plains Indians, who in the early days passively watched emigrants pass by, began to wonder if there were any white people left on the eastern side of the Missouri River.

Diarists, and there were many, reported seeing hundreds of wagons nearly every day. One logged passing two hundred in the morning and being overtaken by another hundred at noon and, on another day, passing five hundred. For wont of anything else to do, those stationed at Fort Kearny, Nebraska, kept count of the passing parade and recorded more than one thousand wagons on a single day in May 1850.

There were numerous reasons for wagons to travel in groups. First, there was the greatly overstressed fear of Indian attack. Though there were attacks by hostile tribes, the majority of emigrants never saw an Indian, and those they encountered generally were helpful and non-threatening. Second, in case of accident or difficulty fording rivers there would be plenty of help around. And, finally, confronted with the boredom of trudging through a bleak landscape day after day, there were social contacts around the campfires at night.

Whether travelers started in Pennsylvania, Ohio, or Illinois, the journey eventually led them to one of four centers: Saint Joseph and Independence in Missouri, Omaha/Council Bluffs (then known as Kanesville) in Iowa, or Leavenworth, Kansas. The booming towns were awash with wagons, stock, and supplies, all available at high prices. As with any gathering of humanity, not all those who filled these towns were upstanding. Prostitutes, gamblers, pickpockets, and other wastrels preyed on the hopeful travelers. "It would astonish you," one man wrote to his wife in the East, "to see the number of people going to California.

The vast numbers of emigrants heading west led to traffic jams like this crossing at Kanesville (now Council Bluffs, Iowa), on the east side of the Missouri River. Modern-day images aside, the wagon travelers were rarely alone on their trek west.

The people are of all kinds, some of the first people in the United States are a-going and some of the meanest are along also."[7]

Though eager to get on the road, travelers were advised to wait until April, when grass would be greening up and plentiful enough to supply feed for stock. The goal was to cross the Sierra Nevada in far-off California before winter and snows set in.

Those who waited to buy what they needed in the far reaches of civilization faced exorbitant prices. Colonel George W. Stokes, who made the crossing in 1862, reminisced in 1923, "Dealers furnished harness, yokes and other supplies; all over the town, horses, mules and oxen were being sold or fitted out for the journey across the plains. Every vacant lot had a wagon exhibit or was filled with hay; and I reckon nobody ever saw, up to that time, so much corn and oats for sale."[8]

Mules and oxen were favored over horses for the long haul, but oxen were preferred because they were more docile than mules, could live off the native grasses, and, in an emergency, could be eaten. Indians, who sometimes raided the trains for stock, shunned oxen, which were difficult to handle and painfully slow. In the States, a good mule could be bought for $100. In the frenzied days on the frontier, prices rose as high as $200. Oxen, on the other hand, sold for $40 to $75 a pair, but the necessary yokes could run as high as $160. Oxen were sturdier, but they traveled at a monotonously slow pace, about two miles an hour. Plus, those who had to drive the oxen complained that it could take thirty minutes or more just to wrestle them into their yokes.

The outfits were a collection of just about any mode of transportation the emigrants could buy, borrow, or throw together. Some people were woefully unprepared, like the man ready to set out from Saint Joseph pushing a wheelbarrow filled with his belongings all the way to California. The popular image is the family gathered up in a massive Conestoga, a large wagon bowed outward like a ship on both ends, which came to be known as a "prairie schooner." But the wagons, capable of carrying two or three tons of goods and favored by freighters headed from the Missouri River to settlements in Kansas and New Mexico, were too expensive, too massive, and too unwieldy for the average traveler to handle. The smaller covered wagon thus became the preferred mode of transportation. It was slow and difficult to maneuver across rivers and mountain trails, but it was sturdy, could carry large loads, and provided shelter. And, if need be, the wagons in a train could be circled at night as a fortress against Indian attacks.

The average wagon was four feet wide and about ten feet long and made of hardwood to withstand severe weather. Enterprising emigrants often built false floors a foot or two off the bottom of the wagon to stash supplies. The top, which gave the rig its popular "covered wagon" name, was canvas waterproofed with paint or linseed oil and held up by hickory staves.

The living space was cramped and often filled with household goods, meaning the human occupants were forced to walk alongside or behind the wagon, prodding the four to six oxen to keep moving. At its highest point, the canvas rose to about five feet, making the wagons top heavy and prone to tipping over on uneven grades. Every wagon carried a vital piece of equipment: a tar bucket, used to grease the wagon wheels, which broke frequently and required numerous repairs. A breakdown could mean death to all stranded.

Those who rode inside, usually women and children, were periodically subjected to stifling heat and the accumulated, smothering smells from traveling for weeks on end. If it rained, the wagon's flaps remained closed, making the fetid air even worse.

The wagons traveled from sunup to sundown, usually hitting the road about 6:00 AM. At midday, the train rested so animals and passengers could be fed. "Nooning" usually lasted about an hour—time enough, noted one woman, for "cold coffee and a crust of bread"—then it was off again on the dusty trail. At night, wagons bunched up in a defensive posture against expected nighttime attacks (which rarely materialized) from Indians and wolves, plentiful on the prairie, and guards were posted to sound the alarm. The lead wagon would turn to the right, the next to the left, and so on until they formed a circle. Tents were raised within the confines and oxen gathered up. Despite the difficulties of the day's travel, including walking all day, women were expected to cook dinner, clean up the wagon, and get the kids to bed. Often, there was socializing around the campfire with dancing, music, storytelling, and general lighthearted fun.

Sunday was designated a day of rest and a celebration of the Sabbath, although observance seems to have faded quickly. On May 11, 1862, William Smedley, who had yet to leave the Missouri River behind on his way to Oregon, noted in his diary, "This was the first Sabbath I had spent in a region where its sanctity was entirely disregarded. We seemed to have gotten beyond the realm of devotion. Pistol shooting and other such amusements were resorted to to break the ennui of the occasion."[9] It probably wasn't because they had become less religious, but because there were extensive repairs to be made and many trains were in a hurry to get to their destinations before winter set in.

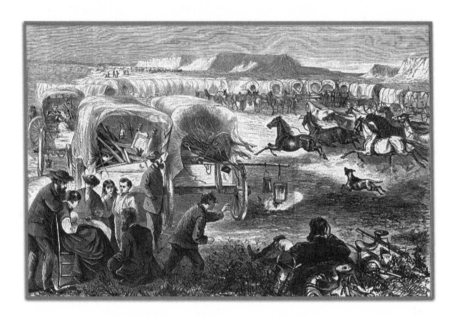

After trudging all day through dusty, barren terrain for sixteen to twenty miles, emigrants circled their wagons at night, huddled around cooking fires, and discussed the day's events. Music and dancing sometimes broke out.

DICK KRECK COLLECTION

At the outset, the trip was a walk in the country. The road was a hard surface, grass and water were plentiful, and a carnival atmosphere of setting off on a great adventure blinded the travelers to the problems they would face before reaching the West Coast.

It wasn't long before reality and boring repetition took hold. Though surrounded by other wagons, one woman lamented, "We would travel for days and never see a soul, other than our own people. Then, sometimes when we came to a stream of water there would be a few families trying to make homes. They were brave people to stay there."[10] Oxen plodded across the landscape barely at the walking speed of a human, hour after hour, day after day. Covering sixteen miles in a day was considered productive. When the trail got too chopped up by the wheels of passing trains, the drovers simply moved over, sometimes as much as a half mile, to find secure footing again.

Though they sometimes broke into trains that were four tracks wide, those in the back of the trains inevitably were forced to battle the dust kicked up by those in front of them. On some trains, individuals took turns riding at the head of the train to get relief from the choking dust that got in their clothes, their hair, their boots, and their lungs.

Ignorant of the great distances ahead of them and the fact that oxen or mules could haul for only so many miles in a region of diminishing water and feed before giving out, pioneers brought too much stuff, whether it was from nostalgia to carry with them what they could of their old life or because they might need it along the way. A typical wagon might carry as much as two thousand pounds. Excess baggage was dumped alongside the trail until the route looked like one long garage sale. "We were compelled to throw away a quantity of iron, steel, trunks, valises, old clothes, and boots," wrote one forty-niner. "We found the road lined with cast-off articles, piles of bacon, wagons, groceries, clothing, and various other articles which had been left, and the waste of destruction of property was enormous. A wanton waste of valuable property."[11]

Francis Parkman, one of the most-read chroniclers of the period, who crossed the prairie in 1846, observed,

> The reader need not be told that John Bull never leaves home without encumbering himself with the greatest possible load of luggage. Our companions were no exception to the rule. They had a wagon drawn by six mules and crammed with provisions for six months, besides ammunition enough for a regiment; spare rifles

and fowling-pieces, ropes and harness; personal baggage, and a miscellaneous assortment of articles, which produced infinite embarrassment on the journey. They had also decorated their persons with telescopes and portable compasses, and carried English double-barreled rifles of sixteen to the pound caliber, slung to their saddles in dragoon fashion.[12]

Stansbury detailed discarded items tossed aside. "The road has been literally strewn with articles that have been thrown away. Bar-iron and steel, large blacksmiths' anvils and bellows, crowbars, drills, augers, gold washers, chisels, axes, lead, trunks, spades, ploughs, large grindstones, baking ovens, cooking stoves without number, kegs, barrels, harnesses, clothing, bacon, and beans were found along the road in pretty much the order in which they have been here enumerated."[13] He apparently didn't see other items dumped along the way, like a safe, a diving bell, and law books.

In 1847, another group of sojourners set out for "the promised land." Urged on by their spiritual leader, Brigham Young, a small group of Mormons, members of the still-young Church of Latter-day Saints, who had survived conflicts and condemnation in Ohio, Illinois, and Missouri, left from the encampment they called Winter Quarters, near present-day Omaha, to find a new Zion.

There were 143 men and boys, 3 women, and 2 children in the party. As thousands of others would do, they followed the Platte River west, but they stayed on the north side of the river on what became known as the Mormon Trail to avoid gentiles, nonbelievers with whom they clashed wherever they tried to establish themselves.

Young encouraged Europeans to join the Saints in their new settlement, Great Salt Lake City. At first, the church gave them financial assistance, but so many were pitifully poor that the burden became too great. Finally, Young decreed that the new emigrants could use handcarts to make the crossing. The first wave of handcart pioneers (each handcart was usually pulled by one person and pushed by others) began their trek on July 17, 1856; there were five hundred people in the party. Five companies made the trip that year and faced enumerable hardships, including severe weather and starvation. A third of their number perished.

A man traveling east along the Platte who passed the group slowly making its way westward described the wretched condition of the Mormon group:

Mormons like these, photographed on the trail in 1867, often traveled in large groups in their quest to "reach Zion" in what was to become Utah. Western travelers mistrusted the Mormons, who were clannish and suspicious of outsiders.

It was the most motley crew I ever beheld. Most of them were Danes, with a sprinkling of Welsh, Swedes, and English, and were generally from the lower classes of their countries. Most could not understand what we said to them. The road was lined for a mile behind the train with the lame, halt, sick, and needy. Some were on crutches; now and then a mother with a child in her arms and two or three hanging hold of her with a forlorn appearance, would pass slowly along.[14]

Many of the emigrants who started west with enthusiasm and high hopes would never get to the imagined land of riches and a new life.

Between 1843, when westward emigration began in earnest, and 1866, when it began to wind down, as many as thirty thousand of the half million who set out for the West died en route.

The greatest threat, one among many, was disease. Beginning in 1849, cholera swept westward from Saint Louis, carried by pioneers ignorant of germ theory. Poor sanitation, rotting trailside animal carcasses, exposure to brackish water and human waste, and close contact with fellow travelers allowed the disease to spread rapidly through wagon trains. Nature's call was not a subject any diarists mentioned. "Toilets"—a term unknown to pioneer travelers—were wherever overlanders happened to be at the time, and the general rule when wagons paused for a break was women to one side, men to the other. Campsites became trash-laden, filthy germ factories. Because rolls of toilet paper had not been invented (although sanitary "waste paper" was available), travelers in need used leaves, cornstalks, or rags for cleaning. "Washing these rags in streams and waterholes was probably done frequently, with predictable results for sanitation."[15]

One doctor theorized that the presence of disease was the result of camp food, "often a perfect mass of indigestible filth too crude even for the stomach of an ostrich." He was partly correct. Good sanitation, even the simple task of washing one's hands before preparing a meal, was absent. One man observed that only the camp cook was filthier than the surroundings in which he worked.

Cholera was a fast-acting disease, often claiming victims hours after their symptoms became obvious. It began with diarrhea, followed by cramps in the victim's calves. Sweating and coldness of skin evidenced advance cases. In the disease's final stages, vomiting occurred, a clear indication that the victim was beyond saving. Repeated—and increasingly larger—doses of laudanum, a powerful soup of opium and alcohol, were recommended, but the travelers also brought a chemist's closet of home remedies, most of which were useless. You either died or you didn't.

John Wood, whose train and body were attacked by cholera, recalled "the sickly course to the promised land":

> We are not alone in the calamity, thousands are around us sharing the same fate. The sick and the dying are on the right and on the left, and in the rear and in our midst. We, ourselves, are nearly all sick—I feel very weak myself. Hundreds are on their way home, faint-hearted and terror stricken. Death is behind as well as before. Many are stalking their way through pestilence, unmoved while others view each step with consternation. A number of our company now feel determined to go home.[16]

Victims were given hasty burials, and graves littered the roadside—one every eighty yards, according to one witness. Graves were sometimes only a foot or two deep, leaving the deceased to be dug up by wolves, or by Indians who wanted the victims' clothes. To discourage these raiders, unfortunates sometimes were buried *on* the trail, where wagon wheels and animals' hooves would cover traces of newly dug earth. Wagon trains could not tarry, because they might miss the fall deadline to cross over the mountains to safety in California or Oregon. Some victims were simply left to die alone on the prairie because surviving members of the train were fearful of contracting the disease. As an extra precaution, they would burn a dead victim's clothing and wagon.

Cholera raged as an increasing number of emigrants crossed; in 1852, an estimated forty thousand made the trip, and some trains lost two-thirds of their members en route. In addition to cholera, they fell victim to smallpox, measles, mountain fever, open sores, typhoid, or dysentery. The following year, as the rush to California and its gold subsided, so did cases of the dread cholera.

Accidents, particularly at river crossings where freezing waters and rushing currents lay in wait for the unwary, were a serious threat. Drowning claimed almost as many travelers as did Indians; the idea of the vast region between the Missouri and California as one large desert overlooked the fact there were numerous streams and rivers to cross, and that they could be especially dangerous during the spring runoff. Some travelers, either too cheap to pay for crossing bridges or riding ferries or full of their own bravado, plunged into rivers and were swept away. Even bathing in a fast-moving river could prove fatal.

The Platte, which most of the overlanders followed, was especially dangerous. Placid, shallow, and muddy most of the year, the river's bottom was akin to quicksand. Stuck wagons could capsize, tossing their occupants and goods into the chilly water. The Green River in western Wyoming, another treacherous, muddy waterway, claimed thirty-seven lives in 1850.

Self-inflicted gunshot wounds were frequent. Inspired by tales of Indian attacks and massacres, and the necessity of hunting along the way, overlanders were better armed than many armies: they carried rifles, pistols, and shotguns. A military official at Fort Kearny in Nebraska described them as "walking arsenals." The problem was, many of them didn't know how to handle weapons. Guns were often stored loaded in case of emergencies and were prone to firing without warning. One man tossed his gear out of his wagon, hitting his gun, which discharged with a blast that hit him in the knee. Another pulled his shotgun out of the wagon muzzle first and it went off, striking him in the foot. One man was shot down when he wandered into camp at night without identifying himself. There were so many weapons about the wagons that some in the train complained that they were more worried about being accidentally shot by one of their companions than they were about attacks from Indians.

There are numerous accounts of children who toppled out of the family wagon and were crushed or wounded severely by its heavy wooden wheels. Traveling with her family in 1856, Katherine Dunlap paid special attention to the loss of children. "A little girl was jostled out of a wagon, run over and killed," she wrote in her diary. On July 16, she saw the grave of an infant. "Oh, what a lonely, dark desolate place to bury a sweet infant."[17] Another young girl, Mary Ackley, recorded, "My two brothers were playing in the wagon on the bed, the curtains were rolled up and front wheels went down in a rut which jarred the wagon, throwing brother John [age seven] out. A hind wheel ran over him, breaking one of his legs. He was confined to the wagon for the rest of the long journey."[18] Diarist J. Goldsborough Bruff, one of the earliest argonauts, wrote, sadly, of twelve-year-old John Hoover, buried on the Platte, who "died June 18, '49 ... Rest in peace, sweet boy, for thy travels are over."[19]

Once across the flat plains of Nebraska, covering what would become the main line of the Union Pacific Railroad in the late 1860s, emigrants could choose whether they would take the Oregon Trail, which veered northwest from the Platte River at what was to become

Independence Rock on the Oregon Trail in western Wyoming was a landmark travelers aimed to reach by the Fourth of July and where many carved their names in the rock. Visible at left in the background is another key point, Devil's Gate.

Ogallala, or continue west, eventually to cross South Pass and on to the deserts in Nevada and the impressive altitudes of the Sierra Nevada.

Whichever route they chose, the travails and misfortunes of those making the crossing between the 1840s and the coming of the railroad in the 1860s are compelling reading, but the fact is, the majority bravely endured endless days and nights and lived to enjoy it. Grandmother Harriet Ward exclaimed, "The scenery through which we are constantly passing is so wild and magnificently grand that it elevates the soul from earth to heaven and causes such an elasticity of mind that I forget I am old."[20] Diarists, their enthusiasm for the journey battered but still breathing, often commented on the beauty of the vast plains, "that boundless, undulating prairie," the weirdness of geological formations, the wonderment of sunsets, the power of thunderstorms and snow that swept across the prairies and their trains. Because many of them were farmers, they also marveled at the richness of the soil and growing conditions. A sense of humor apparently helped too. "Pikes Peak or Bust" was the most well-known lettering on westward wagons, but the wagoneers often decorated their rigs with lively nicknames, among them "The Sensible Child," "Cold Cuts and Pickled Eel's Feet," "Red Rover," "The Pirate," "Mind Your Business," and "Hell-Roaring Bill from Bitter Creek!"

Frequently, those who encountered trouble did so because they were ill-prepared or ignorant about how to deal with breakdowns, reluctant stock, blistering heat and heavy thunderstorms, or even getting along with other members of their parties.

It certainly wasn't an easy jaunt. An anonymous overlander philosophized in 1852,

> To enjoy such a trip along with such a crowd of emigration, a man must be able to endure heat like a salamander, mud and water like a muskrat, dust like a toad, and labor like a jackass. He must learn to eat with unwashed fingers, drink out of the same vessel with his mules, sleep on the ground when it rains, and share his blanket with vermin, and have patience with musketoes, who don't know any difference between the face of a man and the face of a mule but dash without ceremony from one into the other. He must cease to think, except as to where he may find grass and water and a good camping place. It is a hardship without glory, to be sick without a home, to die and be buried like a dog.[21]

In *The Plains Across*, a wide-ranging and in-depth study of the social upheaval of the emigration, John D. Unruh Jr. wrote, "Because this epic westering experience has become so enveloped in myth and stereotype, the reality of how it was accomplished remains historically elusive." The wonder is that so many, perhaps ignorant of what lay ahead, launched themselves on the journey in the first place. Accidents, illness, and privation took a fearful toll, but, in the main, overlanders remained focused on the prize: a new and glorious life in Oregon or California, despite naysayers and rumors of failure spread by those who gave up the quest and sullenly turned back to the States. Walking two thousand miles, probably a good deal farther than many of them could imagine, through torrential rain, long days of isolation, brutal manual labor, hailstorms, and scorching sun is beyond the understanding of modern-day travelers, who can drive from Denver to Kansas City in less than nine hours.

The crossing took a terrible toll, especially as they neared their ultimate goal, California. J. S. Holliday, in his riveting account of gold seekers in *The World Rushed In*, noted,

> There were the infirm and aged. Many of the emigrants were palsied by that terrible disease, scurvy. There might be seen a mother, a sister or a wife, winding along the mountain road, packing blankets and other articles, followed by children over every age, each with some article on his back or in his hands, hoping thus to enable the teams to get along by lessening the load.[22]

Diarist Joseph Stuart remarked in the fall of 1849, "A more pitiable and rusty-looking set of footsore, lantern-jawed skeletons could not be found outside the ranks of the California emigrant army than came by this … route."[23]

Isaac Wistar, who survived the six-month crossing, reminisced,

> Our journey is done, and we hardly know what to do with ourselves. There will be no more Indian alarms; no more stampedes; no more pulling, carrying, and hauling at wagons. We are in rags, almost barefooted, without provisions. But however sad for the fate of the poor fellows who fell by the way, we are glad to have got here at all.[24]

Ultimately, the West underwent a massive change. The time period from the days of the trappers in the 1830s to the completion of the transcontinental railroad in 1869 covered less than forty years, during which the wide-open prairie became home to settlers and new towns. The Watkins family made the crossing in four and a half months to reach California in 1865. Four years later, Francis Watkins went back by train to homestead. It took four days for him and his family to travel from Salt Lake City to Omaha. "Everything thing was changed," he wrote.[25] Time and distance had been compressed.

Chapter Two

A WOMAN'S PLACE

One of the most underreported and neglected aspects of the great migration across the prairie prior to the completion of what came to be known as the Pacific Railroad was the role of women.

Hard numbers are difficult to come by, but some historians estimate that after the early years of the migration—the 1840s, when almost all of the emigrants were single men—10 percent of overlanders were women and 5 percent were children. In other words, for every thirty thousand on the trail in 1850, three thousand were women and fifteen hundred children.[1] Each family, according to one historian, consisted of about seven members.

Pioneer women did almost everything men did, and more. In addition to the "womanly" chores of cooking, washing, cleaning up the wagon, and keeping an eye on the children, they drove teams, herded cattle, made repairs to the wagons, walked thousands of miles, buried dead companions, and negotiated for goods purchased along the trail.

Until the last third of the twentieth century, these contributions, and women's perseverance after the deaths of their husbands and children en route, went largely unreported in history books. In the Hollywood movie and popular history view, women in the West were either compliant helpmates or whores with hearts of gold.

Most of what we know about women's contributions comes from the diaries and letters they wrote and from researchers and authors like Lillian Schlissel, James Crutchfield, and many others who have painstakingly pulled together these remembrances. Through them, a much clearer picture of these women's lives has emerged, and it's not always pretty.

The trip west began with preparations for leaving behind homes and friends. While husbands sold their farms or businesses, bought or

A family making its way west paused to have a photo snapped in Nebraska. The woman may have worn the same dress throughout the months-long journey. Two children sit inside the wagon with the sides raised to provide relief from the heat.

built wagons, acquired and trained mules or oxen, and armed themselves, women were pulling together the necessities of a cross-country journey that could consume four, five, or six months under sometimes unimaginable conditions.

Once on the trail, many of these women's experiences were similar: the deaths of husbands and children, the hardships of cooking outdoors, and stress brought on by the endless monotony of trudging across unfamiliar and hostile territory day after day. But their individual stories and how they dealt with these experiences varied, giving a much more complete picture of the "typical" pioneer woman.

Keturah Belknap, whose year-old daughter died in October 1847, wrote that at that moment "everything was out of place and all was excitement and commotion" because they were preparing to leave Ohio for Oregon in the spring of 1848. Despite her grief, there was much to be done. "So now I will spend what little strength I have left getting ready to cross the Rockies. Will cut out some sewing to have to pick up at odd moments for I will try to have clothes enough to last a year."[2]

In ensuing days, she recorded what she did to prepare herself, her family, and the wagon for the journey. Her labors show remarkable foresight and attention to detail. "Now, I will begin to work and plan to make everything with an eye to starting out on a six-month trip," she wrote. Beginning in the new year, 1848, she got more specific:

> My health is better and I don't spend much time with housework. Will make a muslin cover for the wagon as we will have to double cover so we can keep warm and dry; put the muslin on first and then the heavy linen one for strength. They both have to be sewed real good and strong and I have to spin the thread and sew all these long seams with my fingers, then I have to make a new feather tick for my bed.[3]

One month later, she added that she had cut out homemade jeans for her husband, George, and sewn up sixty-two bushel bags for supplies, and in April she reported that she "will begin to pack and start with some old clothes on and when we can't wear them any longer will leave them on the road. This week I will wash and pack away everything except what we want to wear on the trip. This week I cook up something to last us a few days till we get use to camp fare. Bake bread, make a lot of crackers and fry doughnuts, cook a chicken, boil ham, and stew some dryed fruit."[4]

Loading up the household was a chore shared by men and women. Catherine Haun and her lawyer husband set out for the goldfields of California in 1849 as part of a large wagon train. "It took us four days to organize our company of seventy wagons and 120 persons; bring our wagons and animals to the highest possible standard of preparedness; wash our clothes; soak several days' supply of food—and say good bye to civilization at Council Bluffs [Iowa]."[5]

Belknap was superorganized, noting where every item was stored in the four-by-ten-foot wagon, from "four sacks of flour" to "a wall of smaller sacks" and "a corner left for the wash tub and the lunch basket."[6]

After the excitement of the departure, there were difficulties almost immediately. Pamelia Fergus, whose husband, James, left her behind in Iowa with their three children while he went to seek his mining fortune in Colorado and Montana in 1860, set out to join him in April 1864 as part of a thirteen-wagon train of friends and neighbors. Discouraged with covering only 105 miles in seventeen days, she wrote to James, "I can tell you nothing only that were here and its strange. I wish we had never started. I had a great notion to go back when I got to grenell [Grinnell]. Now I wish I had. It seems impossible to get their."[7] The family was finally reunited in Virginia City, Montana, in August 1864.

"We were not as comfortable today as we expect to be; things were just put in every way," wrote Ellen Tootle, married only seven weeks before leaving Plattsmouth on the Nebraska side of the Missouri River in April 1862. "The inside of the wagon is filled nearly to the top with boxes, trunks, comfortables, blankets, guns, a mattress, all the etc of camp life."[8] Ironically, Tootle, like many of her fellow travelers, would jettison part of their goods, including "comfortables," before completing even half the journey.

Mrs. John Berry wrote home to friends, "Oh, you who lounge on your divans & sofas, sleep on your fine, luxurious beds ... know nothing of the life of a California emigrant. Here are we sitting on a pine block ... sleeping in beds with either a quilt or a blanket as substitute for sheets (I can tell you it is very aristocratic to have a bed at all)."[9]

Not unlike today's cross-country travelers, emigrants spent a lot of time thinking and talking and writing about food, but for them it was more than a matter of entertainment; it could be the line between life and death out on the desolate prairie. The most popular foods "to go" were flour, bacon, and beans. In addition, travelers packed canned goods, sausage, sugar (brown, white, and maple), syrup, dried apples, ham, and coffee. Plenty of coffee.

The average pioneer covered wagon was four by ten feet and crammed with household goods and clothing, much of which was dumped trailside as the trip wore on. The canvas top was water-proofed with paint or linseed oil.

There were few gourmet meals, although many overlanders raved about the taste and tenderness of antelope and the heartiness of bison, when available. In general, it was difficult to tell breakfast from lunch from dinner.

Forty-niner William Swain enumerated a typical day's meals:

Breakfast—Meat fried in batter, boiled beans, pancakes, pilot
         bread [hard tack], coffee.
   Lunch—Usually served at midday and consisting of coffee and
         hard bread.
  Dinner—Rice, meat, pilot bread, and tea.[10]

Cooking on the trail could be a challenge unto itself. First, as the wagons moved farther out on the plains there was less firewood, preceding companies having picked the landscape clean. As an alternative, travelers collected dried prairie grasses and twisted them into small bundles called "cats." They burned well enough but produced copious amounts of smoke. Better was a handy and plentiful alternative: buffalo chips, also known to the emigrants as "meadow muffins." As the train approached a likely camping site, there would be a mad dash from the wagons to collect the largest and driest chips because they burned hottest and cleanest. This duty frequently fell to women and children, who used large sacks or baskets to lug their treasure into camp while the men of the train circled the wagons and dealt with the stock. A bushel could be collected in about a minute, and it took three bushels to cook the evening meal. Then there was the chore, again left to women and children, of fetching water from the nearest source, sometimes a mile away, for making coffee.

Even after a day of walking fifteen or twenty miles there was work to be done. "We find a great deal to do," wrote Cecilia Adams, who with her twin sister, Parthenia Blank, trekked to Oregon with their families in 1852. "P[arthenia] done some washing and I baked bread and pumpkin and apple pies. Cooked beans and meat. Stewed apples and baked suckeyes [pancakes] in quantitys sufficient to last some time. Besides making dutch cheese and took every thing out of the waggons to air." As an afterthought, she mentioned, "A birth took place to day in one of the companies near us."[11]

Those who were resourceful or farsighted brought iron cookstoves or forked poles on which a crossbar could be laid and cooking pots hung. In the main, it was incumbent upon the women in the party to dig a pit one foot deep and three feet long, toss in the chips, and ignite them.

Cooking this way meant long periods bent over or on hands and knees, clouded in smoke. "They emit a delicate perfume," joked one cook about the meadow muffins.[12] Another hardy cook who spent three meals a day over the smoking fire wrote, "I have cooked so much out in the sun and smoke I hardly know who I am and when I look into the little looking glass I ask, 'Can this be me?' Put a blanket over my head and I would pass well for an Osage squaw."[13] After dinner, there were still chores to be done: dishes and cooking utensils to wash, food to prepare for breakfast at dawn, unpacking of bedclothes and beds to be made up, wagons cleaned, and mending of clothes and the wagons' canvas.

As time wore on and food supplies dwindled, the menu became even less interesting. "Many companies subsisted on rancid bacon with the grease fried out by the hot sun, musty flour, a few pinoles [cakes made from dried corn flour], some sacks of pilot bread broken and crushed and well coated with alkali, and a little coffee without sugar," wrote Swain.[14] One eleven-year-old said ironically, "You need but one meal a day; you can eat dried apples for breakfast, drink water for dinner, and swell for supper."[15]

In an odd way, the simplicity of the day-to-day menu was a blessing. "Our mothers cooked our meals on campfires made of buffalo chips, which we children gathered for that purpose, as there was no wood," Amanda Hardin Brown, whose family emigrated to Colorado from Missouri in 1864, recalled later. "But the cooking was very easy for the fare was very simple—mostly biscuits and corn bread, coffee, bacon or ham, and syrup."[16]

An exception was the Fourth of July, jubilantly observed by homesick emigrants who no doubt yearned for the celebrations they knew back in the States and enjoyed the connection to their previous lives. "Most companies, heavily armed, used the Fourth as an excuse to fire their guns," wrote Mary Ellen Jones. There was much celebrating, speechmaking, some drinking, music, and a reading of the Declaration of Independence. And there was plenty of food. Dinner, she wrote, "Included ham, beans, boiled and baked, biscuits, johnny cake [flat cornbread], apple pie, sweet cake, rice pudding, pickle vinegar, pepper sauce and mustard, coffee, sugar, and milk."[17]

There were other distractions. At night, when the wagons were circled in camp, women would visit other groups to talk about the homes, family, and friends they had left behind, take part in Bible readings, and sometimes sing and join impromptu dances. Glimpses of humor surfaced. Diarist Rebecca Nutting recounted a wild night for newlyweds in her train:

David Parker and Catharine Hickman was married. Such a Chivarie as they got that night was enough to awaken seven sleepers. The newly married couple occupied a wagon for sleeping apartments. The first notice they had of any disturbance was when most of the men and women in the company took of the wagon, the men at the tongue pulling, women at the back pushing, and run the wagon a half mile on the prairie. Then the fun began. Such a banging of cans, shooting of guns and every noise conceivable was resorted to. The disturbance was kept up until midnight.[18]

Adverse weather could turn the evening unpleasant quickly. A sandstorm swept over their campsite just at dinnertime, Mrs. Isaac Moore recalled, leading her to remember, "Our most intimate friends could hardly recognized us—so dirty were our faces. And our dinner! Who would have eaten it? We could not tell what it consisted of, although before the storm it looked very tempting."[19] Another camp cook added, "Them that eat the most breakfast eat the most sand."[20]

Sudden thunderstorms on the plains played havoc in the camps; the covered wagons with their top-heavy canvas canopies were easy prey for heavy winds and downpours. Mary Elizabeth Munkers, who crossed on the Oregon Trail from Tennessee with her mother, father, and eight siblings as a ten-year-old in 1846, told an interviewer in 1929:

> I remember while we were camped on the Platte the whole sky became black as ink. A terrific wind came up, which blew the covers off the wagons and blew down the tents. When the storm burst upon us it frightened the cattle so that it took all the efforts of the men to keep them from stampeding. It stormed all night. It would be dark as Egypt one moment, then there would be a vivid flash of lightning when everything would be bright as daylight. It seemed as if the sky was a huge lake or an ocean and was slopping over. The rain came down in bucketfuls, drenching us to the skin. There wasn't a tent in camp that held against the terrific wind. The men had to chain the wagons together to keep them from blowing in the river. As the storm increased in violence the wind would catch our bed quilts and other light things and blow them away. Finally, in spite of the efforts of the men, the cattle stampeded. It took all the next day to round them up and get things fixed up to go onward.[21]

Sleeping in wet clothes and bedding or having to hopscotch through mud in their camp to get chores done before going to bed became almost routine. "Our tent was completely drenched," wrote Charlotte Stearns Pengra in 1853. "You who have never experienced the pleasure of being awakened sundry times during the night by the falling of pearly drops into their faces can scarcely imagine the exquisite pleasure."[22]

"I never saw such a storm the wind was so high," recorded Amelia Knight, who had seven children to manage on the journey. "I thought it would tear the wagons to pieces, nothing but the stoutest covers could stand it, the rain beat into the wagon so that every thing was wet, and in less than two hours, the water was a foot deep all over our camping ground. All hands had to crowd into the wagons and sleep in wet beds with their wet clothes on, without supper."[23] Later she joked, "Came to Dry Creek, so called because it is dry most of the year. I should call it Water Creek now as it is out of its banks and we will have to wait till it falls."[24]

Knight had more than the weather on her mind. When she and the family set off from Iowa in April 1853, she was three months pregnant. Pregnancy was rarely mentioned by women on the trail, other than to note the birth of another child. "Sickness" was frequently a code word for their condition. A number of women were pregnant when they set out or became mothers en route, enduring dreary days of "laying in" in a bouncing wagon while tending to their other offspring. In *Women and Men on the Overland Trail*, John Mack Faragher studied 122 families who produced sixteen children on the trail. "Slightly higher," he wrote, "than the general birthrate for the mid-nineteenth century."[25]

The trip over hilly, bumpy terrain did Knight little good. She noted a short way into the journey that she "had the sick headache all night" and, on June 27, wrote, "I am not well enough to get out of the wagon this morning." Even those who weren't pregnant were subject to "seasickness" from the constant rocking motion of the wagons between sunup and sunset. When it rained, the problem was made worse because the enclosed wagons became stifling and the pungent air nauseating.

Even if the air was dry, the wagon trains were not. Several diarists mention consumption of alcohol for "medicinal purposes." Often, the use of the spirits was recorded only in passing, but Ellen Tootle made no secret of it. "The brandy and whiskey were brought for medicinal purposes, but indulged in a little as we had just started on our journey. The first day, the cork came out of the whiskey bottle and spilled more than half, to Mr. Tootle's great disappointment. I don't believe he has recovered from it yet."[26]

Amelia Knight, whose family, including seven children, trekked to
Oregon in 1853 and who was three months pregnant when they set
out from Iowa

Whatever the popular image of pioneer women in the movies and on television, shown wearing full-length dresses with high necks and sunbonnets, the niceties of civilized society soon faded away on the trail. One woman claimed, "[I] never worked without an apron and a three-cornered shoulder kerchief," but another remembered that she wore the same wool dress every day, hot or cold, for five months.[27]

The simpler the clothing the better. Ellen Tootle, a careful recorder of almost everything that happened, wrote, "My traveling suit is a cotton material brown plaid minus hoopes, dark stockings, brown cambric skirt, brown hat trimmed with brown ribbon and blue veil covering head and face leaving a hole through which I could see and breath. For a change I have a blue calico bonnet with a beaux at least ½ yd. long."[28]

For modesty's sake, the hoops in skirts were abandoned almost immediately. Emigrant Helen Carpenter pointed out that she "would not recommend [hoops] for this mode of traveling because, while climbing in and out of a wagon, the wearer has less personal privacy than the Pawnee in his blanket."[29]

In addition, long skirts and sleeves were a potential hazard because they could catch fire while the wearer was cooking or become tangled in the wagon wheels or in the reins of the teams pulling the wagon. Some women, despite their reservations of dressing like men, wore pants or the new fashion rage, bloomers. Others preferred short wool skirts over wool pants and high laced boots with white stockings. A broad-brimmed straw hat topped the ensemble.

Women were less taken with the "adventure" than their husbands, especially wives like the one who had twelve children to take along. Drudgery and ennui soon set in. "Camp life has no charm for me," Pamelia Fergus wrote to her husband. "The children think it is fun, they want to eat all time," as though the journey were one long picnic.[30]

Ellen Tootle discovered on her group's first day on the road that life was rapidly becoming more basic. "[We] did not stop for dinner, but ate a rhubarb pie Mr. Hanna gave us. It was very soft and rather difficult to dispose of having no plates to hold it, no knife or fork to eat with. We took our first lesson in the use of fingers as a substitute."[31]

Gnats and mosquitoes were ever-present, not to mention other miniature creatures, like lice. When one group of argonauts reached Colorado in 1874, after the westward rush by wagon subsided, they stopped for the night at a stage station between Denver and Julesburg. The horrified women chose to sleep in the wagons, shunning the lice-invested buffalo robes offered inside the station. "They quickly lost their appetites when the cook, preparing to slice the meat first wiped the knife on the seat of his pants."[32]

The loss of loved ones to accident or illness showed that the specter of death was always just over the next rise or bend in the trail. The greatest loss of life among westward-bound emigrants struck in 1856 when two companies of the Mormon handcart pioneers, who set out on their journey to Great Salt Lake City far too late in the season, wound up snowbound and starving in the wilderness of western Wyoming. Their folly resulted in the deaths of as many as two hundred forty of their number, many more than perished in the famous Donner Party.[33]

There were many other such tragedies. In the years 1849 to 1852, cholera swept through the trains and killed upwards of two thousand emigrants. Between 1842 and 1866, when emigration was at its peak, approximately 6 percent of the half million travelers died en route. Early on, emigrants whiled away the day counting the graves they passed until graves became so commonplace that the travelers ceased to bother. Disease spread to the native people: in the mid-1850s, when two hundred thousand emigrants crossed the continent, they brought with them cholera, smallpox, and measles that decimated tribes, killing perhaps up to one-half of the Southern Cheyenne in 1849.

Men and children were most vulnerable to accidents, especially during river crossings, which often were attempted during high runoff and were poorly organized. A crossing without a bridge or ferry meant unloading everything out of the wagon, unhitching the teams, and hauling goods across the river to the opposite bank manually because the wagons were so unstable. Frances Fuller Victor, who made the crossing to Oregon, gave a detailed description of a train's typical river crossing:

> The mode usually adopted in crossing large rivers was to spread the lodges on the ground, throwing on them the light articles, saddles, etc. A rope was then run through the pinholes around the edge of each, when it could be drawn up like a reticule. It was then filled with the heavier camp goods, and being tightly drawn up, formed a perfect ball. A rope being tied to it, it was launched on the water, the children of the camp on top, and the women swimming after and clinging to it, while a man, who had the rope in his hand, swam ahead holding on to his horse's mane. In this way, dancing like a cork on the waves, the lodge was piloted across; and passengers as well as freight consigned, undamaged, to the opposite shore.

A large camp of three hundred men, and one hundred women and children were frequently thus crossed in one hour's time.[34]

Drownings, snakebites, Indian attacks, stampedes, gunshot wounds, and being crushed by the wagons' large wooden wheels lay in wait for the unwary. Storms took their toll too. A lamentable accident took the lives of four men in the company led by J. Goldsborough Bruff, whose accounts of crossing to California in 1849 were richly detailed and, at the same time, almost baroque in their language. In his oft-cited book *Gold Rush*, he retold the tale of a windy, rainy night in northern California, a night when a giant oak tree was uprooted and toppled across a tent occupied by a group of men: "There lay a shocking sight! An aged, grey headed man, and his grown son, with their hips buried in the ground, and their ghastly eyes turned up in death! Next another son, and beside him, a young man, his comrade, slowly dying in agony, with broken legs and mutilated bodies—groaning and uttering the name of God, in acute suffering!"[35]

After all four, ranging in ages from fifteen to fifty-four, died, two of them after a night of intense pain, Bruff and others buried them together in a double grave, "fitting very close," and shrouded their bodies with an old wagon cover. The older man's widow asked Bruff to uncover their faces for one last look. "I had the disagreeable task of getting down in the grave, treading between their necks as well as I could, and standing in the middle, supporting myself with one hand on the breast of a corpse while I loosened the sheet & exposed the face of another. Their eyes were wide open, and she was very vehement in her grief, crying out with clasped hand 'Why did He take them all at once—and not leave me one?'"[36]

A good friend wrote a letter back to Missouri to tell of the messy 1864 death of Martin Ringo:

> I write to give you the melancholy information of the death of Martin Ringo. Just after daylight on the morning of the 30th ult. Mr. Ringo stepped on top of the wagon, as I suppose, for the purpose of looking around to see if Indians were in sight, and his shotgun went off accidentally in his own hands, the load entering his right eye and coming out at the top of his head. At the report of the gun I saw his hat blow up twenty feet in the air, and his brains were scattered in all directions. I never saw a more heartrending sight. He was buried near the place he was shot in as decent a manner as possible with the facilities on the plains.[37]

It was left to Ringo's widow, Mary, pregnant with the couple's sixth child just before they began their trek in May 1864, to continue the trip to California alone. She wrote in her diary on July 30:

> And now Oh God comes the saddest record of my life for this day my husband accidentally shot himself and was buried by the way-side and oh, my heart is breaking. If I had no children how gladly would I lay me down with my dead—but now Oh God I pray for strength to raise our precious children and oh—may no one ever suffer the anguish that is breaking my heart, my little children are crying all the time and I—oh what am I going to do. After burying my darling husband we hitch up and drive some 5 miles. Oh, the agony of parting from that grave, to go and leave him on that hill-side where I shall never see it more but thank God tis only the body lying there and may we only meet in Heaven where there is no more death but only life eternally.[38]

Mary's life was touched by tragedy again that October when her son, Austin, was stillborn. Her family connected the child's death to that of his father, saying the boy was "terribly disfigured from mother seeing father after he was shot."[39]

Particularly heartrending were the deaths of young children. "Freemont is no longer a sufferer on this earth," Elizabeth Elliott wrote home to her parents in Iowa. "He died Sabbath afternoon June 21st." A three-year-old victim of dropsy (now called edema), he was painfully ill for weeks before he succumbed. "While one hard fit was on his dear little eyes and mouth jerked as though it would kill him. He looked at me and reached his dear arms out to me and said, 'Oh, Libbie.' Oh dear I never shall forget that pleading look."[40] Dressed in his Sunday best, he was buried beside the trail in two cracker boxes nailed together. "Oh, he was such a pretty corpse," said his mother. "He looked very natural."[41]

Children's deaths were frequent because life around the wagons could be treacherous. One woman reported, "A little girl was jostled out of the wagon and run over and killed." A young girl wrote of her baby brother, "We all gathered around his little bed in the tent to see him die." Another said, "Chat fell out of the wagon, but did not get hurt much." And, more simply, "Little Dolly is no more … He died at seven … His parents took his death very hard."[42]

The irony of the migration was that the easiest part of the crossing came first. From the Missouri to Fort Laramie in present-day Wyoming was along the Platte River route, a well-worn, level trail whether travelers chose the Mormon Trail on the north side of the river or the Oregon Trail on the south side.

As the days dragged on and the terrain became more difficult, tempers frayed. The endless months of travel, confinement with family and strangers in wagon trains that sometimes stretched miles along the trail, and seeing the same people every night at camps took its toll. By the time the trains reached Fort Laramie, about 550 miles from the Missouri, they were less than a third of the way to their goal of Oregon or California. As difficult as the journey was physically it was also a burden psychologically. For women, the stress of caring for children and the miscellaneous chores could prove to be too much.

Crossing the arid, vast desert in the Humboldt Sink in central Nevada was a cruel joke after traveling so many miles. Catherine Haun painted a vivid picture: "The alkali dust of this territory was suffocating, irritating our throats and clouds of it often blinded us. The mirages tantalized us; the water was unfit to drink or use in any way; animals often perished or were so overcome by heat and exhaustion that they had to be abandoned, or in case of human hunger, the poor jaded creatures were killed and eaten."[43]

The optimism so prevalent at the beginning of the journey began to drain away. Amelia Knight told her diary, "It is dusty from morning till night, with now and then a sprinkling of gnats and mosquitoes, and as far as the eye can reach it is nothing but a sandy desert, covered with wild sage brush, dried up with the heat. I have not felt well to day, and the road has been very tedious to me. I have ridden in the wagon and taken care of Chatfield [her son] till I got tired, then I got out and walked in the sand and stinking sage brush till I gave out." They traveled twenty-two miles that day.[44]

As the days wore on, breakups grew more frequent. Teams split over which trail to take. Did they want to go to Oregon or California? The collapse of oxen and mules led groups to dump belongings and carry their goods the rest of the way. Families broke up as when "Mr. Clark turned his brother and children out of his wagon this morning."[45]

In 1847, Elizabeth Smith Geer traveled from Indiana to Oregon with a large party, which began to disintegrate as they neared their destination. "This morning one company moved on except one family. The woman got mad and would not budge, nor let the children go." After a heated discussion, the wife set fire to one of her husband's wagons, destroying valuable supplies. He gave her "a good flogging," Geer noted.[46]

With obvious relief, Knight, whose company safely reached present-day Idaho in the summer of 1853, wrote on August 11, "Three of our hands got discontented, and left us this morning to pack through. I am pleased as we shall get along just as well without them, and I have three less to wait on."[47]

Squabbles, fistfights, and stabbings broke out. One woman wrote, "Some of our company had a regular fight to day but all of our folks kept out of the muss. One or two was knocked down but no injury done only they are obliged to leave our company."[48] There was no explanation of what precipitated the brawl.

Bruff, who shepherded his Washington City wagon train cross-country, saw the worst side of his comrades. "All the bad traits of the men are now well-developed—their true character is shown, untrammeled, unvarnished. Selfishness, hypocrisy, etc. Some, whom at home were thought gentlemen, are now totally unprincipled."[49] Angered by some of his men's desire to break up the train, he referred to them as "miscreants, vulgar and envious."[50]

Keturah Belknap, among the first to go west in 1848, observed,

> In the next wagon behind ours a man and woman are quarreling. She wants to turn back he won't go so she says she will go and leave him with the children and he will have a good time with that crying baby, then he used some very bad words and said he would put it out of the way. After that we had trouble with those folks as long as they were with us; they take things from those that did the most for them and there was others of the same stripe. They seemed to think when they got on the plains they were out of reach of the law of God or man.[51]

Said one discouraged traveler, "If there is anything that tries a man's patience and brings out his combativeness ... it is a trip across the plains. If there is any inclination to shirk or do any little mean trick or the slightest tendency to hoggishness, it will soon develop."[52] Fights broke out over petty slights, including card playing and failure to observe the Sabbath.

On the other hand, many would not be denied. Juliet Brier and her husband, a minister, were struggling across the desert in 1849 when one of their companions suggested that maybe she should stay where she was and wait for them to retrieve her. Her response: "I knew what he had in mind. 'No,' I said. 'I have never been a hindrance, I have never kept the company waiting, neither have my children, and every step I take will be toward California.' Give up! I knew what that meant: a shallow grave in the sand."[53]

It wasn't all drudgery and hardship; there also was an air of optimism, including keeping diaries and writing letters to send home so those left behind would know the traveler's travails and that they were overcome. Whatever motivation it was that set the voyagers off on the trek in the first place remained for many despite the difficulties, deaths, and perils of the road west. Women, while admitting the trek was boring, nevertheless took notice of their surroundings. Mary Ringo took time to mention, "I had such a nice walk over the bluffs and through the canyon and gathered mountain currants and we saw some beautiful flowers."[54]

Children remained children, though they experienced the deaths of siblings or one or both of their parents. Nobody rode free. They, too, were required to perform chores on the road and in camp, rounding up cattle, gathering fuel, cooking, cleaning, babysitting younger siblings. They had to sew, help bury the dead, and drive the team. But they also behaved like kids. At night, they played musical instruments and sang in campfire gatherings. They sometimes wandered off. At Devil's Gate, a prominent rock formation in western Wyoming, fourteen-year-old Sallie Hester and some friends couldn't resist climbing the mountain. "We made our way to the very edge of the cliff and looked down. We were gone so late that the train was stopped and men sent out in search of us."[55]

The vast majority of women who took on the crossing did so successfully, thankful that they hadn't suffered the fate of so many of their fellow travelers. When they reached their goals, they began the process of establishing schools, churches, theaters, and social organizations they enjoyed where they came from. It was a new life, starting over. Ada Millington, thirteen, was relieved when her family reached California in the fall of 1862. "Tonight is the one hundred and forty-first day of our journey. Twenty weeks ago we got into our wagons and left our Iowa home. We are in excellent health, our journey has been prosperous, with as little trouble as could have been expected. No Indian difficulties to speak of were encountered, and none of our stock was lost or stolen. We are indeed blessed."[56]

After her family reached Sacramento, twelve-year-old Elizabeth Keegan, who rode a horse the entire route from Kansas to California, remembered, "No one can picture the feeling of those who have come that wearisome journey; the joy they feel at once more beholding and mingling with their fellow creatures."[57]

Sarah Royce summed it up for all her fellow travelers: "California, land of sunny skies, that was my first look into your smiling face. I loved you from that moment, for you seemed to welcome me with a loving look into rest and safety. However brave a face I might have put on most of the time, I knew my coward heart was yearning all the while for a home-nest and a welcome into it, and you seemed to promise me both."[58]

Chapter Three

BULLWHACKERS

It was time to go. Passengers scrambled aboard the bright red Concord coach, "a redness that could not fail to attract the attentive consideration of the un-read men of the country," said one in the crowd, watching the departure. The tanned and strapping young man climbed up to the driver's box and commanded his team of six horses with a "Yip! Yip!," a crack of his whip, and a more gentle order, "Let's go, ladies."[1]

In a matter of minutes, the Overland Mail stage was tearing off down the road, leaving behind a drifting column of dust and the admiration of bystanders in its wake.

Stagecoach drivers were the rock stars of their generation, known as "whips," "bullwhackers," or "jehus," the last in honor of the ninth-century King of Israel famed for his swift chariot driving. For a brief period between the era of the covered wagons and the coming of the transcontinental railroad they were the undisputed kings of the western routes.

In *Roughing It*, his memorable and highly readable account of riding across the plains in a speeding stagecoach, Mark Twain described the arrogant demeanor of the driver as he guided his team into a station for a change of horses, blowing a warning trumpet and arriving "at our smartest speed," and causing the local hostlers to spring into action:

> The stage driver was a hero—a great and shining dignitary, the world's favorite son, the envy of the people, the observed of nations. When they spoke to him they received his insolent silence meekly, and as being the natural and proper conduct of so great a man, when he opened his lips they all hung on his words with admiration (he never honored a particular individual with a remark, but addressed it with a broad generality to the horses, the stables,

the surrounding country and the human underlings); when he discharged a facetious insulting personality at a hostler, that hostler
was happy for the day.[2]

There was no time or interest in small talk. Stage companies prided
themselves in conquering the wide-open spaces of the prairies between
the Missouri River and Sacramento in twenty days, traveling night and
day at an average of about ten miles an hour, three times the speed of the
emigrant wagon trains. Every minute counted.

The driver was all business and in a matter of minutes doffed his
heavy coat and gloves, splashed water on his face from a basin, and was
ready to hit the road again, "taking not the slightest notice of a dozen
solicitous inquiries after his health, and humbly facetious and flattering
accostings, and obsequious tenders of service from five or six hairy and
half-civilized station keepers and hostlers who were nimbly unhitching
our steeds and bringing the fresh team out of the stables."[3]

Stage drivers came from a variety of backgrounds: farmers disen-
chanted with the rural life, big-city clerks, gamblers, and drinkers. William Henry Jackson, who later gained fame as a photographer of western landscapes, tried his hand at bullwhacking in 1866, the heyday of
freighters. He recalled in his autobiography,

> When times were hard in the East—when there were too many
> children to share the New England farm—when you left the Army
> after serving through a war, and when you were restless and foot-
> loose—when you had a broken heart, or too much ambition for
> your own good—there was always the West. Horace Greeley's
> advice was far too obvious to be startling. Go west? Of course go
> west. Where else?[4]

Most of the drivers had spent their previous working lives as bullwhackers, laboring behind six to twelve yoke of oxen used to pull the
heavy Conestoga freight wagons that hauled goods from food to lumber
in the mid-1850s until the late 1860s. They were armed with sixteen-
foot-long whips attached by buckskin to an eighteen-inch stock, which
they used to incite their teams to action. It was not a chore easily learned.
One young bullwhacker admitted it took him two hundred miles of driving "before I became proficient enough in handling it to prevent its going
around my neck and hanging me." Just wrestling the oxen into their
yokes was a chore. An experienced crew could do it in thirty to forty

minutes. But a raw recruit like Jackson and his pals struggled. "Our first try on the morning of June 17, 1866 ... we required nearly eight hours and found ourselves almost weary to death before we swung the line at high noon."[5]

Each man was his own traveling armory with a revolver on his hip, a lethal knife stuffed in his boot, and the latest-model rifle nearby. Many could get by in the languages of the Sioux, Pawnee, Cheyenne, Arapaho, and Comanche.

The standard freight wagon train consisted of twenty-six large Conestoga wagons loaded with three tons of goods and one mess wagon. It took a crew of thirty men to herd the three hundred cattle required to supply the train. Each train was run by a wagon master, his assistant, the teamsters, a man to look after the extra cattle, and two or three men as a reserve to take the place of any man who might be disabled or sick. A well-organized train could average twelve to fifteen miles a day.[6]

Both bullwhackers and the stage drivers who succeeded them were rough frontier characters, bearded, hard drinking, and rowdy in their ways, as evidenced in this description from Theodore Davis's *Harper's* article, "A Stage Ride in Colorado": "His hirsute and unclean appearance indicating a cat-like aversion to water. He is more profane than the mate of a Mississippi River packet, and, we have his word for it, 'ken drink more whiskey.'"[7]

They were not the best keepers of sanitation, according to one-time stage messenger Frank Root, who rode thousands of miles with them. "It is a notorious fact that many of the overland stage drivers and stocker tenders ... were inhabited by species of vermin known as *pediculus vetimenti*, but on the plains more vulgarly called 'graybacks.' Some of the boys were fairly alive with them. It is not at all surprising however, for they slept from year to year on ticks filled with hay— they called it 'prairie feathers'—and their blankets were seldom washed from one year's end to another."[8] To cure such infestations, the victims lay their clothing and blankets atop teeming anthills, whose residents eagerly devoured the tiny vermin.

Whatever their personal habits, drivers and the messengers who rode with them as guards were well turned out. Each was issued a gum coat, a buffalo robe, a pair of blankets, a blue overcoat of the type worn by Civil War solders, a pair of flannel overalls, a fur muffler, a shawl, a buffalo coat, a breech-loading Wesson rifle, a Colt revolver, and "plenty of ammunition."

Drivers who labored for Ben Holladay's Overland Stage Company dressed like dandies compared to drivers with other companies.

Bullwhackers, rugged men who drove freight wagons and stagecoaches across the barren and often dangerous prairies before the advent of the Pacific Railroad, used a sixteen-foot-long whip with an eighteen-inch stock to urge their animals on.

Holladay outfitted his drivers in a company uniform made up of high boots with western heels, velvet-trimmed corduroy trousers, a wool-lined overcoat, a wide-brimmed sombrero, and the ubiquitous long whip for use on his teams.

Demas Barnes made the trip from Omaha to Denver in 1865. He was appalled by the drivers' treatment of their animals:

> I have omitted to speak of one feature in our travels which curdles the blood at every step. The cruelty to animals by the brutal drivers is perfectly awful. Each teamster carries a rawhide lash about nine feet long, one and a half inches in diameter at the belly, attached to a short stock or handle, folded over his shoulder, which he uses upon the poor, willing, overworked dumb beasts with apparent delight, and frequently draws blood at every stroke. The concussion is like the snap of a pistol. I wish the drivers—the most blasphemous wretches that ever disgraced a language—might have one good blow to see how they would like it.[9]

The stage driver, with four or six horses on his reins, rode high above the passenger compartment with a storage area, called the shoe, at his feet for mail and special packages. At the back of the coach was a boot for freight and luggage, although the top of the coach frequently held storage as well. It was considered an honor, and a respite from the cramped interior of the coach, to be invited to ride alongside the driver on his perch overlooking the team. There were pluses and minuses.

First, it meant escaping the enclosed confines of the coach, where nine passengers were required to cozy up in the cold of winter or in the heat of summer. From the driver's seat, a passenger could get a spectacular view of the prairies falling away in all directions and observe the herds of bison that dotted the plains.

On the other hand, the drivers, happy for the company, loved to tell stories, jokes, and tall tales. "After awhile," wrote rider and author Henry Stanley, the traveling journalist who went on to find Dr. David Livingstone in Africa in 1871, "the driver's stories cease to be interesting, the scenery is deadly dull, the novelty of stage-riding has already been worn away, and the dreadful monotony of earth and sky becomes distressing."[10] For a time, Stanley, as many passengers did, rode on the roof of the rocking coach. "Thirty hours of imprisonment on a stage roof before me—it is horrible! And now the sun has risen; it is high in the heavens, and the stage appears to be a powerful focus to draw the entire heat upon me; buffalo gnats add to my torments, stinging and buzzing, determined to draw blood-toll."[11]

Passenger comfort was not a selling point. The average trip from Missouri to California took twenty-five days and cost about $150; early coaches had seating for six. Barnes could find almost nothing good to say about the experience:

> The conditions of one man's running stages to make money, while another seeks to ride in them for pleasure, are not in harmony to produce comfort. Coaches will be overloaded, it will rain, the dust will drive, baggage will be left to the storm, a passenger will get sick, a gentleman of gallantry will hold the baby, children will cry, rations will give out, potatoes become worth a dollar each, and not to be had at that, the water brackish, the whiskey abominable, and the dirt almost unbearable.[12]

Catharine Wever Collins, the wife of an army colonel, made the crossing by stage to Wyoming in 1863. She wrote a letter from Fort Laramie, Wyoming, to her sister in Ohio, describing the ups and downs of her journey. "I reached here after a fatiguing ride of 65 miles, along the whole of which I did not see a house, and met so warm and cordial a welcome that I forgot my fatigue." Her trip required connecting by train to a Missouri River ferry to another train and then to a coach. She took the time to describe her fellow passengers on the coach, consisting of a "very pleasant-looking lady" and her daughter, her son, and "a very pleasant young man who was going with her to Denver City, two great Irishmen and a red-headed Missourian."[13]

The companies laid down strict rules for their drivers. Profanity, plentiful and frequently overlooked, was punished by a month-long suspension without pay. Drunkenness was likewise frowned upon but rarely charged against a driver. George E. Vanderwalker, a bullwhacker in his younger days, reminisced in 1909, "It was often remarked that the 'bullwhacker' was more generally addicted to the use of profane language than men in other occupations, but this I deny." It was, he argued, circumstance:

> I admit there were occasions when a manipulator of the wild bulls ran out of plain English and used words he hadn't been taught in the "primer class," but put any man in his place during a sudden Indian attack while on the road and he trying to work six yoke of "irresponsibles" into an improvised corral, at the same time trying

to do a little execution with an old "muzzle-loader," the Indians all the time pouring in basketfuls of arrows into the outfit, making it appear like a traveling feather duster—if there is a man living who wouldn't say "turkey red" with the frills to it, why all I've got to say is that the individual has a right to claim his harp at once.[14]

Once drawn into the staging life, drivers, who led nomadic existences, rarely strayed. "There seems to be a strange fascination with stage driving," wrote a correspondent for *Harper's New Monthly Magazine*. "Though it is one of the most toilsome of lives, a man once located on the box of such a coach seldom or never leaves it for any other employment."[15]

They were intensely dedicated to their task: getting mail and passengers across the prairies safely and on time. Drivers risked their lives and earned respect from the public; some became household names among their peers. Enoch Cummings, Rodney P. West, Bill Trotter, Bill Hooker, Nath Williams, and Ned Baker were immediately recognizable as skillful men of intelligence and honor. Some drivers were known only by their colorful nicknames, such as "Whisky Jack," "Rowdy Pete," "Smiling Tom," "Pap," or "Fish Creek Bill."

An oft-told tale of dedication and courage concerned Ned Baker, "the bravest and the best." Baker and his coach were scheduled to make a run from Julesburg in northeastern Colorado to Denver in 1868, but repeated Indian attacks on the road made the trip perilous. After several freighters and stage drivers were murdered and scalped in the area, Baker was warned not to go, but told the commanding officer at nearby Fort Sedgwick, "Hostiles or no hostiles, general, the coach goes through. I carry the United States mail. It must be delivered on the other side of the Rockies on time."

As he prepared to leave the safety of Julesburg, Baker warned his three passengers, "I will do my best to land you in Denver, but mind, if attacked, we must fight our way through or be scalped." A mere twenty miles down the road, Baker and his charges were set upon by an unusually large band of Indians. The coach's three passengers were killed outright (he refused to let a fourth passenger, a woman, ride along). Troops from the fort raced out to rescue them but found Baker dying beside his burning coach and returned the revered driver for burial at Antelope Station, forty yards off the stage route just west of Julesburg.[16]

Stage drivers were tough young men, tough enough to endure frostbite, recalcitrant stock, long days and nights at the reins, and the constant threat of attacks by Indians and highwaymen. They usually were

The bright red and yellow of the Concord stagecoaches made them attractive targets for Indian raiders. Former bullwhackers gained fame as stage drivers, often regarded as the rock stars of their generation for their courage and aloof behavior.

called upon to drive for forty miles, unless the next man failed to appear for his turn at the reins and they had to take another stretch—all for a monthly salary of $75 to $100, up to $200 a month on more hazardous routes. Alone and speeding through the night in isolated locations, their coaches were particularly vulnerable to attack, and several drivers were killed in the line of duty. Not surprisingly, drivers were virulently anti-Indian and against the government's attempts to "make peace" with the natives. Bill Hooker, famous in Wyoming history for his exploits as a bullwhacker and, later, his written accounts of his experiences, told of a secret society formed by his cohorts. Members of the Buckskin Militia took an oath:

> I (John Smith) do solemnly swear that I will shoot on sight any male Indian, no matter whether he is attacking me or other white men, stealing or attempting to steal my property or the property of others, or whether he is approaching or moving from me. Furthermore, I will answer any call from another member of this band, or any other good white citizen, for assistance in the destruction of any male Indian found on the south side of North Platte River; and will join in any raid upon any Indian camp when called upon by the Chief Buckskin. So help me God.[17]

Considered quaint today, stagecoaches were works of the modern age. The most popular were what came to be known as Concord stages, so named because they were built by the Abbot -Downing Company in Concord, New Hampshire. There were other makes, but the light weight and durability of the Concord made it a favorite among stage companies. The fact that they were painted bright red with a brilliant yellow under-carriage also made them easy targets for Indian assault. Abbot-Downing sold almost four thousand of their coaches between the 1840s and 1866, at an average cost of $1,000.

Unlike their over-the-road brethren in the East, the new Concords were lighter and faster yet still able to carry up to four thousand pounds of passengers and freight at relatively (for the day) high speeds. Their familiar egg shape, turned up at the ends, provided added stability on rough roads. Thoroughbracing, four-inch-wide leather straps at each corner that held the body of the coach off the undercarriage, gave passengers a gently swaying trip, although "seasickness" was not unheard of. The coach was solidly built with oak axles and wheels of hickory and white oak with an iron rim, able to handle rough riding and long runs.

The ubiquitous Concord coach was the backbone of western travel before the arrival of the transcontinental railroad. The overcrowded coaches often put passengers, like this group of African American buffalo soldiers acting as guards, atop the coach.

The rear wheels stood five-foot-one and the front wheels were three-foot-ten. The smaller front wheels let the driver turn tighter circles.[18]

Starting a stage company was expensive; many tried and many failed. The business required crews—superintendents, division agents, stock buyers, drivers, stock tenders, station keepers, blacksmiths, messengers, guards, and conductors (who rode along to tend to the needs of passengers and, when necessary, use a shotgun to fend off Indians and holdup men)—and food to feed them. The main line required 2,750 horses and mules bought at a cost of about $500,000. Feeding them was a major expense, $700,000 a year for hay and grain hauled to the stations. The Holladay Overland Mail and Express Company's original investment included one hundred Concord coaches and ownership in about half the one hundred stations along the route.

Several regularly scheduled coach companies emerged in 1849, offering passenger service along the early western trails. Most died young, but one of the first, the Pioneer Line, survived long enough that it eventually reached California from Leavenworth, Kansas, charging $200 for a thirty-day ride and food along the way. It was left to two companies to dominate the coaching business across Nebraska and Kansas to the goldfields of Colorado and the rapidly expanding territories of California and Oregon between the late 1850s and the coming of the transcontinental railroad in 1869.

Lack of mail service to the West was a major concern for the US government, which was interested in maintaining contact with the vast area on the far side of the Missouri River. In 1857, the government sought bids for running the service. The Butterfield Overland Mail Company run by John Butterfield was the winner over eight other bidders and began service from Tipton, Missouri, (then the end of the railroad tracks) on September 15, 1858. The trips ran over a route across southern Kansas and covered the distance between Tipton and San Francisco in an average of twenty-two days.

Another Butterfield, David (no relation to John), backed by one hundred investors, operated his Butterfield Overland Despatch on the Smoky Hill route through central Kansas between Atchison, Kansas, and Denver from September 1865 to March 1866, until it eventually merged with the stagecoach giant Holladay Overland Mail and Express Company. The problem for the Butterfield was that its route ran through the heart of Cheyenne territory, and the Indians didn't appreciate the increasing traffic crossing their land, causing the company financial hardship because of stolen stock and burned-out stations.

The merger of the Overland Despatch and Holladay created the Central Overland California and Pike's Peak Express Company, a staging behemoth running from Atchison to Placerville, California. It was the largest and most important of the many stage companies, "the greatest stage line on the globe."[19] Holladay eventually controlled more than thirty-three hundred miles of coach routes in the West. He was the ideal man to run cross-country stages but was reviled as a predator among his competitors. Frank Root and William Connelly, whose massive *The Overland Stage to California* is the definitive work on the subject, praised Holladay effusively:

> His long and successful career on the frontier was of great advantage to him. He had crossed the plains many times with oxen and mules long before the first stage line was dreamed of, and had "roughed it" on the frontier in pioneer days.
>
> He had been all over the great West and Northwest and enjoyed a wide acquaintance in the territories and on the Pacific slope. He employed the most skillful and experienced stage men in the country; he bought, regardless of price, the finest horses and mules suitable for staging that money could secure; he purchased dozens of first-class Concord coaches; he built additional stations and storehouses at convenient distances on the plains and in the mountains for storing hay and grain, and added many extra features to make the long, tedious overland trip of nearly 2,000 miles by stage an easier and more pleasant one.[20]

A shrewd businessman, Holladay sold out his interests to Wells Fargo & Co. just ahead of the completion of the transcontinental railroad in 1869 and the inevitable death of staging.

Riding a stage not only required a certain amount of tolerance for fellow passengers and their habits; it also was helpful to have an iron stomach to survive the rocking of the coach and often gruesome food served at stations. Horses usually were changed at stops called "swing stations," about twelve miles apart; changing teams required less than five minutes. Every forty or fifty miles there was a "home station," where passengers could stretch their legs, wash up, and get something to eat.

Though stages were faster than their covered-wagon predecessors, they were no picnic for riders. Later versions of the Concord sat nine passengers, three facing forward and three riding backward on two cushioned benches, and an additional three riders on a bench in the center of the coach. It was crowded, noted Root. "Being jostled about when the road was rough, it would be anything but pleasant for nine crowded passengers, inside a coach, riding six days and nights between the Missouri and Denver."[21] To make matters worse, not all passengers were of equal size. "It occasionally happened that there would be a fat woman among the passengers, perhaps weighing two hundred fifty pounds. A person weighing perhaps less than one hundred twenty-five pounds, while being crowded by a fat fellow would think it an imposition to be obliged to pay as much for passage as a man twice as heavy. Still the stage company made no distinction."[22]

Those with courage could find space to ride atop the coach, sometimes leading to as many as fourteen passengers crammed into and on one coach. Henry Steele recalled riding as a youngster in 1867: "At night two of my brothers and myself were laid snugly between buffalo robes and lashed to the roof to prevent rolling off."[23]

No passenger began his cross-country journey without a blanket or two. Even in summer, the plains could be chilly at night, and coaches were drafty with only canvas flaps over the windows to keep out the weather and dust. In addition, travelers might unexpectedly be forced to sleep on the floor at stations if weather or fear of Indian attack halted their travel. Some travelers were farsighted enough to bring their own food, given that dining at stops along the route could be a threat to digestion. One woman brought along a dozen hard-boiled eggs and enough ham for several days.

The broad span of the countryside became wearisome, without a tree or even a bush of any note for hundreds of miles across "this limitless expanse of grassy land," wrote Twain. He also found the accommodations limited, at best:

> Our coach was a great swinging and swaying stage, of the most sumptuous description—an imposing cradle on wheels. It was drawn by six handsome horses, and by the side of the driver sat the "conductor," the legitimate captain of the craft for it was his business to take charge and care of the mails, baggage, express matter, and passengers. We three were only passengers, this trip. We sat on the back seat, inside. About all the rest of the coach was full of mailbags for we had three days' delayed mails with us. Almost touching our knees, a perpendicular wall of mail matter rose up to the roof. We had 2,700 pounds of it aboard.[24]

As the days wore on, tempers shortened. Passengers elbowed each other for more room and often pushed sleeping travelers off themselves. There were, observed travel writer Bayard Taylor in one of a series of reports he filed for the *New York Tribune*, "no corners to receive one's head." Little more was expected. "The fare of one hundred and twenty-five dollars which one pays the Holladay Company is simply for transportation. It includes neither space nor convenience, much less comfort."[25]

After an all-night ride in the rain, he mused, "By eleven at night ... we were all so cramped and benumbed that I found myself wondering which of the legs under my eyes were going to get out of the coach. I took it for granted that the nearest pair that remained belonged to myself."[26]

"Persons who have never tried sleeping in a stagecoach may wonder how sleeping was possible when sitting bolt upright and traveling at speed," said a woman traveler who rode in 1861. "I can assure you that on our first night out from Omaha precious little sleep fell to our lot. But before our trip ended everyone could settle back from a lurch of the coach, or a halt for change of horses, and in a remarkably short time be seemingly in a Rip Van Winkle slumber."[27]

Mealtime was hit or miss. The speeding coach stopped three times every twenty-four hours to give passengers a respite from the cramped conditions and to feed their hunger. Meals could be quite satisfying, given the state of the passengers and the location of the stops, or could be excruciating. The usual meal was biscuits without butter, coffee (always coffee) without milk, beans, bacon, and, when available, jackrabbit, antelope, or bison. Dessert almost always consisted of pie made from dried apples. For this repast, passengers paid fifty cents to $2, depending on the distance from civilization. A "square meal," that is, one that was the worth the price paid for it, was a rarity.

Food was dispensed at home stations, two or three times larger than the swing stations where horses were swapped out. They had room for lodging and eating, a ticket and post office, store, barn with stable, and staging equipment and livestock. They were very often isolated and primitive in construction (of adobe or sod), though they looked like oases to weary travelers. New York newspaperman Alexander K. McClure covered three thousand miles in 1867 and found the stations "devoid of cleanliness." At one overnight stop, he reported, he battled bedbugs all night. "They do be awful," admitted the innkeeper, whose bare feet showed they had not been washed for months.[28]

At some stations, sanitation was nonexistent, "indescribably filthy." A passenger complaining about the meal put before him because it contained a good deal of dirt was told by the proprietor, "Well, sir, I was taught long ago that we must all eat a 'peck of dirt'" to which he replied, "I was aware of that fact, my dear sir, but I don't like to eat mine all at once."[29] Another turned down his meal after watching the cook fondling the station's dogs and cats before putting her hands into flour to make biscuits.

Nor were passengers' eating habits, driven by extreme hunger, always the best. "Westerners ate to fill the belly, not for pleasure. Food was food." An early-day traveler commented on the primitive eating arrangements:

> We are now ready to replenish the inner man. The bar is convenient for those who wish to imbibe. Breakfast is announced. We seat ourselves at the table. Before us is a reasonable quantity of beans, pork, and flapjacks served up in tin plates. Pea tea, which the landlord calls coffee with a bold emphasis, is handed to us. We help ourselves to such other things as may be within reach. Neither spices, sauces, nor seasonings are necessary to accommodate them to the palate. Our appetites need not nursing.[30]

Others described such meals and their participants as "a feast of wild cats" or "perfectly prodigious." It was every man for himself. "The spoon strikes every now and then and a quick sucking-up noise announces the disappearance of a mouthful of huckleberries on the top of a bit of bacon, or a spoonful of custard pie on the heels of a radish. It defies description. The 'feed' is most distasteful—all noise, dirt, grease, mess, slop, confusion, and disorder."[31]

Haste was the order of the day. "Before you had time to look at your meat, a piece of very flat pie, with a doughy crust, and dried fruit inside is placed under your nose, on the same plate with your meat. Men pick their teeth with forks and jackknives, gobble down gallons of water and slide."[32] At one mealtime, a diner found that the tablecloth was the same sheet he had slept on the night before.

As a correspondent for his *Springfield* (Massachusetts) *Republican*, Samuel Bowles found the meals at least tolerable. "Our meals at the stage stations continued very good throughout the ride; the staples were bacon, eggs, hot biscuit, green tea and coffee; dried peaches and apples, and pies were uniform; beef was occasional, and canned fruits and vegetables were furnished at least half the time. Each meal was the same: breakfast, dinner and supper were undistinguishable save by the hour; and the price was one dollar or one dollar and a half each."[33]

Others were not so enthralled. After stopping for a meal at a station that had been burned out by Indians, a young woman noted, "We sat down to a breakfast of coffee without milk, bacon swimming in fat, stewed canned tomatoes, stewed dried apples and biscuit yellow with soda." But, she added with an upbeat note, it was "the first hot food we had tasted for two days."[34]

Speaking of the food set out for his fellow bullwhackers, former driver Vanderwalker recalled in 1909, "Only a stomach capable of digesting feathers in a wad could long survive the stuff before indigestion took a fall out of it. Taos Lightning or the 'Mule Skinners Delight' was frequently used as an antidote."[35]

If the food and conditions were frequently substandard, one thing travelers could count on at even the most remote station was whiskey, even if some of it was barely drinkable. On a stop along the Platte River in central Nebraska keepers set up a makeshift bar with a board over two barrels, featuring "some of the vilest stuff under the name of 'old Bourbon whisky' that ever irrigated the throat of the worst old toper. To a few gallons of 'sod corn juice' the proprietors ... would add a quantity of tobacco and some poisonous drugs and thus manufacture a barrel of the worst 'rotgut' ever produced ... sold to thirsty customers at enormous prices." They didn't mind as long as it "had even a faint smell of liquor about it."[36] "Tourists" were a good source of income. One enterprising fellow set up a shop at a stage stop, offering wine, whiskey, cigars, tobacco, and pipes to the traveling public.

The coming of the railroads across Nebraska and Kansas in the late 1860s and early 1870s spelled doom for the staging companies, although they continued to serve isolated settlements beyond the reach of iron tracks until the turn of the twentieth century. They tried to keep one jump ahead of the advancing rails, connecting the end of track with towns still unserved. Speed was against them. As an example, it took freighters two weeks to go from Omaha to Kearney; the railroad did it in fourteen hours. Just as the stagecoach sped along the road at seventy to one hundred miles a day, far outranging the covered wagons that were able to make only eight to fifteen miles a day, the iron horse took speed to another level, making the trip from New York to San Francisco in only seven days.

In a few short years, innovations from freighters to the Pony Express to the telegraph, stagecoaches, and railroads turned what had been a vast unknown into a rapidly developed landscape. The breadth of the change was not lost on at least one coach passenger: "We pass with pity the emigrant's slow wagon and the mule train—hot and dusty and parched by day, cold and shivering and parched by night. It is a wonder how people can go alive through this country at the rate of only twelve and fifteen miles a day, and finding food and drink as they go. But they do, year by year, thousands and thousands."[37]

The flush days of staging, a rugged and romantic era in the American West, covered only eight years. The "old West" was becoming a thing of the past. In 1864, the farsighted editor of the *Leavenworth (Kansas) Daily Conservative* editorialized, "The West! The West! Where is the West? Where is the West of today? Cities, towns, and farms are springing up and spreading forth. The Great American Desert is a myth. Can our statesmen of today look upon the horizon of the golden West and realize half its vastness?"[38]

Chapter Four

INDIANS!

Millions of acres of land lay between the Missouri River and the Rocky Mountains. The Arapahos, Sioux, Cheyennes, Kiowas, Comanches, Pawnees, and more than two dozen other tribes roamed the prairies, if not always peaceably, with the understanding that there was plenty of room and buffalo, even for the oncoming whites. Even when trappers began to trickle westward in the 1840s, the Indians were not alarmed, because the incursion consisted of so few whites that their presence was, if not insignificant, at least tolerable.

With the discovery of gold in California in 1848 and the subsequent rush the following year, there began a tidal wave of emigrants— more than a half million by 1870—from which the Indians would never recover. Early on, relations between the Indians and overlanders were generally cordial. "It was quite natural, for example, for overlanders to solicit route information from Indians, especially during the early 1840s and the initial gold rush period," noted historian John D. Unruh.[1] But more and more kept coming—an endless stream it seemed to the watchful Indians—not only passing through Indian country but staying to establish towns and farms and, most devastatingly, constructing two railroads: the Union Pacific through Nebraska and Wyoming and the Kansas Pacific across Kansas and Colorado.

The Indians, who first viewed the westward-trekking whites with the same curiosity the emigrants had for them, were rarely a threat to the lives of those riding the covered wagons, despite the images of savagery in the popular media. The cinematic portrayal of bands of whooping warriors galloping around and around wagon trains is false; when the emigrants circled their wagons in a defensive position, it was almost impenetrable. Clever in fighting techniques, Indians were not foolish enough to expose themselves to rifle fire from behind barricades. Most of the attacks took place when the wagons were stretched out on the trail or when emigrants wandered from the train and were caught alone.

When it came to aid and trade, both sides benefited. Women diarists were terrified by rumors of attacks and kidnappings but found, as Nancy Hunt did, "We always treated the Indians well and with respect, and they never molested us."[2] In fact, it was the Indians' kindnesses (showing where water and grass could be found) and guidance (pointing out the best routes) that saved emigrant lives.

Whites did not understand the Indian ritual of exchanging gifts. "Virtually every overlander met at least a few Indians anxious to 'swap.' Most encountered a great many. Indians were not easy marks in the bargaining process. Indeed, the traditional stereotype of the easygoing Indian, victimized in his every dealing with the white man, is simply not accurate," wrote Unruh.[3] Some whites compared the Indians to "wily British merchants," especially when it came to dealing horses. Sometimes the horses traded weren't even the Indians' property, having been stolen a short while before from other emigrants.

Goods passed back and forth. Indians prized clothing, particularly shirts, and blankets, mirrors, and liquor, while the travelers wanted moccasins, pelts, and food. Some Indians were enterprising enough to set up checkpoints along the Smoky Hill route in Kansas, where they demanded tribute for crossing their land. Emigrants sometimes bristled at the idea and attacked the Indian sentinels or simply crossed anyway.

Indians quickly discovered that wagon trains were targets of opportunity. Emigrants and traveling newspapermen often described the Indians they met as beggars. Theft was a far greater threat than death. "While arrows were infrequent, pilfering was not," wrote Unruh, quoting overlander Byron McKinstry, who said, "They will put their hands into one's pockets if you are not resolute with them, especially squaws."[4] When haggling and begging failed, Indians resorted to outright thievery or assault. But it wasn't just Indians who robbed the emigrants. Roving bands of whites—"a tribe of Indians who have blues eyes and light hair, who wear whiskers, and speak good English"—masqueraded as Indians and committed vicious crimes, especially on the California end of the trails.

By the mid-1860s, Indians' attitude toward the emigrants turned more hostile. The more perceptive of their leaders saw the trend: more whites arriving daily, the region's most vital asset, bison, beginning to disappear or becoming harder to find, and the tribes being pushed off their homelands into smaller and smaller spaces. All this was abetted by the Homestead Act of 1862, which gave 160 acres or more of land to those who would settle on it for five years. Much of the land given away was Indian land west of the Missouri River. Taxpayers had more value to the federal government than autonomous tribes.

The summer of 1864 marked the start of the Indians' push back. Frequent raids were made on white settlers, and stagecoaches became targets for attacks. Supply wagons and stagecoaches ceased running across the plains for six weeks for fear of Indian attack. Supplies of grain, merchandise, and provisions were cut off, and stages carrying mail ceased to run. Some encounters were memorable. The Sioux roamed the Platte Valley in present-day Nebraska but remained out of sight of most emigrants. Isaac Fisher wrote in his diary during the crossing, "They are much wilder than the buffalo and antelope. The traders have told them that the emigrants have the cholera and smallpox, and they keep shy of us." But not entirely. Another member of his wagon train commented after an encounter with the Sioux, "The pretty young squaws certainly are beauties of Nature and will compare very well with some of the young ladies of the States who think themselves handsomer … They are what Nature designed them to be, women without stays or padding."[5]

The US military, still occupied with fighting the Civil War and Reconstruction that followed in the South, was unable to devote sufficient men or resources to the "war." Lieutenant General William T. Sherman, whose job it was to protect the builders of the Union Pacific and the rising numbers of emigrants in the territory, was badgered on all sides to do something. Confronted with limited military options and an enemy that seemingly vanished after lightning attacks, Sherman fought a war on two fronts: against the Indians who repeatedly evaded his troops in the West, and against carping politicians in the East, who wondered why he wasn't doing more to subdue the Indians. The bothersome politicians were, wrote Robert G. Athearn, "like cockleburs under the saddle blanket, annoying and distracting, but only superficial."[6] Sherman wrote a letter to army headquarters in August 1866, warning, "We are in no condition to punish the Indians this year, for our troops are barely able to hold the long thin lines that are traveled by daily stages and small parties of emigrants."[7]

Everybody had advice for Sherman. In October 1866, he received a letter from General James Henry Carleton in Santa Fe, New Mexico:

It was Civil War hero William T. Sherman's job to protect railroad builders against Indian attack.

To spin out this war with Indians year after year through the country to "play hardly an even game" with the Indians, leads to no decisive results and is a "penny wise and pound foolish" system. The true economy, in my opinion, is to put troops enough in the country to drive the Indians to the wall at once; to exterminate them if they won't give up; to put them on reservations if they do give up, and have done with it.[8]

Among the many problems facing the army was chasing down its opponent. "The regular troops can fight Indians when they get a chance, but the difficulty with them is to find the Indians," reasoned the much-traveled journalist Henry Stanley.[9] Troops very often "found themselves chasing after only thirst and starvation, sometimes coming very close to wiping themselves out when supplies collapsed."[10] The Indians knew the territory, fought in small groups, and frequently seemed to be one step ahead of the troopers, whose leaders were West Point trained in set-piece battles but often inexperienced in frontier warfare.

Drunkenness was rampant among the officers assigned to lead their men, volunteers in the Regular Army, into the vast country west of the Missouri River.

At a time when the army was officially concerned about alcoholism among the rank and file, the sight of their officers reeling and staggering under a load of liquor did not encourage temperance. Nor were attempts to keep prostitutes away from the soldiers and to raise the standards of sexual morality facilitated when a married officer was known and observed to be having an affair with another's wife.

A fair example is a Seventh Cavalry captain who had long borne a reputation for being extremely foul-mouthed and who was unpopular with both his men and other officers. A list of charges and specifications was drawn up against him, consisting of incidents sworn to have taken place between August 1 and the last of December 1878. It was charged that he had been drunk on duty six times, once as officer of the day, and that he had been absent without leave for two days on an extended spree in Deadwood, Dakota Territory. He was also accused to having twice broken arrest and of attempting to persuade the post trader at Fort Meade to lie on his behalf; of drinking with a company laundress in an ambulance while on the march and later carousing with her in her tent; and of ordering a soldier to drive him and two laundresses, in an army ambulance, to a nearby road ranch, where he staged another protracted debauch.[11]

None of this did much to raise the morale or morals of the rank-and-file soldier.

Given the size of the military units and the dust and din they raised on the march, there was little chance of sneaking up on Indians. Supplying such an army in the wide-open spaces also presented problems: the soldiers needed to be fed, kept supplied with arms and ammunition, and clothed. "We have no business to put men out here unless we give them food and shelter, and all things but sand and water must be hauled from one to four hundred miles," Sherman reported in 1866.[12]

A regiment of one thousand mounted men required three hundred wagons for provisions and another three hundred for forage, ammunition, and clothing. Each soldier was outfitted with forty to sixty rounds of ammunition, a blanket or overcoat, extra pants, socks, drawers, and a scarf "worn from the left shoulder to the right side in lieu of a knapsack." He also toted bread, cooked meat, salt, and coffee. All told, he carried about fifty pounds.[13] Sherman reasoned,

> There is no better food for man than beef cattle driven on the hoof, issued liberally, with salt, bacon and bread. Coffee has also become almost indispensable, though many substitutes were found for it, such as Indian corn, roasted, the sweet potato, and the seed of the okra plant prepared in the same way.
>
> I would always advise that the coffee and sugar ration be carried along, even at the expense of bread, for which there are many substitutes. The potato, both Irish and sweet, forms an excellent substitute for bread.[14]

Real or imagined attacks, especially by the Sioux and Cheyennes, kept soldiers and settlers in a state of high anxiety. If men were uneasy, women were more so because of two threats related to their gender: fear of sexual assault and fear that their children would be carried off. One emigrant woman carried a locket containing cyanide in case of capture by Indians. There were repeated reports of nervous emigrants shooting their own stock or elk or each other in the mistaken belief that there were Indians lurking about; a small band of Indians became "a horde."

Sherman found the dangers overblown, taking an optimistic stance in a letter from Fort Sedgwick, Colorado, to General John Rawlins:

> I see little danger of Indians. The telegraph is unmolested; the stage passes daily; and I find the road filled with travellers back and forth,

with ranches every ten miles; yet there is a general apprehension of danger though no one seems to have a definite idea of whence it is to come. I have met a few struggling parties of Indians who seemed pure beggars, and poor devils, more to be pitied than dreaded. This does not look like danger, and I feel none at all.[15]

In spite of Sherman's assurances, paranoia was rampant. Denver was a good example of the rising and irrational fear of attack. Rumors and exaggerated accounts of Indian attacks out on the plains—and some reports of settlers' murders that were true—fueled fear in the isolated city. It was, in part, what led Colorado's territorial governor John Evans to whip up sentiment for eliminating Indians' presence in the area. Cross-country travelers were fond of retelling stories of emigrant graves lining the wagon routes.

Some assaults were real enough. A large force of Sioux, led by Red Cloud, harassed troops and travelers along the Bozeman Trail in Montana in 1866 and 1867. Repeated attacks on military forts along the vital route killed sixteen soldiers and fifty-six civilians in less than five months. Nearly every wagon train and person was prey, halting travel along the route.[16]

In April 1868, a band of Sioux led by Two Strikes killed five railroad section men near Elm Creek Station in Nebraska and ran off their stock. Later that year, two conductors, Tom Cahoon and William Edmunson, out fishing on Lodge Pole Creek, were surprised by a group of Sioux who ran them down and shot Cahoon, scalped him, and left him for dead. Edmunson, meanwhile, made a dash for a nearby post and safety, but not before he took eight arrows and several bullets. Both men, to everyone's surprise, survived the attack.[17]

The tipping point in the deterioration of white-Indian relations came on November 29, 1864, when Colonel John Chivington and US volunteers under his command used the cover of a cold and still-dark morning to sweep down on a Sand Creek village of six hundred Southern Cheyennes and Arapahos, brought together near Fort Lyon in southeastern Colorado by the promise of protection from attack.

More than two hundred Natives, two-thirds of them women and children, were slaughtered in a matter of minutes in a raid that led to the condemnation of Chivington, even by some of his own officers. Outraged tribes immediately went on a killing and pillaging spree in eastern Colorado, western Kansas, and up into Nebraska and Wyoming. Beginning in January 1865, Cheyenne and Sioux war parties swept over the

Platte River area and controlled the vital route for several hundred miles, cutting off supplies and mail, burning stage stations, stealing horses, and killing both settlers and emigrants. Travel on the Platte was paralyzed.

A second incident of destruction by the military in the spring of 1867 did little to calm the Indians' anger. General Winfield Scott Hancock, a hero in the Civil War at the Battle of Gettysburg and the man who had overseen the executions of the conspirators in the plot to assassinate Abraham Lincoln, and his troops surrounded a Cheyenne village on Pawnee Fork near Fort Larned, occupied the village for three days and ultimately burned the camp and its goods in retaliation for a series of raids on the nearby Smoky Hill route. "He would brook no insolence from these red rebels, for his Civil War experience had taught him that only decisive action would suppress rebellion. Taking the war to every Indian lodge would crush resistance and force the Cheyennes to accept government control."[18]

Hancock's assault on the village followed a bungled series of meetings at Fort Larned designed to convince the Dog Soldiers, a Cheyenne military society that had evolved into a separate division of the Cheyenne Nation, to give up their warring ways. Hancock, popularly known among his fellow officers as "Hancock the Magnificent," harangued the chiefs, to their obvious displeasure. He warned them that "if the Cheyennes wanted war ... his army would give it to them in full measure."[19] Angered by their treatment at the hands of Hancock, the tribes immediately went on a destructive rampage.

The human toll was a two-way sword. According to one accounting, 362 overlanders were killed between 1840 and 1860. The storytellers were less concerned with Indian deaths, which may have added up to 426.[20] In one gory example, stagecoach riders arriving at Kelly's Station, 150 miles northeast of Denver, were greeted by the sight of the bodies of two Indians riddled with bullets, one tied to a building and the other to a fence. Left behind by their comrades a few days earlier during a heated gun battle with the occupants of the station, they were stripped nearly nude, pieces of them hauled off as souvenirs, and their eyes gouged out. One had his nose chopped off and his intestines pulled out.[21]

Repeated incidents of murder and thievery, sanitarily referred to as "depredations," did nothing to salve settlers' enmity toward Indians. Businessman Nathaniel Hill wrote from Denver to his wife in the East, "There is no sentimentality here on the frontier respecting Indians. Indians are all the same, a treacherous, villainous set. I would rejoice, as would every man in Colorado, to see them exterminated."[22] The editor of the *Montana Post* warned, "It is high time the sickly sentimental-ism about humane treatment and conciliatory measures should be con-signed to novel writers, and if the Indians continue their barbarities, wipe them out."[23]

Noted New York newspaper publisher Horace Greeley trekked west by stagecoach in 1859 and, like a lot of his fellow travelers, had little regard for those already living on the vast western prairies. "The Indi-ans," he wrote, "are children. Their arts, wars, treaties, alliances, habita-tions, crafts, properties, commerce, comforts, all belong to the very low-est and rudest ages of human existence. They are utterly incompetent to cope in any way with the European or Caucasian race." And, he added, "God has given this earth to those who will subdue and cultivate it, and it is vain to struggle against His righteous decree."[24]

Henry Stanley reflected on the expansionist attitude of the time. "What has taken place was inevitable. It is useless to blame the white race for moving across the continent in a constantly increasing tide. The whites have done no more than follow the law of their nature and being. Moreover, they had as much right to the plains as the Indians, and it would not be a difficult task to prove that they had a better right."[25] This rationale was known as Manifest Destiny, the idea that the white man was chosen to spread civilization across the continent, multiply, and defeat whatever or whoever crossed his path. Historian Athearn takes a dim view of the policy. "The only explanation anybody had for the ceaseless white expansion was a lame, high-sounding phrase, an easy principle called 'Manifest Destiny.' If any people ever had a manifest destiny, it was the American Indians."[26]

The Indians were not without their victories in the ongoing con-flict. In 1865, Cheyenne, Arapaho, and Sioux warriors launched a series of attacks in Colorado, Kansas, Nebraska, and Wyoming in retaliation for Chivington's assault at Sand Creek. The tribes held a war council in January 1865 and decided to attack Julesburg in northeastern Colorado, a major supply depot for the military and area ranches.

Up and down the Platte River, the Indians attacked ranches and stage stations and made off with large numbers of cattle and horses. On February 2, 1865, they returned to Julesburg. At the first attack, on January 7, George Bent, a half-breed who traveled with the tribes during their sweep through eastern Colorado into Nebraska, had told the chiefs not to torch the warehouses because in a few weeks the soldiers would fill them again. After a second round of pillaging, they burned Julesburg to the ground.

In March, the united tribes regrouped—some estimated there were as many as two thousand warriors—in a string of camps along the Powder River, where they decided to launch attacks on the Platte River route used by emigrants and trains of freighters.

In June 1867, troops commanded by Captain Albert Barnitz had "quite a desperate little fight" near Fort Wallace in extreme western Kansas. Spurred on by sightings and signs that they were only hours behind a large force of Indians. Barnitz and his men suddenly found themselves set upon. In a letter to his wife, Jennie, Barnitz gave one of the most colorful accounts of a military-Indian encounter:

> They turned suddenly upon my line, and came literally sailing in, uttering their peculiar Hi!—Hi!—Hi! and terminating it with the war-whoop—their ponies, gaily decked with feathers and scalp-locks, tossing their proud little heads high in the air, and looking wildly from side to side, as their riders poured in a rapid fire from their repeating arms, or sending their keen arrows with fearful accuracy and force.[27]

The Battle of Beecher Island in 1868 demonstrated that the Indians, superb horsemen and strategists who were on their "home field," could match the army's finest. In August, a troop of fifty-one hand-picked scouts led by Major George A. Forsyth and armed with the latest in military weaponry, Spencer repeating rifles and Colt revolvers, left Fort Hays, Kansas, for the Republican River, where Indians had been congregating and creating havoc for whites. In mid-September Forsyth's men were camped on the Arikaree River when they were attacked and chased onto an "island," little more than a sandbar covered in brush and a single cottonwood tree in the middle of the river. Scout Chauncey B. Winney wrote in his diary, "The ground on which our little squad was fighting was sandy. We commenced to scoop out the sand with our hands to make entrenchments for ourselves."[28] The battle, really a series of skirmishes, lasted off and on for almost a week, ended only after relief troops—the famed African American buffalo soldiers under the command of Colonel Louis Carpenter—arrived to save the scouts.

Forsyth wrote twenty-five years later that his men killed thirty-five Indians; Indian accounts say it was more like six. The greatest loss for the Indians was the death of Roman Nose, a Cheyenne leader, though not a chief, "a man of great courage, a splendid fighter, and looked up to by the whole tribe. He was a brave, possessed great influence, and was an acknowledged leader in war."[29]

There also were devastating losses for the Indians, including at Washita River in present-day Oklahoma, where Lieutenant Colonel George Custer's Seventh Cavalry decimated a Cheyenne village and killed Black Kettle, who had survived the massacre at Sand Creek. This was followed by another crushing defeat at Summit Springs, where fifty-one Dog Soldiers were killed, marking the beginning of the end for the warrior societies. It was here that the army's chief of scouts, William F. "Buffalo Bill" Cody, shot and killed Tall Bull, leader of the Dog Soldiers.

The Union Pacific Railroad set off from Omaha, Nebraska, on July 10, 1865, on its inexorable trek west. It almost immediately ran into trouble with tribes, mainly Cheyennes and Sioux, along the route, which paralleled the Platte River across Nebraska and Wyoming that emigrants and other travelers had trekked for two decades.

Between 1866 and 1868, there were repeated attacks against the UP and its workers, particularly among surveyors and graders who labored in small groups in isolated areas well ahead of the onrushing construction. Some were murdered, but usually the raiding parties only stole their stock.

Beginning in late 1867, the raids diminished when emigrants poured into the country and the military stepped up its presence in the region. Until then, raids along the line became so frequent that UP officials despaired of completing their work. For a time, they were forced to run trains only during daylight hours. Oliver Ames, a key figure in the building of the Union Pacific and, later, governor of Massachusetts, raged in the spring of 1867, "I see nothing but extermination to the Indians as the result of their thieving disposition and we shall probably have to come to this before we can run the road safely."[30]

One of the most written and talked about attacks on the railroad took place in August 1867 when a group of Cheyennes, led by Spotted Wolf (some accounts say their leader was Turkey Leg), reached the railroad line near Plum Creek in what is now Lexington in central Nebraska and wrecked a freight train. A handcar running just ahead of the freight was thrown off the tracks and the following train derailed. Probably the most accurate account of the ambush came from Porcupine, a young Cheyenne warrior who was there that day:

> We had a fight with the soldiers [near] Ash Creek, which flows into the Arkansas. There were Sioux and Cheyennes in the fight, and the troops had defeated us and taken everything that we had, and had made us poor. We were feeling angry.

Encounters between Union Pacific workers and marauding bands of warriors became so frequent in the mid-1860s one railroad official proclaimed that only extermination of the Indians could ensure completion of construction.

One of the most recounted attacks by Indians on the railroad occurred in August 1867 when Cheyennes ambushed a handcar carrying workers in southern Nebraska. The band also successfully derailed a speeding freight train.

Not long after that we saw the first train of cars that any of us had seen. We looked at it from a high ridge. Far off it was very small but it kept coming and growing larger all the time, puffing out smoke and steam; and as it came on, we said to each other that it looked like a white man's pipe when he was smoking.

Not long after this, as we talked of our troubles, we said among ourselves, "Now the white people have taken all we had and have made us poor and we ought to do something. In these big wagons that go on this metal road, there must be things that are valuable— perhaps clothing. If we could throw these wagons off the iron they run on and break them open, we should find out what was in them and could take whatever might be useful to us."[31]

Porcupine related how he and Red Wolf laid a log across the track just before sundown and waited for the next train. Shortly, six railroaders riding on a handcar came pumping down the line. When their cart struck the log, the car sailed off the rails and the men were scattered on the right-of-way. Two of the men, though stunned, were able to escape into the darkness. William Thompson, an Englishman riding the handcar, recalled that the Indians rose up from the grass and began shooting:

We fired two or three shots in return, and then, as the Indians pressed on us, we ran away. An Indian on a pony galloped up to me. After coming to within ten feet, he fired. The bullet passed through my right arm but seeing me still running, he rushed up and clubbed me down with his rifle. He then took out his knife, stabbed me in the neck, and making a twirl round his fingers with my hair, he commenced sawing and hacking away at my scalp.

Though the pain was awful, and I felt dizzy and sick, I knew enough to keep quiet. After what seemed to be half an hour, he gave the last finishing cut to the scalp on the left temple, and as it still hung a little, he gave it a jerk. I just thought then that I could have screamed my life out. I can't describe it to you. I just felt as if the whole head was taken right off."[32]

In a bizarre stroke of luck, Thompson's attacker dropped the scalp as he galloped away and the Englishman retrieved it. Later, he filled a bucket with water and dropped the scalp, nine inches of his own hair, into it before making his way to Omaha, where a doctor tried unsuccessfully sew it back on. Thompson took the scalp back to England, had

Englishman William Thompson lost his flowing locks in an Indian attack in 1867 but got them back and tried, unsuccessfully, to have them sewn on. In 1900, he donated the scalp with its reddish-brown lock of hair to the Omaha Public Library.

COURTESY OMAHA PUBLIC LIBRARY

it tanned and sent to Omaha, where it is periodically put on display at the Omaha Public Library.

Buoyed by their success with the handcar, the Indians spied a speeding freight train coming down the line. They deftly bent the rail, and when the locomotive struck the break it leaped into the air and left the track. The Cheyennes plundered the train's boxcars, and what they didn't want or couldn't carry they scattered across the prairie, but not before they killed and scalped the engineer, fireman, and brakeman and set the train ablaze.

In a letter to ethnologist George Bird Grinnell in 1914, George Bent, son of William Bent, the builder of Bent's Fort in what is now southeastern Colorado, and Owl Woman, the daughter of the Cheyenne arrow keeper who rode with the Cheyennes during this period of upheaval, wrote,

> The party of Cheyennes that wrecked (the) freight train on ... [the] Platte River in 1867 was mostly Northern Cheyennes. Spotted Wolf ... and Crazy Wolf were leaders of the wrecking party. They were both braves and not chiefs. There were seven in this party. The front part of the train was on fire, the whole train went off the track, so the Indians had no trouble to get out what they wanted.
>
> Just as they got their animals packed they seen smoke down the railroad track. Men told everybody to hurry off. The train stopped near the wrecked train and seen soldiers taken off their horses from the train. Old men and women drove off the pack animals fast as they could.
>
> They tell me Spotted Wolf's party left there at midnight, their horses all loaded with lots of stuff. All of them were walking and driving their loaded down horses. They traveled all night. After they got to their village, next morning men and women, [a] few boys went to plunder, then they camped there.[33]

The following April, as mentioned earlier, a small band of Sioux killed five workers near Elm Creek Station and made off with their animals. They then mounted an unsuccessful attempt to derail a train near Ogallala, but well-armed passengers and railroaders drove them off. As the railroad made its way through Nebraska and Wyoming at a rapid pace—a mile of track laid a day in the summer of 1867—supplies and military units, including artillery, gained greater access to the territory, forcing Indians farther and farther north and south from their traditional home.

A two-headed solution to the Indian issue by whites—the Peace Commission in the East and more aggressive behavior of the military in the West—left the Indians confused. Treaties between the US government and the Indians were violated frequently. The Peace Commission, established by Congress in 1867, believed that the Indians could be subdued and best served by being moved onto reservations, mainly in Oklahoma and the Dakota Territory, as the commissioners put it, "endeavoring to conquer by kindness."

At the same time, those living on the frontier had little patience with the tribes whose land they had overrun. To them, the obvious solution was extermination. The *Daily (Georgetown) Colorado Miner* editorialized:

> It is not necessary to sit down and discuss the Indian character. We all know how that is. Those who never saw him think he is a high-toned chivalrous character—loving his friends, hating his enemies, never doing a dishonorable action and in every way worthy of the highest respect.
>
> Those of us unfortunate western people, who have met the gentleman, don't believe anything about it. We know him to be a dirty, drunken, ignorant, lousy, treacherous, thieving scoundrel. Born a thief, he thinks it is high talent to lie, and to kill his enemy when asleep is his glory.[34]

There were other, even more pointed, voices. Secretary of the Interior James Harlan wrote to President Andrew Johnson:

> The attempted destruction of three hundred thousand of these people, accustomed to a nomadic life, subsisting upon the spontaneous productions of the earth, and familiar with the fastnesses of the mountains and the swamps of the plains, would involve an appalling sacrifice of the lives of our solders and frontier settlers, and the expenditure of untold treasure. All the military operations of last summer have not occasioned immediate destruction of more than a few hundred Indian warriors. Such a policy is manifestly as impracticable as it is in violation of every dictate of humanity and Christian duty.[35]

At least as dangerous to the Indians' survival as the ongoing encounters with the military was the whites' penchant for "saving" them by bringing them "civilization." Whites, especially women, saw the success of the Omahas as proof that Indians could be trained to farm, taught to be productive citizens, that "civilization is no fanciful theory, but, under proper care and influences, is within the grasp of all the Indians."[36] Religion, they believed, could elevate the Indians out of "savagery."

General John Pope, one of those whose job it was to keep the Indians and whites away from each other, reasoned in 1865, "The Indian, in truth, no longer has a country. He is reduced to starvation or to warring to the death. The Indian's first demand is that the white man will not drive off the game and dispossess him of his lands. How can we promise this unless we prohibit emigration and settlement? The end is sure and dreadful to contemplate."[37]

The coming of the railroads doomed the Indians' way of life. The rails severed the traditional migration paths of the buffalo and brought tens of thousands of settlers into the region, leading one Nebraska traveler to comment, "They are covering the territories like a swarm of locusts."[38] It led to the building of hundreds of settlements, and eventually, the rise of states that joined the Union from ocean to ocean, but there was no time or sentiment to consider the fate of the Indians, driven from their homes and ancestral lands onto reservations. Travel writer Bayard Taylor, who crossed the plains via stagecoach in 1867, predicted:

> No one of us will live to see the beauty and prosperity which these States, even in their rude, embryonic condition, already suggest. The American of today must find his enjoyment in anticipating the future. He must look beyond the unsightly beginnings of civilization and prefigure the state of things a century hence, when the Republic will count a population of two hundred millions and there shall be leisure for Taste and Art. We have now so much ground to occupy, and we make such haste to cover it, that our growth is— and must be—accompanied by very few durable landmarks. Not until the greater part of our vacant territory is taken up, and there is a broad belt of settlement reaching from ocean to ocean, will our Western people begin to take root, consolidate their enterprise, and truly develop their unparalleled inheritance.[39]

More bluntly, as Sherman told an assembly in Cheyenne, Wyoming Territory, in 1880, "We used to call this the West. You are no longer in the West, boys; you are in the middle."[40]

Chapter Five

"A GREAT PURPOSE"

Building the transcontinental railroad was the obvious step. Talk of a railroad to girdle the nation began in earnest in the 1830s, so it wasn't a new idea when talk of the Union Pacific and the Central Pacific teaming up to traverse the two thousand miles from the Missouri River to San Francisco—one of the original plans had it starting on the Mississippi—gained avid followers in the 1850s. It was improbable but no longer a wild pipe dream.

The expansion of the country's rail system had been nothing short of phenomenal. An average of 2,160 miles of new track was spun out annually in the 1850s, and by 1870 the eastern half of the nation was crisscrossed by almost fifty-three thousand miles of track. The population of the United States exploded from 12.8 million in 1830 to 31 million in 1860, most of it east of the Mississippi. Americans were looking for new lands to conquer and settle, and the wide-open spaces of the American West beckoned; the railroad and the steam locomotive were going to get them there because the future lay in the West and in technology.

Who first suggested the idea of a transcontinental railroad is open to debate. Rumblings of the idea stretch back to the mid-1800s, when the nation's first American-made steam locomotive, The Best Friend of Charleston, made its inaugural run from Charleston to Hamburg, South Carolina, at the astonishing speed of more than fifteen miles an hour, on Christmas Day in 1830. Two years earlier, William Redfield, a New England saddle and harness maker and a meteorologist, produced a pamphlet proposing a railway from New York City to the Mississippi and beyond. Redfield was an interesting fellow. Besides his careers as saddle maker and meteorologist, he devised a system wherein canal steamboats towed passenger barges at a distance to protect riders from boiler explosions. He took a deep interest in street railways in cities and was one of the first supporters of the Hartford and New Haven Railroad. He also received an honorary degree from Yale and was a member of the Association of American Naturalists and Geologists.

Surely one of the first public advocates of a transcontinental railway was Samuel Dexter, editor of the *Western Emigrant* in Ann Arbor, Michigan, who wrote in his newspaper on February 6, 1832:

> It is in our power ... to open an immense interior country to market, to unite our Eastern and Western shores firmly together, to embrace the whole of the fur trade, to pour those furs into India and in return enrich our interior with the spices and silks and muslins, and teas and coffee and sugar of that country. It is in our power to build up an immense city at the mouth of the [Columbia], to make it the depot for our East India trade and perhaps for that of Europe—in fact to unite New York and Oregon by a railway by which the traveler leaving the city of New York shall, at the moderate rate of ten miles an hour, place himself in a port right on the shores of the Pacific. It is one of those great projects which none but a great nation could effect—but peculiarly adapted to the enterprising character of the people of the United States.[1]

One of the most active proponents of the transcontinental in the 1840s was merchant Asa Whitney, who saw the possibilities, and profit, in moving goods and people long distances by rail. He called getting it built his "great purpose." After going bust in the Panic of 1837, he traveled to the Orient and saw the trade possibilities there. His idea was that a transcontinental railroad would more closely link the United States with the markets in Asia, so he roamed the country, spending his own dollars to carry on a one-man campaign for the road. Running out of money and frustrated that he couldn't get lawmakers to consider his idea after five years of campaigning, in 1849 he published a brochure for general distribution that outlined his scheme. It was a thorough document pinpointing the reasons the road should be built, possible routes, and the coming gold rush to California. It did not discuss Whitney's early plan that he be allowed to sell land on either side of the route in exchange for helping get it built. Rejected repeatedly by Congress in his efforts, Whitney finally gave up, married a wealthy widow, and lived out his life as a gentleman farmer in Maryland. Fifteen years later, his name was virtually unknown among rail advocates; no railroad even bothered to name a station stop for him.

In the 1850s, support grew to almost universal proportions. The question was, where should the route run? Regional wrangling pitted the North against the South. Trying to settle the issue, the government sent teams of surveyors west between 1852 and 1854. Its findings, "Reports of Explorations and Surveys to Ascertain the Most Practicable and Economical Route for a Railroad from the Mississippi River to the Pacific Ocean," a title almost as long as the eventual railroad, pinpointed five possible routes: a northern route along the 47th and 49th parallels, where the Northern Pacific and Great Northern Railways eventually were built; a central route between the 41st and 42nd parallels through Nebraska and Wyoming, the route chosen; a middle route between the 38th and 39th parallels through Kansas; and a southern route near the 32nd parallel, later followed by the Southern Pacific.

Many argued, based primarily on weather, that the most southern route was the best, but when the southern states bolted the Union they gave up any chance of getting the line.

Some, like New York newspaper editor Horace Greeley, an avid booster of the West, didn't have a favored route but wanted to see a transcontinental railroad built. A bit of a romantic but also a hardheaded businessman, Greeley looked at the numbers, which, he said, showed that 381,107 passengers traveled by ship to San Francisco between 1849 and 1857. In 1859, he calculated, thirty thousand emigrants crossed the prairies. "I estimate that twice to thrice the number who actually did go to California would have gone, had there been [a railroad], and that the present Anglo-American population of the Pacific slope would have been a little less than two million."[2]

In 1860, Fred W. Lander, one of those hired by the government to survey possible routes, stated his preference in a letter to Congressman Reuben Fenton, a member of the select committee studying the Pacific Railroad. He was all for it. "I have but one view upon the subject, and that is guided by the simplest, the strictest possible construction of the Constitution of the country—a construction by which we can alone remain a prosperous, a united and a happy country."[3] Lander, for whom the Wyoming town is named, favored what was known as the central route, across the Platte Valley. "The country is a flat, gravel plain. It unites the traffic of numerous sections, and will soon become a self-sustaining road."[4] This recommendation must have pleased Fenton, who represented Iowa, a vital link between the East and Omaha, the eventual jumping-off place. Unfortunately, Fenton, forty, died of pneumonia on March 2, 1862, while serving in the Union army, a year and half before the construction on the Pacific Railroad got under way.

Greeley saw the country with his own eyes when he made his famous trek across the continent and wrote about it in *An Overland Journey*. He came back convinced that the nation needed a transcontinental road. "Is there a national need for a railroad from the Missouri to the Pacific?" he asked rhetorically. Everybody, he believed, would profit. "Everything that can be eaten or drunk is selling in the Kansas mines [actually Pikes Peak in the extreme western edge of the Kansas Territory, a "gold rush" that fizzled] at far more than California prices. A railroad ... would reduce ... the average cost of food at least half."[5]

There were many reasons advanced to get the railroad built. Politicians were concerned that people in far-off California and Oregon, places farther from New York City than England, might get it into their heads to form their own countries; the railroad would bind the huge distances into one nation.

Denver, one of the largest cities between the Missouri and the West Coast, was nowhere in the discussion about routes and construction schedules. Early on, the Union Pacific management looked at passing through Denver but, unable to find a suitable route through the Rockies, opted for Cheyenne in Dakota Territory. Community leaders in Denver were devastated. William Byers, a cheerleader for the burgeoning Colorado city and owner of the town's *Rocky Mountain News*, used his newspaper's columns to advocate for his city to be included on the transcontinental route. In 1859, he wrote on page one of his paper:

> The road must pass through the South Platte gold fields and this, our consolidated city at the eastern foot of the Rocky Mountains, will be a point which cannot be dodged. The route ... may continue from here directly westward, entering the mountains by the Platte Canon, following up the stream to the junction of the North and South Forks, thence up the North Fork to South Park. This route we consider entirely practicable, presenting less obstacles—if we except the first fifteen miles after entering the Platte Canon, and even there they are not at all insurmountable.[6]

And then he told a little white lie: "For hundreds of mile through the mountain region on the route indicated, the profile of the country is fully described when we say *hilly*."[7]

The railroad wasn't buying it. Its surveyors and engineers discarded any such routes through the Rockies and opted instead to head straight west out of Cheyenne over Lone Tree Pass (also known as Evans Pass and Sherman Pass and, later, as Sherman Hill) and into Utah and the ultimate meeting with the Central Pacific at Promontory Summit.

Businessmen saw the country's financial future in the Far East, where vast markets, they thought, awaited American goods. It turned out that the growth was not in foreign trade but in filling the western expanses with farms, towns, and, eventually, cities whose goods and services would be spread at a hefty profit by the railroad. Everyone would benefit, said Greeley. "The first need of California today is a large influx of intelligent, capable, virtuous women. With a railroad to the Pacific, avoiding the miseries and perils of 6,000 miles of ocean transportation, and making the transit a pleasant and interesting overland journey of ten days, at a reduced cost, the migration of this class would be immensely accelerated and increased."[8] To the government's advantage, he noted, the road could move large numbers of military troops at a reduced cost and cut the delivery time of mail from months to a few days.

At the time, there were two ways of getting to California or Oregon: by trudging two thousand miles across a desolate and hostile territory between the Missouri River and the coast or by sailing via Panama (seven thousand miles) or around Cape Horn (fifteen thousand miles). The latter voyage took almost five months to complete.

The railroad and its steam locomotive captured the public's fancy. "The day of mere visionaries had passed," wrote Maury Klein in his massive three-volume history of the Union Pacific. "To breathe life into the project, promoters were needed, tough, practical, persistent men capable of lobbying for what they required, organizing a vast enterprise, and pushing it in the face of every obstacle."[9]

Those "persistent men" appeared in the forms of two very different visionaries: Grenville M. Dodge and Dr. Thomas C. Durant. Dodge was in it for the adventure; Durant was in it for the money.

Durant lived to make money. Born in 1820 in Massachusetts, he obtained a medical degree from Albany Medical College but never practiced medicine, though he kept the "doctor" title throughout his life. He was a master manipulator. He founded the Mississippi and Missouri Railroad and convinced towns along its projected route across Iowa to vote bonds to build it, then went to work for another railroad, cashed the M&M bonds, and began the process all over again, which ultimately led him to the Union Pacific.

His interests came first; everything else was secondary. He engendered no love among his associates. One went so far as to brand him

Thomas C. Durant

incompetent to lead such a massive undertaking as the Union Pacific. He bombarded employees with memos, demanding that they work longer, harder, and cheaper. As the last word on everything that went on with the railroad, he could be capricious and contradictory.

For all his personal faults, and they were plentiful, Durant had an eye for hiring competent people. He brought in the Casement brothers, Dan and Jack, to run the track-laying operation; hired Samuel B. Reed to oversee procurement and disbursement of supplies; saw Peter Dey's genius as a surveyor (until Dey got fed up and quit); and, most important, had the good sense to hire Grenville M. Dodge.

Dodge was only twenty-two when he was hired as a railroad surveyor and engineer in 1853 under the tutelage of Peter Dey. He set off from the Missouri River and what was to become Omaha, Nebraska, to look for the quickest, least expensive route across the plains. "No other man would be more important to or more closely identified with the history of the Union Pacific than Grenville M. Dodge," Klein raved. "He would influence its destiny from the first survey to its reorganization thirty years later."[10]

Dodge is alleged to have met with lawyer Abraham Lincoln, a stout believer in rail travel, in Council Bluffs, Iowa, in 1859, when Lincoln was visiting there on business. Some historians doubt Dodge's account in his memoirs of that meeting, in which Lincoln is said to have probed him for details on where he thought the transcontinental route should go. Dodge, who would have been twenty-eight years old at the time, said he laid out his plan for the Platte Valley to the future president.

Born in Massachusetts in 1831, Dodge, who loved the outdoor life, left Dey's surveying party to explore on his own twenty-five miles up the Platte River Valley, in what ultimately became the transcontinental route. Ever farsighted, Dodge bought land on the Elkhorn River, a tributary of the Platte, a move that would solidify his belief that the tracks should run through his property.

In 1861, he walked away from Durant's employ to serve with the North when the Civil War broke out. He became friends with Generals William T. Sherman, Phil Sheridan, and Ulysses S. Grant, associations that would serve him well later. Near war's end, Dodge was made commander of the army's Department of the Missouri, which covered a large chunk of the West, and set about doing what he thought needed to be done: ridding the potential rail route of Indians. In 1865, Cheyennes and Arapahos wreaked havoc with supply lines. Dodge, who spent five years in the territory as a young man, a time that included a thrilling

Grenville M. Dodge

encounter with Indians intent on stealing his horse, believed that there could be no railroad while the Indians were threatening the lives of workers laboring on it. He was a "savage exponent of search-and-destroy tactics against the Indians."[11]

Durant lured him back to work on the UP in May 1866. He was, wrote historian Keith Wheeler, "the ideal man for the assignment. He already knew [the route] like the back of his hand. Dodge, the engineer, wanted to construct the shortest, cheapest line possible; the financiers, it sometimes seemed, were intent on mapping out the longest line possible in order to qualify for increased government loans that were based on total track mileage laid."[12]

In this, and a lot of other ways, Dodge was a polar opposite to Durant; he inspired loyalty in his employees and worked tirelessly. If he had a flaw, it was a total lack of a sense of humor; he was all business. Among his many puzzling decisions, Durant hired Silas Seymour as "consulting engineer," less an engineer than a spy to keep an eye on Dodge. Seymour, forty-eight, was a government engineer in the Interior Department who had some experience with railroading. After he went to work for the Union Pacific (he lobbied furiously for the job), his main contribution was second-guessing the work of others and reporting back to Durant.

Dodge was beloved. Seymour was derided as a meddler. "Colonel Seymour, the consulting engineer of the road is here," young surveyor Samuel Chittenden wrote from Echo Canyon, Utah, in 1868. "He is a regular old 'granny' and we may be switching around here for some time yet."[13]

Seymour's sharp tongue earned him the enmity of others in the company and the sobriquet "Insulting Engineer," but he was a man to be reckoned with because he had Durant's ear and happily fulfilled his assigned chore of keeping an eye on Dodge. Nevertheless, Dodge maintained his position and the respect of Durant for the work he did.

It was Seymour who, after work began on the initial route out of Omaha, suggested a newer, longer—albeit flatter—path that became known as the Oxbow, which added nine miles and additional construction costs because not only did new work have to be done but work on the previous line had to be dismantled. The idea appealed to Durant because it added $144,000 and another 115,200 acres of land to the Union Pacific's coffers. Furious, Dey quit the company in December 1864, citing "the undigested views of Mr. Seymour." Some forty-five years later, Dey's original line became the new route.

When he arrived in Omaha in the spring of 1866, Dodge found a company in disarray. No one could agree on which route was the best, either in terms of time or money. He demanded of Durant that he be given total control over the building operation, a demand that was agreed to but was violated frequently. He always had Seymour at his back.

The basic problem was money: the railroad and Durant were living on credit. Certainly no private entrepreneur could afford or was willing to take a risk on a project that was expected to cost $100 million and forge a path across sparsely populated land as foreign to eastern investors as Mars. "The men of business did not believe the scheme was practicable," wrote Grace Raymond Hebard. "An investor had no money to invest in two thousand miles of railway, declaring that the Indians would tear up the track and make bonfires of the flag stations along the line. In all the six hundred fifty miles between Reno, Nevada, and Corinne, Utah, there was only one white man living. How could a railroad pay across such deserts?"[14] Even if the transcontinental proved successful (and there was no guarantee that it would), return on investment would be years in the future. The immediate return would have to be in building, not operating.

Government aid was an obvious necessity. The Pacific Railway Act of 1862, designed to encourage investors, was a huge boost. Robert E. Riegel enumerated the government largesse:

> The aid granted to [the Union Pacific and Central Pacific] was extremely generous. Each was to receive five odd sections of land on each side and within ten miles of the road, and also the right to use necessary building materials from the public domain. In addition, a government loan was provided on the basis of a mortgage on the railroads. It was to be for $16,000 a mile over the greatest part of the route, $48,000 in the Rockies and Sierras, and $32,000 in the region between the two ranges.[15]

The reaction among potential investors was practically nil, so in 1864 the act was amended (with behind-the-scenes manipulation by Durant) to sweeten the pot. The new act allowed the UP to issue first mortgage bonds, making the government's bonds a second mortgage. It also allowed bonds to be issued every twenty miles instead of every forty. And the land grant provision was doubled to 12,800 acres per mile and included rights to coal and iron on the land.

American schools have taught for years about the corruption of Crédit Mobilier, and there was plenty of corruption to learn about. But the reality is it is unlikely the transcontinental railroad could have been built without the government's financial backing. The simple yet ingenious scheme that raised millions of dollars for the railroad and for its principals and their friends sprang from the head of Durant.

Riegel outlined how Crédit Mobilier worked:

> Durant evolved a brilliant solution which would not only provide for the raising of the necessary capital but would also allow the insiders to make their fortunes. Joining with his friends in the Union Pacific he bought a Pennsylvania corporation called the Crédit Mobilier of America, which was particularly available because of the leniency of its charter provisions. The plan was then simple—at least after it was put into operation. Members of the Crédit Mobilier, who also controlled the Union Pacific, voted construction contracts to dummies who transferred them to the Crédit Mobilier. Construction contracts were paid by the Union Pacific in cash [actually by check], which was immediately returned to the railroad for its stock and bonds at par. The Crédit Mobilier then sold the stocks and bonds on the open market for whatever they would bring. The final receipts from these sales were the only real money that appeared in the transaction.[16]

In other words, members of the Union Pacific board would let construction contracts to the Crédit Mobilier, which they also controlled, make money off the building of the road, then use the cash to buy low-cost UP stocks and bonds and sell them at a higher rate. It was brilliant.

Of course, there were abuses. American business interests operated almost without controls in the late nineteenth century, and the Union Pacific was no exception. Klein pointed out, "For Crédit Mobilier to succeed, there had to be a generous spread between the contract price and the actual costs of construction. Part of the difference was of course profit to the contractors for the work, but that was only the beginning."[17] Further, he explained, bookkeeping included mysterious charges, for promotion, lobbying and legal fees, office overhead expense, travel and other expenses, and advertising. Congressmen were gifted with stocks and bonds for their votes on key issues. It was a system tailor made for abuse. The scheme later exploded into a full-blown Washington scandal. Careers and lives were ruined. In the long run, the government made a good return on its loans, giving the railroads $64.6 million and receiving $168 million in principal and interest.

John "Jack" S. Casement

It was left to Dodge and the Casement boys to keep the railroad rolling forward. Despite the financial sleight of hand and the squabbling among the principals, a ceremonial groundbreaking for the launching of the Union Pacific trackage was staged in Omaha on December 2, 1863, but because the railroad was woefully underfunded, the first rail wasn't put down until July 10, 1865. With high hopes and a sunny outlook, Durant predicted that the first hundred miles, required by the government under the Pacific Railway Act of 1862 to be completed by June 1866, would be done by the end of the year. It wasn't even close. By October 1865, only fifteen miles of track were in place, twenty-eight miles in November, and by the end of the year backers saw only forty miles laid.

Despite years of optimistic predictions and the investment of thousands of dollars, it appeared Major General Sherman's gloomy forecast, made during a visit to the nascent railroad in October 1865, might be depressingly correct. "This is a great enterprise," he said to start an excursion of influential political and newspaper figures to the end of track, only fifteen miles distant. "But I hardly expect to live to see it completed."[18]

Chapter Six

"THE GRANDEST ENTERPRISE UNDER GOD"

It was an ill-timed launch for what one admirer anointed "the grandest enterprise under God." There was a Civil War on. The builder was short of cash and laborers. Management was in turmoil. And yet, launch it did. By the time the Pacific Railroad was finished it would require more than five years to build, involve thousands of laborers, cost hundreds of lives, and forever change the political and cultural face of America.

Another miracle of the age, the telegraph, preceded the railroad across the prairie by almost a decade. In 1860, Congress authorized the building of a telegraph line from Missouri to San Francisco. Expected to cost $40,000 a year and be completed in ten years, it was in operation to Omaha by that September and carried news of Abraham Lincoln's election as president to Fort Kearny. Crews quickly strung wire through Nebraska and Wyoming, and down to Salt Lake City, where the Western Union linked up early in 1869 with the Pacific Telegraph Company, working its way east. But the telegraph could transmit only information; the railroad moved people and freight.

The telegraph line followed the route of the Union Pacific Railroad, which lacked leaders who fully understood the task before them—not necessarily, it turned out, a bad thing.

On December 2, 1863, a blustery day in Omaha, Nebraska, one thousand of the populace of the nascent Missouri River town turned out for an elaborate 2:00 PM groundbreaking ceremony accompanied by bells, whistles, mortar fire, fireworks, and so many long-winded speeches that most of the crowd went home before the festivities ended. No one even bothered to record who spiked the first rail. So effusive were the many speakers at the groundbreaking that the dignitaries' post-ceremonial banquet at Herndon House, the city's finest hotel, didn't begin until 1:30 AM.

The principal speaker of the day was a peculiar promoter named George Francis Train, a man of endless schemes, a believer in psychic telepathy, and possessor of a wild mane of curly hair and an apparently marathon pair of lungs. He never tired of hearing his own oratory. Train was a man, said celebrated travel writer Albert Richardson, known among his friends for his own peculiarities, "curiously combining keen sagacity with wild enthusiasm, a man who might have built the pyramids, or been confined in a straight jacket for eccentricities. He drinks no spirits, uses no tobacco, talks on the stump like an embodied Niagara, composes songs to order by the hour ... is intensely earnest, and has the most absolute and outspoken faith in himself and his future."[1]

Always the enthusiast, Train, thirty-four years old and clad in a dazzling all-white suit that day, let loose a verbal barrage that would stir any patriot's soul. "This is the grandest enterprise under God!" he thundered. "Man has made this great line of railway to run east and west; but God, thinking man might blunder, was his own topographical engineer and took the precaution to build the mountains and the rivers north and south, and what God has put together, let no ambitious plebian in the North or rebel traitor in the South dare to tear asunder!"[2] Those gathered by the river roared their approval. The crowd loved him, but when he predicted during his speech that the Pacific Railroad would be finished before 1870, they broke into derisive laughter.[3] Train was so sure of the success of the endeavor that he bought five hundred acres of Omaha (albeit at rock-bottom prices) from where the railroad would set off on its westward journey. One of the original shareholders in the Union Pacific, Train was the most colorful of an array of colorful characters involved in the company. He was a key figure in the establishment of the Crédit Mobilier, the construction company set up to reap benefits from the building of the railroad. He ran, unsuccessfully, for president as an independent against Ulysses S. Grant in 1872.

In his 1902 autobiography—dictated, not written—he made full use of his oratorical skills:

Many persons attribute to me simply an impulsiveness, and an impressibility, as if I were some erratic comet, rushing madly through space, emitting coruscations of fancifully colored sparks, without system, rule, or definite object. This is a popular error. I claim to be a close analytical observer of passing events, applying

Eccentric stock promoter George F. Train was the most colorful character among many colorful characters involved in building the Union Pacific. He was brash, self-confident, and, said one observer, "talks on the stump like an embodied Niagara."

the crucible of Truth to every new matter or subject presented to my mind or my senses.[4]

It was signed "Citizen George Francis Train," an affectation he took on late in life. He also refused to shake hands with people, preferring to shake his own hand in the manner of Far Eastern potentates.

In November 1872, Train found out that the women's rights advocates Victoria C. Woodhull and her sister, Tennie C. Claflin, publishers of their own newspaper, had been arrested for printing "obscenity" over an account of clergyman Henry Ward Beecher's adulterous affair. "I immediately said, 'This may be libel but it is not obscenity.'" As a defense, Train published passages from the Bible "worse than anything published by these women."[5]

He, too, was arrested, but the court chose to declare him a lunatic, although he was never admitted to an asylum. Always odd, Train became a recluse and lived out his remaining years at the Mills Hotel in New York City, talking only with children and animals before his death on January 4, 1904, after he contracted smallpox.

After Train's stirring oration at the groundbreaking ceremony, what happened next was unexpected—nothing. Plagued by a shortage of funds (the backers barely scraped up enough cash to pay for the cost of the groundbreaking gala) and of rails and ties, the project went into a semi-slumber.

By December 1864, a year after the public hoopla at Omaha, a work crew led by Peter Dey had graded only twenty-three miles west from Omaha. And it cost the company $100,000. Not a single rail had been laid; internal strife was eating away at efforts to get building. Dey, who spent five years scouting the Platte Valley and knew the territory better than anyone, laid out what he thought was the most direct and cheapest route. Others in the company, looking at government cash for number of miles laid, preferred a more meandering course. Eventually Dey, a man of high principles, got fed up and quit.

Things were in such disarray that the first track wasn't laid until July 10, 1865, a mere three months after the end of the Civil War. Only a mile and half was in place by August, and by November of that year twenty-eight miles of track were down, although one hundred miles were graded.

Enter the Casement brothers.

The hiring of Jack Casement and his brother, Dan, changed everything. The boys ran their own company, J. S. and D. T. Casement, and were hired to oversee construction in February 1866, just before the legendary Major General Grenville M. Dodge joined the company as head engineer. Jack, who served as an officer for the Union during the Civil War, brought military discipline and tactics to the chore; "the best organized, best equipped, and the best disciplined track force I have ever seen," raved Dodge.[6] As bookkeeper and supply manager, Dan kept the ties, rail, and other supplies coming on a more regular basis.

The diminutive brothers—Jack was just five feet four and Dan "five feet nothing"—breathed life into the track-laying process, which had been painfully slow during the first year of construction. Their stroke of genius was the creation of work trains that both speeded up the work and gave their workers, mostly Civil War veterans, more comfortable lodging and better food. It was a compact city on wheels.

E. C. Lockwood, the Casements' brother-in-law and a paymaster for the UP, traveled with them on an 1866 excursion to the end of track. In a reminiscence written in 1931, he recalled,

> When we reached there, I was surprised to find a train of boarding cars all ready for us. They had been built under the supervision of Dan Casement the previous year. There were four of them, each 85 feet long. One whole car and half of another were used for dining cars, with the office and kitchen in the end of one of them. The remaining half car and the other two were bunk cars. Across the ceilings in racks were about 1,000 U.S. rifles, to be used in case of attack by Indians.[7]

There were boxcars for supplies, a butcher's car (a herd of cattle followed the construction train to supply fresh beef), flatcars for rails and ties, and a bakery car. A large tent was set up trackside to feed the crews at long tables and benches. "Tin plates were securely nailed to the tables," wrote Oscar Osburn Winther. "After one group of men had eaten and departed an attendant with a pail of water and a mop 'swabbed out' each plate in rapid succession and thus prepared the tables for the next round of eaters. 'If we don't nail 'em down they'll pile one plate on another and take up too much room. This way we kin crowd 'em in,' said the man with mop."[8]

The support crew included two conductors, two engineers, two foremen, a wagon master, a financial manager, a storekeeper, a physician and surgeon, a chief steward and sixteen assistants, a telegraph operator, a draughtsman, and a civil engineer and seven assistants.[9]

Graders, work gangs made up largely of rugged Irish-Americans who labored to clear the way for track-laying crews coming on a hundred miles behind them, take a meal break at their usual table, the ground.

COURTESY UNIVERSITY OF WYOMING, AMERICAN HERITAGE CENTER, 160364

Despite the "comforts" of bunks and ample meals (bacon, ham, beans, and fresh-baked bread were staples), it was not an easy life. At its peak, the railroad employed ten thousand men, including surveyors, graders, tracklayers, supervisors, teamsters, and support crews. Though it has come down that most of the men were Irish, that's only partly true. The largest portion was Civil War veterans, many of them former Southern soldiers. But there were also Swedes, Danes, and Finns recruited out of Chicago, and hundreds of African Americans, who worked as mule whackers and graders. All were up at 5:30 AM, fed and on the job by 6:30 AM, and worked until nightfall six days a week, more when the Casements pushed their daily production from one mile a day to as much as five miles a day. All this for $3 a day and all they could eat.

In withering summer heat while the men toiled across Nebraska and Wyoming, the bunk cars grew unbearably hot, forcing workers to build makeshift tents and sleep on the ground trackside or atop the cars, where there was a chance of catching a cooling breeze. It wasn't just the stifling heat that drove some to sleep outside the cars. "To tell the truth, we were troubled by 'cooties,'" remembered Lockwood. "A companion and myself escaped them by making our bed between skylights on the roof."[10]

The work could be exceedingly dangerous. Because there were no air brakes, car men worked atop the cars to apply brakes by hand. Scurrying over the freight cars in icy conditions was no picnic. "All couplings were made by hand," recalled W. L. Park, a superintendent for the UP. "Wrecks were frequent. Cattle frequently got onto the bridges as there were no fences; washouts swept away the frail bridges; there were many 'break-in-twos'; occasionally there was misunderstanding of orders which resulted in collisions."[11]

Samuel Chittenden, a graduate of Yale and a member of one of the railroad's surveying parties, which worked far in front of the construction crews, gave an intimate peek into the daily lives of the men working on the line. "Things are pretty rough and to be comfortable is about all one can expect," he wrote home in March of 1868, adding, "It is a rough and dirty life but no worse than I expected."[12] He looked on the bright side: "My woolen drawers have lasted just long enough," he cheerily wrote in May. "They are completely worn out and I have just put on the cotton ones. I have enough of them to last all summer. My stockings held out bravely. I have not one with a sign of a hole in it, my shirts are in the same condition."[13]

He and the other men toughened up. "To show you how tough I am getting I will tell an incident," Chittenden wrote. "We got into camp late night before last, ate our supper, rolled down our bed, went to bed and slept till morning. When we rolled it up we found a *pickaxe* under it. We had slept all night without finding it out."[14]

The following month he wrote to his mother, "No one in the East can imagine the amount of whiskey that is drank in this country. Every ranch and farm house along the road always have a keg of whiskey and all the natives think it necessary to take four or five drinks a day of the vile stuff."[15]

Nothing happened without the surveyors, rugged and adventurous men who worked out in the wilderness hundreds of miles ahead of the graders; it was their job to lay out the line, the course the graders and tracklayers were to follow. Rivers, ravines, and steep grades were taken into consideration. They did their work in the wildest of settings, much of it previously untrod by white men. Dodge, who replaced Dey as chief engineer, recalled, "Each of our surveying parties consisted of a chief, who was an experienced engineer, two assistants, also civil engineers, rodmen, flagmen, and chainmen, generally graduated civil engineers but without personal experience in the field, besides axmen, teamsters, and herders. Each party would thus consist of from eighteen to twenty-two men, all armed. Each party entering a country occupied by hostile Indians was generally furnished with a military escort."[16]

Not only did they have to deal with capricious weather—broiling in the summer, freezing in the winter—but they were constantly under the threat of attack by hostile Indians, mainly Cheyennes, Sioux, and Arapahos. Almost from the day the surveying crews set out from Omaha in 1864, attacks and the threat of attacks were a constant source of concern. Because of their isolation, surveyors were the most vulnerable of the crews. "The Indians are everywhere," Sherman wrote during a trip along the line. The military commanders had only seven or eight companies of infantry to watch over three hundred miles of track work. Percy Browne and his surveying crew were 150 miles west of Fort Sanders in Wyoming, searching for an acceptable course for the rail builders coming up behind them, when suddenly a band of perhaps three hundred Sioux overtook the party in a typical attack—"from every sandhill and ravine the hawks of the desert swoop down with unrivaled impetuosity," wrote one observer—near Bitter Creek. Browne, his men, and a few soldiers took cover on high ground but were overwhelmed. Browne took a bullet to the abdomen and told his men to leave him behind since he was sure he was going to die. They stayed with him and the Indians gave up the attack. He later died.

There are dozens of other stories about crews set upon, killed, and scalped. Surveyor Arthur Ferguson recounted in his diary that his party was roused early one morning by cries of "Here they come, here they come, boys!" Ferguson and his compatriots, many clad only in their underwear, opened fire on what he called "the most daring Indians that I ever saw or heard of." One galloped into camp amid a storm of bullets and made off with the company's horses but was shot and killed as he rode away.[17]

Since the days of emigration by whites, the plains tribes were being squeezed off their homelands, and it only grew worse with the discovery of mineral riches in California, Colorado, Nevada, and Montana. The Indians recognized that the coming of the rails meant more white invaders and an even more restricted lifestyle. They became more hostile and the attacks on the railroad more frequent as the Union Pacific rails moved westward through Nebraska and Wyoming.

The Indians' general method was to hit and run in small bands before the US military forces, thinly spread through forts in the West, could respond. The attacks usually took place on isolated homesteads or on work crews laboring alone with minimal support from the army. It was livestock, not lives, that usually were taken. Bridges and way stations were burned. A successful derailment of one of the UP's trains was carried out at Plum Creek in central Nebraska in 1867; woodcutters in the Laramie Mountains were assaulted for their stock; two members of a Mormon wagon train were killed when attacked by Cheyennes; young C. H. Sharman was working as a civil engineer in western Nebraska in 1867 when he and his companions were set upon. "A band of Cheyennes swooped down on us and captured about seventy head of stock, mules and horses, in spite of the soldiers who were supposed to protect us."[18]

Rumors of Indian depredations and murders of railroad workers and settlers, spread by newspapers in the East, fueled doubt about the project; reports of attacks were often grander than the actual attacks. At North Platte, armed workmen, who rounded up women and children and stashed them in the partially completed roundhouse, repulsed an assault on railroad workshops. Indians circled for a time, then withdrew without shots being exchanged. H. Clark Brown, working as a carpenter for the railroad from North Platte to Omaha, recalled years later, "We suddenly sighted what we thought were Indians. With guns in hand we dropped to the side of the car and waited for developments. After a short time we discovered the 'Indians' were stumps of trees."[19]

Management grew more and more frustrated. "We've got to clean the damn Indians out or give up building the Union Pacific Railroad," complained Dodge. Sherman, whose job it was to supply troops to protect the line, declared, "The more we can kill this year the less will have to be killed the next year, for the more I see of these Indians, the more convinced I am that they all have to be killed or be maintained as a species of paupers."[20]

As persistent as Indian raids seemed to be, especially in the summer of 1867, the workers' own carelessness was ever present. Some drowned after toppling from incomplete bridges. There were snakes, illnesses, and on-the-job injuries and deaths among the track-laying crews. Not to mention their own foolishness. Ferguson, whose carefully kept diaries are a frequent source for railroad historians, logged at least a half dozen shootings: "A sad accident occurred at Hall's grading camp before dinner, which was [the] accidental shooting of a man through the body"; "Two men were shot this evening in a drunken row"; "another man shot this evening. All well."

He feared for his well-being. On August 3, 1868, his diary entry read,

> While sitting in one of our tents a few days ago, a bullet entered the canvas, making quite a hole through it, and struck near my side and within about one foot or 14 inches of me. It was quite a narrow escape from receiving an ugly wound. About a day or so previous to this, while I sat at the table eating, quite a number of bullets whistled over my head and within rather close proximity to my person. I rushed out of the tent, and Mr. Upham, who stood nearby, informed me that the last shot struck in the ground between the two tents. It is no unusual thing to hear bullets nearby and at times overhead whistling with their shrill, demoniac sound—yelling like real demons. It is all owing to the carelessness of individuals in our vicinity whose reckless disregard of life and limb in their promiscuous shooting [is] perfectly outrageous and alarming.[21]

Such difficulties aside, the men were making progress, and Durant loved to show off the work that had been completed. He ordered underlings to lead numerous excursions by rail to the end of track. They served multiple purposes: wooing potential investors, gaining approval from government inspection teams, and getting reams of free publicity from newspaper reporters. The last wrote breathless accounts of the building and the vast land it was passing through, encouraging support from a skeptical public.

The excursions were a hassle for railroad managers. Every few months, it seemed to those who had to shepherd politicians, potential

Union Pacific vice president Thomas C. Durant posed heroically along the line of the Pacific Railroad, which disappears to the horizon on the flat plains of Nebraska, in 1866. The rough-hewn ties illustrate how haphazardly the line was set out.

JAMES L. EHERNBERGER COLLECTION

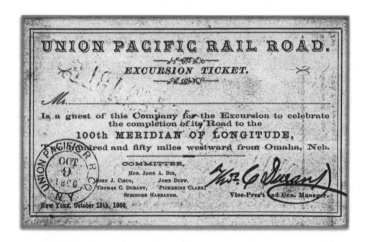

The Union Pacific ran frequent excursions to the end-of-track for publicity and for raising monies from wealthy individuals. This ticket for the October 1866 trip, complete with plenty of champagne, was signed by Thomas C. Durant himself.

JAMES L. EHERNBERGER COLLECTION

investors, and newspaper correspondents to the end of track, Durant authorized an excursion that featured the railroad's best passenger equipment, sumptuous meals, plenty of refreshments, and demonstrations by work crews of the speedy laying of track.

The Grand Excursion in October 1866 was made up of more than one hundred guests, including railroad directors, UP engineers Grenville Dodge and Silas Seymour, government commissioners, politicians, and representatives from fifteen newspapers, many of them from large East Coast cities. Among the more notable guests were Congressman Rutherford B. Hayes of Ohio (misidentified on the passenger manifest as "R. B. Hays"), who would become president ten years later; the secretary of the French legation at Washington; Abraham Lincoln's son Robert; and Scotland's Earl of Airlie. They even brought along an official photographer, John Carbutt. There was plenty of money on board. An unnamed correspondent reported, "The capital represented by a limited number of individuals on board amounts to over $50 million." The trip out to the 100th meridian, near today's Cozad, Nebraska, aboard a special train that included three Pullman sleepers and a "sumptuous director's car" began with a bountiful dinner for the guests at the Hoxie House in Omaha with roast beef, mutton, lamb, brazen ox, antelope, tongue, macaroni, sardine salad, and four kinds of pies (strawberry, damson, peach, and cherry) for dessert.

En route, the train, which, reported one amazed rider, "smoothly made its thirty miles an hour," stopped near Columbus, Nebraska, for a campout. The 155 passengers weren't exactly roughing it. Tents were set up, and mattresses brought by train from Omaha were laid atop beds of straw. Elaborate meals were served in a large tent. The excursionists were treated to a dance performance by Pawnee Indians hired by Durant for the occasion (they negotiated a $100 fee for their efforts) and a middle-of-the-night mock Indian attack that terrified the company, particularly the women in the party.

As a finale, before the trekkers got back to Omaha, Durant had his men set fire to the prairie, lighting the pitch-black night along a twenty-mile front.

A similar railroad-sponsored outing a year later was less successful. A trainload of senators and other guests had ventured 360 miles west of Omaha in June 1867 when the camping party was pounded by a sudden and intense thunderstorm. A *New York Times* reporter wrote, "The romance of camping out had by this time lost its charms for such of the ladies as had not been entirely overcome by the fatigues and excitement of the day, and quite a number of them were willing to brave rain, mud, and rattlesnakes for the sake of again finding the shelter of the sleeping cars."[22]

Such outings were disruptive for the men trying to meet the company's tight schedule of a mile or more of track laid a day. After one such Durant-ordered outing for professors from Yale and eastern journalists, all of whom had a splendid time, Webster Snyder, the UP's general superintendent for operations, complained to management that the visitors "have interfered with our work very much and have worn me out."[23]

The man who ran many of the outings was Luther Bent, who carried his head at a peculiar angle from a wound he had received while serving as a major in the Union army. He was, remembered fellow UP man A. P. Wood, "intelligent and a fine talker [with] an affable manner and a good joker. He knew how to arrange for the comforts of his guests, and handled the *very necessary* liquid refreshments with such skill and care that he knew at all times where he was and what he was doing, while some of the guests did not know either."[24]

On a trip to end of track in 1865, a reporter for the *Omaha Weekly Herald* wrote that the excursion included an extremely interesting speech given to the travelers by General William T. Sherman, but he failed to record most of it because "the frequency with which the wine bottle had come around had somewhat numbed his reportorial facilities."[25]

Newspapermen and other visitors frequently expressed their surprise at the beauty and fertile nature of the landscape they saw along the route. Almost all commented on the dizzying pace of the laying of track by the Casements' crews, conducted at a walking pace and carried on with military precision. One mile of track required forty cars carrying ties, fastenings, rails, fuel, and supplies for crews and animals, all of it hauled from the Missouri River. Crews laid a new rail that was thirty feet long and weighed 560 pounds every thirty seconds. One correspondent raved, in exquisite detail,

> A light car, drawn by a single horse, gallops up to the front with its load of rails. Two men seize the end of a rail and start forward, the rest of the gang taking hold by twos, until it is clear of the car. They come forward at a run. At the word of command the rail is dropped in its place, right side up with care, while the same process goes on at the other side of the car. Less than thirty seconds to a rail for each gang, and so four rails go down to the minute ... The moment the car is empty it is tipped over on the side of the track to let the

next loaded car pass it, and then it is tipped back again; and it is a sight to see it go flying back for another load, propelled by a horse at full gallop at the end of 60 or 80 feet of rope, ridden by a young Jehu, who drives furiously. Close behind the first gang come the gaugers, spikers, and bolters, and a lively time they make of it. It is a grand "anvil chorus" … It is in triple time, three strokes to the spike. There are 10 spikes to a rail, 400 rails to a mile, 1,800 miles to San Francisco … 21 million times are those sledges to be swung; 21 million times are they to come down their sharp punctuation before the great work of modern America is complete.[26]

Not everyone shared Durant's vision of a transcontinental railroad and the new American West. Even before the central route was chosen, a congressional committee voiced skepticism. Senator George Duffie of South Carolina dismissed the plains as "a desert … which no American citizen should be compelled to inhabit unless as a punishment for a crime."[27] *The New York Times* wrote, guardedly, in December 1867, when the road was ten miles west of Cheyenne, "We are assured by the directors of the Union Pacific Railroad that the railway from the Missouri to the Pacific will be completed in 1870, so that in three years from this date the time from New York to San Francisco will be less than a week. It is hard to realize that so great a distance may be accomplished in so short a time."[28]

The drumbeat against the grand project was so persistent, Dodge complained in his autobiography, "[The] lack of confidence in the project, even in the West, in those localities where the benefits of its construction were manifest, was excessive and it will be remembered that laborers even demanded their pay before they would perform their day's work. [He neglected to mention that the cash-strapped railroad was sometimes tardy paying workers.] Probably no enterprise in the world has been so maligned, misrepresented and criticized as this."[29]

Even after the mammoth undertaking was completed, the popular journal *Harper's New Monthly* worried, "Of the commercial value of this road it is yet too early to speak with confidence. The heavy articles which enter into commerce will not pass over the line; a great part of the road runs through a region which will always be thinly populated." The editors conceded, however, "nearly all the passengers between the Pacific and the Atlantic will pass over this road" and "the political uses of the road are incalculable."[30]

Naysayers aside—"rancid little men," snapped one supporter—the support for the road and what it meant for the growth of the country

Brothers Jack and Dan Casement revolutionized the railroad's track-laying operations by organizing work gangs into military precision. They could lay a 560-pound section of rail every thirty seconds, sometimes covering a mile or more a day.

was generally positive. S. D. Page, a writer for the *New York Herald*, after riding a railroad-sponsored excursion for eastern newspapermen in the summer of 1868, looked past the rickety, crime-ridden towns to a bright future: "In time all this will give way to an intelligent civilization, and in place of the gambling house and the brothel we will see the school house and the church. The advanced guards of civilization are the railroad, the gambler, the liquor seller, and the prostitute, who in turn give way before the approach of a healthful community."[31]

The New York Times correspondent who also rode one of the many railroad-sponsored outings west of Omaha was able to write in 1868:

One year ago, there were only three locomotives and 20 platform cars engaged in the transportation of materials. Today there are 23 locomotives, and 250 freight cars employed in the same business—fine first-class cars, with necessary mail and baggage cars, and two magnificent excursion and sleeping cars. Today there are no stages running east of Fort Kearney, and nearly one-half the distance to Denver may be traveled in 10 hours, and in the most luxurious passenger cars.

One year ago the great Union Pacific Railroad was regarded as a myth, and the men engaged in it and controlling it as a set of stock-jobbing Wall Street speculators. Today it is known and felt to be a power and a reality, and Mr. Durant and his associates are believed to be in earnest and fully capable of carrying out to successful completion the mammoth work which they have undertaken.[32]

Chapter Seven

"HELL ON WHEELS"

Every town that popped up along the route of the transcontinental had extravagant dreams. Founders of each ragtag assembly of tents and wooden storefronts were certain that their tiny settlement was destined to grow into a metropolis.

The Union Pacific Railroad helped feed these dreams. It was forever issuing brochures extolling the land beyond the Missouri River, much of which it owned, thanks to the largesse of the federal government, and which it helped populate with emigrants. An example of the railroad's high-flying images:

> The traveler beholds, stretching away to the distant horizon, the undulating prairie, a flowering meadow of great fertility, clothed in grasses, watered by numerous streams, the margins of which was skirted with timber ... During the fall and winter, the weather is usually dry. The heat of summer is tempered by the prairie winds, and the nights are cool and comfortable. The winters are short, dry and invigorating, with but little snow. Cold weather seldom lasts beyond three months, with frequent intervals of mild, pleasant days. The roads in winter are usually hard, smooth and excellent."[1]

From the time track-laying crews set out from the terminus at Omaha, Nebraska, on the Missouri River on July 10, 1865, until May 10, 1869, when the rails of the Union Pacific and Central Pacific were joined at Promontory Summit, Utah, every village along the route saw the coming of the railroad as its savior. Town fathers were effusive in their predictions. Omaha was "the most beautifully situated city in the world"; North Platte was touted as "the fairest city in Nebraska"; Julesburg, its adherents promised, would become the capital of Colorado; Corinne, Utah, its founder vowed, would one day be "the Chicago of the Rocky Mountains."

They weren't just "towns"; they had to be "cities." Bayard Taylor, who roamed large parts of the West at the time, complained,

> I only wish that the vulgar, snobbish custom of attaching "City" to every place of more than three houses could be stopped. From Illinois to California it has become a general nuisance, telling only of swagger and want of taste, not of growth. Why not call it "Goldenport" (as it will become a sort of harbor to which the ores will be shipped) or any other simple name? In the Russian language two unnecessary accents usurp one-seventh of the typography; and in Colorado, when one talks about the mining towns, he must add one-seventh to his speech in repeating the useless word "City."[2]

It wasn't just the towns along the transcontinental; optimism was rampant everywhere in the rapidly expanding West. An avid supporter of Greeley, Colorado, which wouldn't see a passenger train until 1870, proclaimed to a gathering of fellow townspeople, "My friends, it is all right; this thing is bound to succeed, and Greeley will be one of the finest farming regions on the face of the Earth!" To which one skeptic in the crowd replied, "Oh, yes, I bet that feller gets four dollars a day for lying."[3]

In their turn, Schuyler, Plum Creek, Granite Canyon, Lookout, Benton, and Red Desert became pinpoints on the UP's route map, marking the progress of the greatest building project of the nineteenth century then fading away. Bryan, founded in 1868 in Wyoming, was a "near-miss." Green River was to have been the terminal, but when the UP directors found that speculators had squatted on land there, the UP established Bryan thirteen miles to the west, where the railroad built an eating station, shops, and roundhouse; it also was a shipping point for the Sweetwater mines. The town remained an important stop into 1871 and, like other towns on the line, was a raucous place:

> There was such dancing and fiddling, such drinking of health's, shuffling of cards and rattling of dice as we never saw before. From the dance saloons came the sound of hurdy-gurdies, violins and banjos, the rattle and clatter of the double shuffle and plantation breakdown, mingled with shouts and oaths, the jingling of glasses as the rude men, wild with whiskey, and ruder women, decked

Saloons and dance halls welcomed railroad workers. There, wrote
one newspaperman, "rude men, wild with whiskey, and ruder
women, decked in silks, satins, flounced and ruffled ... went whisking in each other's arms 'round the room."

Green River, Wyoming, with tents and false-front businesses
moved from the previous temporary stop, was typical of the rough-
and-tumble towns that sprung up as the Pacific Railroad worked its
way west to Promontory Summit.

in silks, satins, flounced and ruffled, and glittering with trumpery jewelry, went whisking in each other's arms 'round the room.[4]

Bryan was the scene of one of the more bizarre instances of frontier justice when a drunken stranger ordered a section man's wife to give him some food. She refused, and he knocked her down in front of her husband. A court was convened and the jury voted to hang him. He was taken outside of town via locomotive, and a rope was thrown over a telegraph pole. The condemned man was helped up to the top of a box and barrel and the noose put around his neck. He appealed from his precarious perch, "I am falling, gentlemen." Someone in the crowd kicked his rickety perch from under him and he was dispatched.[5]

Rampant lawlessness and a lack of reliable water led the railroad to move the division point back to Green River, where the railroad had established its own town (and real estate sales). By 1872, Bryan, which had five thousand inhabitants at its height, was extinct.

Some towns, such as Omaha and North Platte in Nebraska and Cheyenne and Laramie in Wyoming, did grow into sizable cities. Most never lived up to their promoters' dreams. Once they had served the railroad's purpose—a place to winter over or a depot for the ever-increasing flow of supplies arriving from the East, or a stopping-off place for the thousands of men, graders, and tracklayers working on the road—their existence became superfluous.

Columbus, Nebraska, was shunned by the railroad for its many "whiskey ranches," places, one observer noted, where the five thousand inhabitants were "having a good time, gambling, drinking, and shooting each other." Sidney, Nebraska, which had such a reputation as a lawless village that trains that stopped there for fuel and water wouldn't let their passengers debark for fear of violence by town toughs, was dismissed by one wag who said there wasn't anything at Sidney but climate, "but there was a great deal of climate."[6] Benton, Wyoming, "by day disgusting, by night dangerous."[7]

The most notorious of the towns have come down to us as "Hell on Wheels," a term first applied by writer Bowles to these wide-open gatherings of saloons, whorehouses, and casinos, although some historians aren't so sure Bowles was the first to use the expression. It has become so ubiquitous in the language that it now refers to a difficult-to-deal-with personality.

As towns go, they weren't much to look at, and even less inviting to live in. The societal flotsam that flowed into these towns wasn't interested

Writer Samuel Bowles is generally cred-
ited with hanging the moniker "Hell on
Wheels" on the upstart towns.

in farming or settling or developing the West. Their main function was to pocket the wages of the ten thousand or more men toiling on the construction of the railroad. "Wherever a large number of men are employed in work of this kind, a swarm of men and women will be found who serve the needs of the men doing the hard work," wrote historian John Galloway.[8] Far from home, without wives, families, or churchmen to rein them in, graders and tracklayers who were working hard and getting paid regularly needed some place to vent. To be sure, there were legitimate businesses, but the vast majority were intent only on making a fast buck off the men.

The new towns were largely temporary, hastily thrown together, and consisting of tents and false-front businesses. What looked like brick or stucco buildings were, on closer inspection, merely wood fronts painted to look like something more substantial. These crude structures came to be known as "shebangs" and housed the plentiful saloons filled with thieves, gamblers, and prostitutes. Each dance hall and saloon competed vigorously for business. Brightly lit halls, some with lanterns shining through colored glass panels, beckoned with seductive billboards.[9] Benton, one of the worst of the hellholes, had its share of watering holes and quickly built hotels. The Buffalo Hump Corral advertised free drinks to go with its gambling operation. The rival North Star upped the ante: "A dash to cut the water in the drink." The Desert Hotel sold meals for $1 and rented beds for $3.

It was no secret why they were there: to relieve workers of their pay. "There is no attempt to conceal vice; the faro table is as public as the workman's bench, and more frequently seen, and the current saying that there is not a virtuous woman west of Cheyenne, is fearfully near the truth."[10] The Union Pacific crews were willing and able to spend their pay on such diversions. A company photographer complained, "Verily, men earn their money like horses and spend it like asses."[11]

These pop-up towns were murderous environments without organized law enforcement until the locals grew tired of the violence and established vigilante committees. Men were strangled for a day's pay, and "a man for breakfast" was a common phrase among townspeople who woke up to find another body sprawled on their dirt streets. To be sure, there were legitimate businesses (bakeries, jewelry stores, and mercantiles), but it was the saloons and brothels that ran day and night with scarcely a pause. The accommodations themselves were none too welcoming. When a hotel patron complained about the dirty roller towel in his room, he was told that there had been "twenty-six men that went before you and you're the first one that complained."[12]

Keystone Hall in Laramie was a fine example of the "Big Tent," which provided liquor, gambling, and fun-loving female companionship in towns across Wyoming. Poker, chuck-a-luck, three-card monte, and faro—and whiskey—were popular.

The predators calculated where construction crews would pause, then rushed to set up their operations at the next end of track, using the railroad's flatcars to move their tents and flimsy storefronts. The most famous structure was the Big Tent, which hopscotched along the route, gathering "scum and wickedness," from North Platte, Nebraska, to Corinne, Utah, during the five years it took to complete building the transcontinental. Its opulence dazzled those who entered it. The Big Tent was one hundred feet long and forty feet wide, complete with a large dance floor and dozens of tables. There was a bar, of course, fitted with cut-glass goblets and pitchers, shelves crammed with liquor bottles, all surrounded by mirrors and paintings imported from the East. A band stood by night and day to amuse patrons. There was ample whiskey; it cost a good-time Charlie fifty cents for a shot, and another fifty cents for a shot for his "date" (with a dance thrown in). The girls drank tea and the whiskey was cut with water, but it was still a good time.

There was gambling in the front of the tent: faro, three-card monte, high-low, chuck-a-luck, black and white, roulette. If things went well for the "sucker" and his companion for the night, the tent was attached to canvas cubicles in the back. And, just in case, a physician manned a small clinic to prescribe cures for whatever ailment might have been carried away from the cubicles. *New York Herald* correspondent Henry Stanley caught up with the Big Tent in Julesburg, Colorado:

I walked on to a dance house. Gorgeously decorated and brilliantly lighted. I was almost blinded by the glare and stunned by the clatter. The ground floor was as crowded as it could well be … Mostly every one seemed bent on debauchery and dissipation. The women were the most reckless … expensive. They come in for a large share of the money wasted. Soldiers, herdsmen, teamsters, women, railroad men, are dancing, singing or gambling. There are men here who would murder a fellow creature for $5. Nay, there are men who have already done it. Not a day passes but a dead body is found somewhere in the vicinity with pockets rifled of their contents.[13]

Safely ensconced in the East, far from the action, the *Pittsburgh Commercial Gazette* scoffed at the notion that these towns were all that special when it came to crime and vice:

The horrors of these places are greatly exaggerated by the excessively virtuous newspaper reporters, who keen on a stirring item draw a fearful picture of the depravity of frontier life. There is no form of crime known in the West which is not daily seen in New York, Philadelphia, or any large city, and nearly always under a more squalid garb. In Eastern cities, gambling and other kinds of vice are conducted by better dressed people, and under some veil of secrecy, in direct violation of the law; but in the West all these same enormities are done openly on the streets by the roughest and hardest looking specimens of humanity, where there is no law."[14]

They were wrong. The cattle and mining towns in the West were among the toughest anywhere; the hellholes that sprung up along the Union Pacific were no less so. Statistically, frontier towns were extremely violent, with high rates of homicides comparable to the worst parts of big eastern cities. Because the railroad towns were so fluid, it is difficult to find exact homicide figures, but sometimes "a man for breakfast" was no idle boast.[15]

Meanwhile, the Central Pacific, working its way eastward from Sacramento, California, experienced no such turmoil. The vast majority of the CP's workers were Chinese who kept together in their own camps, gambled only among themselves, sent part of their wages back to China, and stayed healthy on a diet of rice, vegetables, and hot tea. James Strobridge, who acted as the construction whip on the CP, the same job held by Jack Casement on the Union Pacific, viewed the Chinese as superb workers. "They learn quickly, do not fight, have no strikes that amount to anything, and are very cleanly in their habits. They will gamble and do quarrel among themselves most noisily—but harmlessly."[16] And they did it for $35 a month.

The UP, on the other hand, employed thousands of Civil War veterans, tough, battle-hardened men who knew the joys of whiskey-drinking and fighting and partook of both whenever they could. It was a young man's game. The laborers were generally between eighteen and thirty years old, and their bosses weren't much older. Thomas C. Durant, who ran the company, was the "old man" at forty-five when construction began at Omaha. Chief engineer Grenville Dodge was thirty-four; the Casement boys, Jack and Dan, in charge of construction, were thirty-seven and thirty-three, respectively, and promoter/gadfly George Train was thirty-four.

A large percentage of workers on the line were Irishmen, many of whom migrated to the United States in the 1840s and were employed in building trades, including helping to construct canals in the East where, twenty-five years before the construction of the transcontinental, they were paid $1 a day for thirteen hours of back-breaking labor. Employers hit on the idea of feeding their employees whiskey as part of their pay, which led to brawling and alcoholism. These traits easily transferred to work on the transcontinental.

When the railroad moved on to the next end of track, so did the predators. Down came the tents and flimsy storefronts, to be loaded on flatcars and reconstructed perhaps one hundred miles away. It was said that two boys armed with screwdrivers could put up a store in three hours. Crews could throw up an entire block in one day.

Town fathers, many infused with more enthusiasm and greed than common sense, laid out grids for vast townships, often with a main street that ended at the depot on one end and at a public building, like a courthouse, on the other. The first settlers in could buy 320 acres for $1.25 an acre under the federal Townsite Act of 1844. Whatever they could resell to those who followed was profit. The railroad itself enjoyed a healthy cash flow from the sales of plots in would-be towns. Unscrupulous promoters and land men were happy to take advantage of town founders who knew that a railroad link was vital to their future success. "Paper railroads," consisting of nothing more than stock certificates and bonds, lined the pockets of such con men.

Newspapers and other boosters were complicit in the hype. Editors churned out stories and pamphlets about the vigorous growth of their communities. Sometimes they flat-out lied. An 1858 brochure for landlocked Sumner, Kansas, on the route of the Kansas Pacific Railway, pictured steamboat docks, a waterfront business district, four churches, a college, and tree-lined streets. In truth, the town could boast of one graded street and two hundred houses.

Like most of the towns that appeared out of nowhere along the route, Benton and Bear River City, at opposite ends of Wyoming, didn't live past their rambunctious days. Benton, eleven miles east of present-day Laramie, exploded to a population of three thousand in a few weeks, then vanished two months later, in September 1868, leaving behind few signs of habitation beyond spent cans and a few unknowns buried in the local cemetery.

But in its brief heyday, Benton was the epitome of a Hell on Wheels town, "by day disgusting, by night dangerous, almost everybody dirty, many filthy, and with the marks of lowest vice," said the well-traveled Samuel Bowles. Denizens could choose entertainments among twenty-five saloons and five dance halls. Bowles, who had covered essentially

Jack Morrow, a thief and swindler and "a convivial, jolly fellow," sits atop a barrel, center, in front of a liquor store/bank in the hard-scrabble town of Benton, Wyoming, which boasted twenty-five saloons and five dance halls before it vanished in 1868.

COURTESY DENVER PUBLIC LIBRARY, WESTERN HISTORY COLLECTION, Z-5803 the same route via stagecoach in 1865, was appalled by what he found three years later.

> One to two thousand men, and a dozen or two women were encamped on the alkali plain in tents and board shanties; not a tree, not a shrub, not a blade of grass was visible; the dust ankle deep as we walked through it, and so fine and volatile that the slightest breeze loaded the air with it, irritating every sense and poisoning half of them; a village of a few variety stores and shops, and many restaurants and grog shops; by day disgusting, by night dangerous; almost everybody dirty, many filthy, and with the marks of lowest vice; averaging a murder a day; gambling and drinking, hurdy-gurdy dancing.… Like its predecessors, it fairly festered in corruption, disorder and death, and would have rotted, even in this dry air, had it outlasted a brief sixty-day life.[17]

Ankle-deep in alkali but thriving as a major freighting center for wagon trains heading to Montana, Idaho, and Oregon, Benton was a toxic soup of railroad men, Indians, gamblers, prostitutes, saloonkeepers, merchants, miners, and mule whackers.

If Benton was the "wickedest," Bear River City wasn't far behind. Established in the fall of 1868, Beartown, as it was also known, supplanted Bryan as a way station in western Wyoming. Bryan faded because of violence and general lawlessness, but Bear River City turned out to be not much better; in a lot of ways, it was worse.

Its start was promising. When he and his crew were camped near Bear River in western Wyoming in the fall of 1868, surveyor Samuel Chittenden wrote to his mother in East River, Connecticut,

> There is great excitement here about towns. Some men have bought a claim here and we staked out a town on it for them. [In return, we receive] a lot, and if the lots do not sell for $100, they are going to make up the balance and this they will have to do for I have heard today that the Company are to lay out another about six miles from here and this will be the death of this one.
>
> This town has been in existence only three days still at an election for May, Common Council, etc. today there over 800 votes and there is twice the business done here than is done in Guilford, there are six groceries and three cloth stores and whiskey shebangs ad infinitum.[18]

Rapidly moving west, the transcontinental never failed to draw a crowd when it pulled into town. The platform at the large depot in Rawlins, Wyoming, was busy with men, women, children, and a dog as they awaited a train's arrival.

The phrase "the other side of the tracks" fit Bear River perfectly. The better class of folks occupied the north side of the tracks while the criminal element prevailed on the south side. Bear River was one of the most rough and tumble of the Hell on Wheels towns. Following the lynching of three unsavory fellows, rioters trashed the offices of the *Frontier Index,* the roving newspaper that followed the railroad's course from North Platte, Nebraska, resulting in the deaths of probably sixteen men. The Union Pacific, which had seen enough violence and bad behavior in the towns it spawned, moved its support facilities to nearby Evanston. By 1872, Bear River City was no more. Today, there is a historical marker and little else at the windswept site ten miles east of Evanston.

Some of the town boosters' high hopes came true. After the railroad builders and their freewheeling brethren moved on to the next Hell on Wheels, towns like North Platte, Cheyenne, Laramie, and Ogden became more livable. Vigilantes chased off the scum; settlers brought their families, who brought with them government, churches, schools, legitimate businesses, hotels, and, vital for a town's survival, regular rail passenger service, which carried in waves of farmers and stockmen and sightseers. And come they did. In 1869, when the two railroads closed the gap at Promontory, thirty thousand rode the UP. The following year, the number jumped to 150,000, many of whom weren't planning to stay but merely wanted to ogle the wonders of the West that they read about in eastern newspapers and magazines.

A *New York Times* reporter, partaking of one of the many press excursions, noted after a stopover in Cheyenne in September 1870, only three years after the city's founding, "That once famous place, boasting its hordes of desperadoes, numerous gambling 'hells' and intensely wicked dance houses and like places of entertainment, has lost much of the vigor which it possessed ... The change is a happy one. If Cheyenne should never recover its lost greatness, its moral gain will more than counterbalance its physical loss."[19]

All along the line, vice merchants and their hangers-on preyed on the young, rambunctious young men who worked hard, had plenty of cash on payday, and were eager to spend it. As the railroad moved west, it was a new venue many times over but the same old entertainments. Demas Barnes mused in *From the Atlantic to the Pacific, Overland* in 1866 about where it would all end: "I often speculate on what will finally become of all that rolling scum which the locomotive seems to blow onward as it presses westward. One is gradually surrounded by the same faces in each successive town, the same gamblers, the same musicians playing the same old tunes to the same old dance, the same females getting always a little more dilapidated."[20]

As time passed, trappings of the new towns that survived the hellacious early days changed. Upstanding citizens replaced the denizens of old. The West as Americans knew it vanished in the space of thirty years from the time of the early trappers and emigrants crossing in covered wagons to riders gliding along in passenger trains.

Chapter Eight

MILEPOST 0.0: OMAHA

The term hadn't been coined, but Omaha was the first of the Hell on Wheels towns, "a terror" where painted ladies paraded the streets in open carriages and houses of prostitution and gambling parlors flourished.

Founded in 1854, Omaha was an important staging area for westward travelers even before the arrival of the Union Pacific, its railroad shops, and hordes of workers in the 1860s. Thanks to the influx of railroad workers and supplies ferried up the Missouri River with which to build the railroad, the town doubled its size to fifteen thousand between 1864 and 1869. Freighters, adventurers headed for the newly discovered goldfields in the Pikes Peak region of present-day Colorado, emigrants, and riverboats found the small town a convenient stopping-off place. Among those heading west was a group of Mormons, whose condition shocked a *New York Times* correspondent in August 1868:

> We encountered a lot of Mormon immigrants, some 450 in number, waiting to be forwarded over the [rail]road as far as Cheyenne or Benton, where they take the overland route for the promised land. A motley crowd they were—men, women and children, old and young, all haggard-looking and travel-soiled. I should judge most of them were English, and certainly from their dull, stolid appearance, they must have been selected from the lowest strata of society. Their condition certainly must be improved, both mentally and physically ... A more woebegone and wretched-looking set of human beings I trust I shall never see again.[1]

The living was primitive. Mail delivery, for example, was a sometime thing. There was no post office; the town's postmaster carried letters in his hat and delivered them if he happened to run into the addressees on the street.

Weather was a constant source of discussion. "No town on the Missouri River is more annoyed, even afflicted, by moving clouds of dust when the wind is up than Omaha. It is absolutely terrific," noted one traveler. "For two or three days people have been obliged to shut themselves up in their houses for protection from the sand."[2] A seasoned traveler commented in the spring of 1867, "They boast greatly of the rare variety of climate—having had snowstorms, thunderstorms, hurricanes, impassable mud, choking dust, earthquakes, floods, hard freezes, and burning suns all in the space of three weeks."[3]

Another New York Times correspondent conceded that the riverside village was "the most beautifully situated city in the world" but then went on to complain that "Omaha has not made provision as yet for a people's park" and "of good fresh water the people here also lamentably deficient, and strange to say, they don't know it, for they persist in telling the stranger that the water of the Missouri is the finest drinking water in the world." And, he added for good measure, "there is not one first-class hotel in the place."[4]

Reverend Joseph Barker, who arrived in the settlement in 1856 with his wife, two sons, and a daughter, described it with a jaundiced eye. "At that time," he later wrote, "the city consisted of a few huts, two or three decent houses, a bank, the State House, a saw mill, and a few stores. The population would be about three or four hundred. The country round was one vast wild."[5]

Remoteness aside, the populace knew how to party, given the primitive facilities. An executive ball, the first in Nebraska Territory, was thrown in honor of Governor Mark W. Izard in the winter of 1855, barely one year after the city's founding. Izard was a large, blustery man who enjoyed the trappings of his office. He insisted, for example, that an African American servant be hired to announce him when he approached the legislative chamber. He was happy to be honored with a ball.

The party in what passed for the town's best hotel turned out to be a debacle. First, the dance floor, made up of rough-planed boards and a definite trip hazard, was washed down prior to the festivities, and, because the room was so cold, the water froze. Second, only nine women could be rounded up for the dance, and two of them didn't know how. The combination led to several pratfalls.

Given the primitive nature of the settlement, it was grand celebration, topped off by a midnight dinner of sandwiches made of thick bread and bacon, coffee, and dried-apple pie, all "passed around" because there were no tables at which to sit.[6]

Rival towns took the occasion to mock the Omahans' attempt at social graces:

> A group of splendid ones is on the floor, and loving mated—the gents encircle their partners' waists with one arm. That ladies and gentlemen closely face to face. They are very erect and lean a little forward. (Music.) Now all wheel and whirl, circle and curl. Feet and heel of the gents go rip rap, rip rap, rip. Ladies' feet go tippity tip, tippity tip tip, tip. Then all go rippity, clippity, slippity, flippity, skippity, hoppity, jumpity, bumpity, thump. Ladies fly off by centrifugal momentum.
>
> The ladies' faces are brought against those of the men or into their bosoms, breast against breast, nose against nose, toes against toes. Now they are again making a sound, like georgy-porgy, deery-peery, didy-pidy, coachey-poachey.[7]

As was typical with these early towns, optimism was rampant. A promotional map put out in 1854 looked into a bright future: "Lots will be given away to persons who will improve them—private sale will be made on the premises. A newspaper, the *Omaha Arrow*, is printed weekly at this place; a brick building, suitable for the Territorial Legislature, is in process of construction, and a steam mill and brick hotel will be completed in a few weeks."[8]

Omaha, billed as the "Gate City to the West," had long been a magnet for travelers. The discovery of gold in the Pikes Peak region in 1859 made the town a center for supplies and a jumping-off place for adventurers headed to the Rockies. Steamboats plying the Missouri used Omaha as a major stopping-off point. When the Union Pacific's intentions to start the Pacific Railroad on the west side of the river became known, other railroads—the Chicago and North Western; Chicago, Rock Island and Pacific; the Saint Joseph and Council Bluffs; and Chicago, Burlington and Quincy—all ran rails to the town.

The arrival of the UP vaulted what was a frontier town into a full-blown city. Omaha's population of a few hundred, living in rough conditions on the edge of the frontier, rose to 1,883 in 1860 and exploded to twenty thousand after the coming of the railroad. By the 1880s, it was home to two daily newspapers, eleven hotels, several breweries, fifteen churches, and a thriving school system.[9]

The population of Omaha, jumping-off place for westward emigrants and the Union Pacific, doubled between 1864 and 1869.
This view at Twelfth and Farnum in 1867 shows the *Daily Herald*
newspaper offices conveniently located above a saloon.

In fact, the town, perched on the west side of the river, shouldn't have been the terminus of the railroad at all. An enthusiastic supporter of the railroad, President Abraham Lincoln, carrying out the mandate of the Pacific Railway Act of July 1, 1862, designated the starting point as "the western boundary of the State of Iowa," specifically the riverside town of Council Bluffs. Nevertheless, it was Omaha, not Council Bluffs, that landed the big prize.

The Civil War delayed actual construction, but planning was moving forward. Track, ties, locomotives, railcars, and other construction materials transported by rail to Saint Joseph, Missouri, then carried by steamboat poured into town. By the winter of 1864, supplies piled up, enough rail to lay eighty miles of track, thirty flatcars, coal, iron, and four locomotives. The company built a car house, engine house, and machine shops of brick. At one point, management was putting $250,000 a month into acquisition and construction. Town lots suddenly sold for as much as $5,000.

The Reverend Barker was astonished when he later paid a visit to the UP shops. "I assure you, I was really surprised. The buildings are crowded with men at work. They have no room or means to supply the demands of the road. They are at present in want of 4,000 freight cars & though they turn out ten cars a day they cannot supply the present demand."[10] By 1868, the railroad was in full bloom. The shops at Omaha were manufacturing freight and passenger cars, churning out twenty-four flatcars a week, along with first- and second-class coaches, baggage cars, and cabooses.

The job market flourished. As would be repeated time after time for five years along the route of the Pacific Railroad, Omaha also took on a darker demeanor as workers, gamblers, prostitutes, whiskey sellers, con men, camp followers, and hangers-on joined more upstanding citizens, legitimate businessmen who supplied the town's clothing, food, household needs, and built substantial buildings and stores. Even as the railroad worked its way west, slowly at first, then picking up speed, Omaha remained the primary jumping-off point for military supplies to western forts, and, later, for passenger trains.

Primary among those who preyed on workers were saloonkeepers, gamblers, and prostitutes, who would follow the railroad and its workers all the way to the road's completion at Promontory Summit in Utah. The railroad's need for laborers seemed insatiable, but job opportunities in the West were less available to women because men also filled the occupations of clerk, secretary, and office worker. Some women took to operating boardinghouses, hard to do because it required a large investment of capital unless they took boarders into their own homes. There were jobs for teachers, but the pay was poor and locals closely watched teachers for moral infractions. Nevertheless, women, married, single, divorced, or widowed, joined the trek westward to work as milliners, dressmakers, waitresses, and laundresses. But the small towns of the West could accommodate only a limited number of such skills.

Faced with limited choices and the need for employment, some women were forced to turn to prostitution; it has been estimated that upward of fifty thousand women were involved in the trade in the trans-Mississippi West.[11] They were young women from a variety of ethnic backgrounds, including Irish, English, French, Swiss, Mexican, Asian, Native American, and African American. High-end prostitutes worked in brothels, houses where they were paid well, were taken care of by madams, and formed friendships with the other girls. They also could be found in the numerous saloons, places where "the miserable females … have to dance all night till the broad daylight, with about as much hilarity as so many prisoners in the treadmills."[12]

It was not an easy life for *nymphes du pavé*. Josie Washburn, a former hooker who was a madam in her own houses in Omaha and Lincoln, wrote a scathing reminiscence of prostitution in 1909:

> Crowd after crowd come to the different doors and yell for admission. They are drunk, we fear them; WE NEVER GET OVER THIS FEAR, although we have seen the same performances daily year after year. A drunken bunch has arrived, they are young and handsome fellows, they use vile language … They are society dudes and imagining they are making a hit with our girls by exhibiting their toughness, and failing to find an appreciative audience they pinch and hurt the girls just to hear them scream, and curse and call them names.[13]

While the town thrived, visitors to Omaha loved or hated it; there seemed to be no in-between. Making his own grand tour of the West by stagecoach in 1865, writer Bayard Taylor came away impressed:

> The people of Omaha are convinced that their place will be another Chicago. They certainly have a beautiful location. The crescent hills, open toward the east, enclose a high, favorable shelf of land, upon which the city can spread for some time to come. They who reside in the higher part of Omaha enjoy a much broader and more beautiful view than can be had from any other place on the Missouri.[14]

Riverboats plying the Missouri River dumped supplies at the Omaha
landing, "Gateway to the West," in anticipation of the building of
the transcontinental railroad. Track, ties, locomotives, railcars, and
other materials began their trek here.

The *Times* correspondent called Omaha's residents as "plucky and persevering a people as any to be found in the land,"[15] but not all visitors were so impressed. Another *Times* correspondent, stopping off in 1871, conceded that the outpost had "many a substantial building of brick," but he couldn't wait to leave. "Once arrived in Omaha," he reported, "it strikes you as a place where the mind of man has been fertile in suggestions [of] how to get you out of it. The Traveler thankfully accepts the situation, and avails himself of the earliest opportunity to put Omaha behind him."[16]

Traveling salesman Dewitt Weld recalled in 1901 his 1869 visit. "We got into Omaha on a Saturday. Rain was falling in bucketfuls. When the stage got up the hill to the Cozzens Hotel, I volunteered to go to the post office to get the baron's [French ambassador Baron Baudice Boileau, a traveling companion] mail as well as my own. Walking along the plank sidewalk in front of the hotel, I reached the end to find a canal almost, and stepping on what I took to be a plank I landed waist deep in mud and water."[17]

Miriam Leslie, who made the popular viewing excursion west in 1877 with her husband, Frank, for a series of articles titled "Out West on the Overland Train," was even less impressed:

> We took a carriage and set forth to view the town. We found it big, lazy, and apathetic; the streets dirty and ill paved, the clocks without hands to point to the useless time; the shops, whose signs mostly bore German names, deserted of customers.... Returning to the station, we found the platform crowded with the strangest and most motley people it has ever been our fortune to encounter. Men in alligator boots and loose overcoats made of blankets and wagon rugs, with wild unkempt hair and beards.... The women looked tired and sad and were queerly dressed in gowns that must have been old on their mothers.[18]

When he wasn't engaged in church activities, the Reverend Barker hit the social circuit, which had seen considerable improvement since that comical first inaugural in 1855. He wrote in October 1868:

> I was out to a large party at the new house of Mr. Yates, the cashier of the First National, Kountze's bank. Some seventy people were there. It was a very fine affair. I never saw a better dressed party. The larger part of the ladies were young married, and nearly all

dressed in handsome light coloured silks. Very expensive silks with white lace & flowers. There was a band & dancing in the dining room. Supper, the handsomest I have seen, was laid in two rooms. And the table was laid with coffee & tea & sandwiches. Haunch of venison, fine ham, turkeys, chicken salads, buffalo tongues, chickens and oysters, pickles. It was the handsomest party yet.[19]

English journalist W. F. Rae predicted that "Omaha is one of those American cities which seem to spring up, flourish, and wax great in the twinkling of an eye."[20] The marriage between Omaha and the Union Pacific was a perfect match. The railroad poured money into the local economy, which in turn met the railroad's needs. The city's expansion was so speedy that one real-estate dealer furnished its salesmen with fast horses and light buggies to hurry prospective buyers onto the plains quickly so that the new homesites seemed only minutes from downtown. Journalist Albert Richardson saw a bright future: "Now … will rise a great city, heart of a dense population, on the grand highway of travel and traffic for the whole globe. And sixty years hence—what imagination so rich and wild as to paint *that* picture?"[21]

As the railroad rolled westward, the undesirables and lowlifes packed up and left behind a city whose future as an important rail and commercial center was assured. Its reputation as a "terror" soon would be eclipsed by the next Hell on Wheels, North Platte, Nebraska.

Chapter Nine

MILEPOST 291.0: NORTH PLATTE

The Union Pacific reached North Platte, Nebraska, as winter began to set in in November 1866. What had been a gathering of a few primitive shelters grew to 675 inhabitants in a few weeks and exploded into a booming city of five thousand souls in only six months.

The railroad was happy to be there, having covered almost three hundred miles up the Platte Valley since the first spike went down in Omaha in 1865. Winter was coming on, meaning work would have to be suspended to avoid the stinging blizzards and freezing temperatures on the plains. There was little "civilization" beyond North Platte, where the open prairie was still home to tribes trying their best to fight off the growing wave of whites and stave off the slaughter of bison, antelope, and deer.

Supplies and workers stacked up. Fifteen thousand tons of government freight bound for military forts farther west lay stored under acres of canvas. Railroad workers bided their time until the spring thaw. Some lived and cooked their own meals in the UP's shops. Twelve hundred emigrant wagons perched at the edge of town, including those of Mormons waiting to resume the march toward Utah.

And, of course, there was the inevitable tide of ne'er-do-wells who flocked into the newest Hell on Wheels. An early inhabitant, Andrew Miller, made what may be the first mention of the Big Tent, the oversized saloon/gambling house/brothel that was to become infamous in various towns as the railroad worked its way toward its Utah meeting with the Central Pacific.[1] Miller was so sure of the town's future that he had lumber and other building materials freighted in from Denver and opened a general store with partner William Peniston.

There was the usual conglomeration of lesser dens of vices where all manner of frontier types could gather, making North Platte a "lively and somewhat picturesque place."[2] There were fifteen buildings, nine of which were saloons. A shot of whiskey sold for a hefty twenty-five cents; the new arrivals were free spenders. The few upstanding citizens among the seedy pack chose not to venture out after dark for fear of running into a gun-toting desperado, which included almost everybody.

Henry Stanley recorded in May 1867, "North Platte is a gay frontier hamlet, its citizens a motley crowd of construction camp denizens, toughs, roughs, gamblers, and emigrants but a few months from the countries of the Old World. Women from the dance halls, bullwhackers, and teamsters lined the tracks to see the train come in." The Cedar, the town's rough log hotel on Front Street, he said, "charged a lot but gave little in the way of comfort."[3]

Stanley was, in general, unimpressed. "The location is seemingly unsuited for a town site, being intersected by numerous sloughs populated by swarms of mosquitoes."[4] Stanley's description of the town's denizens is one of the best ever recorded:

> Every known game under the sun is played here. The days of Pike's Peak and California are revived. Every house is a saloon and every saloon is a gambling den. Revolvers are in great requisition. Beardless youths imitate to the life the peculiar swagger of the devil-may-care bullwhacker and blackleg, and here, for the first time, they try their hands at the "Mexican monte," "high-low-jack," "strap," "rouge-et-noir," "three-card monte," and that satanic game, "chuck-a-luck," and lose their all. Old gamblers who reveled in the glorious days of "flush times" in the gold districts declare that this town outstrips them all yet.[5]

Unlike other Hell on Wheels stops on the transcontinental route, the founders of North Platte were not satisfied with the usual collection of saloons, brothels, gambling shebangs, and liquor outlets—"infested with reckless desperadoes."[6] Slowly, the town took on some semblance of respectability. The first permanent building in town was a log schoolhouse, built with donations from the citizenry. In early 1867, the railroad started construction on a brick roundhouse and machine shops, as much for protection against Indian attack as an investment in the town's future. Frame houses popped up where tents once stood. On the downside, there wasn't a single church. The first Sunday school didn't meet until August 1868, with three children, and the new school had no teacher.

North Platte, Nebraska, the first major stop along the route, 291 miles west of Omaha, became the prototype for division points, featuring a roundhouse, repair shop, and a thirty-foot-tall windmill to supply water for thirsty locomotives.

There was no courthouse, and each of the representatives on the county commission, who met at the house of W. M. Hinman, kept his records in his home. During the initial term of the district court (there was one judge for the whole state), there were no cases tried and a grand jury was impaneled but no indictments were handed down. There was, however, a crude form of law enforcement. When a jewelry store was broken into and robbed, citizens chased the robbers, caught two of them, and promptly strung them up.

In March 1868, the county commissioners took the unusual step of ordering whiskey peddlers to pay $25 for a one-year license to sell liquor in less than five-gallon lots. Some of the booze peddlers reluctantly went along with the tax, but when the commissioners raised the fee to $150, all hell broke loose. Saloonkeepers and other dispensers of alcohol raised such a ruckus that the commissioners had to rescind the new fee.

The commissioners even took on the Union Pacific, the town's bene-factor, by levying an assessed valuation of $49,000 on its property. The railroad protested, the case went through the courts, and the tax wasn't paid until the sheriff chained the UP's locomotives into the roundhouse.

The first passenger train reached North Platte in the spring of 1867. For a time, it appeared its arrival was years off. In May 1866, the end of track was at Schuyler, 215 miles east of North Platte and named for Ulysses S. Grant's vice president, Schuyler Colfax, whose political career was stained by his involvement in the Crédit Mobilier scandal. Con-struction was proceeding at a snail's pace. It took ten months to cover the sixty-eight miles from Omaha to Schuyler; at that pace, it would take twelve years to reach the West Coast. Those in charge of construc-tion chose to run around Columbus, two hundred miles east of North Platte, because of its many saloons. "It would not answer," Thomas C. Durant, the company's head man, told Samuel Reed, in charge of sup-plies for the transcontinental, "to have men so near whiskey shops as Columbus."[7] Not that things would be any drier in North Platte.

Now the Casement brothers and their work crews were hurrying things along. The company surveyed, graded, and laid two hundred miles of track in less than six months to reach North Platte. By summer, the builders were off and running to the next end-of-track destination, Julesburg, on the Colorado/Nebraska border (now the northeastern cor-ner of Colorado), which it reached in June. Business was booming on the Pacific Railroad. When the railroad left town, so did the "floating class," the gamblers, prostitutes, and hucksters. That fall, the railroad felt confident enough about its service that it announced passenger trains

Desperate for cash to continue construction, the Union Pacific advertised its trains almost as soon as the tracks left Omaha. An eye-boggling multitude of typefaces on this broadside promised "equipment new and road bed in perfect order."

would run on Sundays. And in May 1868, the UP dropped its fares from Omaha to Cheyenne, where the end of track was established in January, from $51.50 to $38.50.

Indian troubles were still prevalent, especially between the fall of 1866 and the end of summer 1868. Major Henry C. Parry, medical officer for the UP's chief engineer, Grenville Dodge, wrote in May 1867: "I found as I passed through North Platte that the Indians had driven all the traders and miners in from the mountains, and at North Platte they were having a good time, gambling, drinking, and shooting each other. I observed that in every establishment the persons behind the counters attended to their customers with loaded and half-cocked revolvers in their hands. Law is unknown here."[8]

Heavily armed workers watched closely for attacks west of North Platte. One alert engineer suspected something was up when he spied telegraph wires cut at trackside. He slowed his train and suddenly saw more than one hundred Sioux gathered on either side of the tracks with a rawhide rope stretched across the rails. He hit the throttle and ripped through the rope, scattering Indians everywhere and killing several, as well as sixteen of their horses.[9]

Threat of attacks by Indians kept the populace of North Platte in turmoil; there were plenty of reasons to think they might. A large band swooped down on workers at Hinman's ranch just outside town, killing and scalping five field hands, then turned their attention to an approaching train and tried to stop it. Engineer Dutch Frank was having none of it. He plowed through the aggressive warriors defiantly standing on the tracks, killing or mangling many of them.[10]

Finally, an attempt was made to reach a peace agreement with the Sioux, Cheyennes, and other tribes. In July 1867, tribal leaders began to trickle into town, camping near the roundhouse, but it wasn't until September that the meetings got under way. Among those in attendance were General William T. Sherman and the railroad's George Francis Train. A good number of Sioux chiefs, including Spotted Tail, Pawnee Killer, Cut Nose, and Swift Bear, aired grievances for the Indians. Indian Commissioner Nathaniel G. Taylor urged them to "speak fully, speak freely, and speak the whole truth." One of the chiefs did just that: "The Great Father has made roads stretching east and west. The country where we live is overrun by whites. All our game is gone. This is the cause of great trouble."[11]

Sherman warned the gathered tribes that his troops could become as plentiful as grasshoppers if they didn't cease their campaign. The speeches went on for two days, both sides saying they wanted peace, but nothing definitive came out of the meeting. The Indians went away dissatisfied and returned a few days later in a warring mood. They circled the town, terrifying the citizens with war whoops "that would make a bald-headed man's scalp itch," remembered carpenter H. W. Guy in 1925. "The women and children were taken to the hotel. Our gang of twenty-seven men barricaded the doors and windows of the uncompleted roundhouse."[12] The Indians gave up the faux attack and departed.

The railroad hired more than one hundred Pawnees, sworn enemies of the Sioux and Cheyennes, to fight off attacks. This, combined with an ever-increasing presence of soldiers due in part to speedy delivery of troops and weapons by the railroad, led to a dramatic decline in assaults on the construction crews and settlers.

By 1873, North Platte, which once boasted a population of five thousand, had shrunk to around 150, most of whom worked for the Union Pacific. Unlike many of its on-line brethren, however, North Platte did not die. A new brick schoolhouse went up in 1873 and a brick courthouse was completed in 1875 at the cost of $20,000. A substantial business district took shape. Though its rough and rowdy ways lived on through gambling parlors and houses of ill repute well into the 1940s (some labeled it "Little Chicago"), the early settlers' ambitions proved in the long run to be the right decision. Today, the city is a major agricultural center whose population is twenty-four thousand, and North Platte is home to the Union Pacific's Bailey Yard, billed as the world's largest classification yard, where freight trains are put together.

Chapter Ten

MILEPOST 377.4: JULESBURG

Location, location, location.

The town of Julesburg is actually a succession of four towns, usually referred to by present-day residents as Julesburg I, II, III, and IV. Julesburg III, the end-of-track version where the transcontinental arrived in June 1867, would not win any beauty prizes; visitors routinely commented on its unsightliness. It was described as a place where "vice and crime stalk unblushingly in the midday sun"[1] and cruelly viewed as "a flea-bitten collection of shacks—unpainted, unwholesome, and thoroughly unlovely."[2]

Like other towns along the railroad's route, Julesburg III boasted its share of bummers and hangers-on eager to take advantage of the Union Pacific work crews who had nowhere else to rid themselves of their hard-earned pay. But unlike those other towns, early-day Julesburg had another reason to exist: it was an important crossroads on the overlanders' Platte River route. In the early 1850s, Frenchman Jules Beni established his trading post near the crossing of the Platte used by the Cheyennes and Arapahos as they trekked to and from their hunting grounds in the fertile Platte Valley. Later, he accommodated the oncoming tide of whites as well.

Beni, also known as Jules Reni, was by all accounts a despicable character, "a liar, a thief and a scoundrel." Travelers complained that his prices were far too high and that the vile liquor he poured, known as Pilgrims' whiskey, a concoction of alcohol, red pepper, molasses, and water, was watered down even further to make it stretch. He would eventually get his comeuppance; gouging travelers was one thing, but stealing from his employer was quite another.

Beni's trading post was well known when Butterfield's Overland Stage Company set up its station there in 1859, and he was named its keeper. When his bosses realized that Beni was stealing the US mail being carried by stage as well as horses, they called in thirty-year-old John Alfred "Jack" Slade, Overland's central division superintendent and a man with a reputation for being genial when he was sober and a cold-blooded killer when he was drunk.

Slade promptly fired Beni and his thieving cohorts. Beni responded by shooting Slade from an ambush with both barrels of his shotgun, then fleeing town. It appeared for a time that Slade would die. After being sent to Saint Louis for treatment, he recovered and returned to Julesburg, determined to square things with Beni.

Two years later, Beni was captured in a gun battle with Overland men near Cold Spring, Wyoming, taken to Chanson's Ranch, an Overland station about twenty-five miles from Fort Laramie, and tied to a corral post. According to legend, Slade, who reportedly had spent the day drinking, shot off Beni's fingers one by one, then cut off his ears with a bowie knife and kept them in his vest pocket, flashing them to barkeeps and onlookers. There is no historical basis for that Wild West tale. More likely is an account that claimed Slade, drinking and playing cards while Jules awaited his fate at the corral, hit Beni in the mouth with his first shot and polished him off with a second bullet to the head. In Slade's mind it was a legal execution because he had taken precaution to stop at Fort Laramie to inform those in charge of the district about "rustlers." He was later cleared of the killing; the execution of a stock thief was considered justifiable.[3]

Satisfied that he had squared things, Slade wound up in Virginia City, Montana, where he established a freighting company and terrorized residents with his drunken antics, including riding his horse into saloons and tearing up the town with his pals. Eventually, the townspeople grew tired of his behavior and vigilantes from nearby Nevada City hanged him in March 1864.[4]

The original Julesburg was on the south side of the South Platte River near what was known as Upper California Crossing, perhaps as early as 1852. Soon, a "town," mostly sod and wood buildings—a blacksmith shop, warehouse, stable, and a large boardinghouse for the stage line's customers—sprang up around Beni's trading post. It was a shabby collection, but it was an important stop for freighters and for the thousands of emigrants slowly making their way across the prairies for California or Oregon. It was not unusual for wagon trains three miles long to pause at Beni's post.

Camp Rankin, a military post, was established a mile west of the stage station in October 1864. It was neither very attractive nor much of a fort. In September 1865, it would be renamed for Major General John Sedgwick, shot in the head by a sniper while arranging his artillery at the Civil War battle of Spotsylvania Court House in May 1864. Known among his admiring troops as Uncle John, he was the highest-ranking Union officer killed during the war.

Primitive buildings constructed from cottonwood and cedar logs hauled in from miles away inside five-foot-high walls of sod or adobe, Camp Rankin was a dusty rectangle 240 by 360 feet that contained stables, a corral, barracks, officers' quarters, a small parade ground, a hospital, and a magazine. In 1866, General William T. Sherman wrote to Secretary of War John A. Rawlins from Fort Sedgwick: "The post was first built of sods, and now looks like hovels in which a negro would hardly go. Surely, had the Southern planters put their negroes in such hovels, a sample would, ere this, have been carried to Boston and exhibited as illustrative of the cruelty and inhumanity of the man-masters."[5]

The fort was garrisoned by Company F of the Seventh Iowa Cavalry, led by Captain Nicholas O'Brien and armed mostly with breech-loading Gallagher single-shot carbines, although those who could afford them purchased their own Henry or Spencer repeating rifles. Two twelve-pound mountain howitzers boosted the troops' firepower.

After the slaughter by Colonel John Chivington and his one-hundred-day Colorado volunteers of more than two hundred Cheyennes and Arapahos at Sand Creek in southern Colorado in November 1864, the vengeful tribes joined with the Sioux and embarked on a rampage of killing, stealing, and burning throughout eastern Colorado, Kansas, Nebraska, and Wyoming. Especially hard hit was the Platte Valley, one of the main routes of travel for the tide of emigrants from the East.

Julesburg I had a star-crossed existence, thanks to Indian raids in January and February 1865. Julesburg was a fat target. By 1865, the Overland Stage Company had established a station house complete with a large storehouse packed with supplies available, at high prices, to travelers.

An estimated one thousand Indians gathered in the sand hills southeast of town, hiding from soldiers garrisoned at Camp Rankin, about a mile away. At dawn on January 7, 1865, a small group of warriors led by Big Crow carefully made their way down Devil's Dive, a rough piece of road used by stages and wagon trains on their way into Julesburg.

The plan was an old one, used successfully by Indian warriors over and over. Big Crow and ten men would draw the soldiers out of the camp, then the main body of Indians would attack and kill them all. On cue, Big Crow's men charged the fort, yelling and firing as they went. It worked. Thirty-seven troopers mounted up and charged out, prepared to do battle. The element of surprise was lost when an incoming stage-coach deflected the attention of the young warriors, who opened fire too soon. The driver, his buffalo coat studded with arrows, reached Camp Rankin safely in his coach.[6]

Nevertheless, the Indians surrounded the troopers only three hundred yards from the fort and killed fourteen soldiers and one civilian. In their biography of George Bent, a half-breed who rode with the Cheyenne Dog Soldiers and took part in the fighting, David Fridtjof Halaas and Andrew E. Masich wrote that "not a single warrior had been killed," although other sources, including soldiers who survived the battle, said that between 30 and 142 warriors died.[7]

With the soldiers chased back into the fort, the Indians turned their attention to Julesburg, the small settlement only a mile away, where large stores of goods waited to be taken. Cornmeal, bacon, flour, sugar, rice, canned meats and fruits, barrels of syrup and molasses, and hardware were loaded up and hauled off. Ten miles of telegraph wire on either side of Julesburg were torn down and the poles used to build an enormous bonfire. The celebrating Indians wanted to torch the buildings, but their chiefs and Bent convinced them that if they left them standing the white men would soon refill them.

Marauding Indians rampaged all along the Platte Valley route that spring and summer, burning ranches, killing whites, and making off with horses and goods. The day after the Julesburg raid, Indians swept down on Valley Station near present-day Sterling, Colorado, killed one man and wounded several others, killed horses, and burned wagons. On January 12, reports reached Camp Rankin that a large group of Indians had attacked Clear Water Ranch, killed nineteen white men, destroyed the mail, and taken $30,000 in cash. So pervasive were the attacks that for a time all freighting and stages along the Platte were halted.

Less than a month after the Julesburg raid, the Indians returned to sack the town a second time and burned it to the ground. Captain O'Brien and his troops were returning to Fort Rankin from a patrol about 2:00 in the afternoon on February 2 when they spotted smoke rising over the town. In a 1914 interview in the *Rocky Mountain News*, O'Brien recounted a thrilling tale of troopers charging through the attacking Indians, sabers flashing and cannon fire resounding, to reach safety at the fort. The reporter's telling appears to be largely based on an account written some years before by Second Lieutenant Eugene

F. Ware, stationed at the camp.[8] A thrilling story, but not true, wrote Colorado historian Doris Monahan. She maintained that O'Brien and his men saw the smoke from the burning buildings and laid low until the fort's cannon cleared the way for them. "The story of the dramatic entrance into Julesburg with guns blazing and horses galloping madly through a crowd of dazed Indians was told so often by O'Brien and Ware that the principals began to believe it. Unfortunately, another exciting tale of the West must be reduced to fact by the testimony of witnesses."[9] Once again, the Indians hauled off what they could carry from the raid.

Less dramatic was a subsequent attack on Julesburg on February 2, although the warehouses were burned to the ground.

Major Henry C. Parry, who served as a surgeon for the Union during the Civil War and traveled westward as medical officer with the Union Pacific Railway Commission, was camped near newly renamed Fort Sedgwick the following June. In a series of letters to his father in Pottsville, Pennsylvania, he described life on the frontier. "I just got back from Julesburg," he wrote on June 10. "The Cheyennes came down on the place last night about 7 o'clock and were handsomely repulsed. They killed two men, scalped and mutilated their bodies in a most brutal manner. Several Indians were wounded, only one killed. I visited five men who were injured by arrows. I never saw an arrow wound before and regard them as worse than a bullet wound. One of the men killed was pinned to the earth by an arrow through his neck. He must have been shot after being scalped."[10]

A public backlash was inevitable. "A Letter from a Soldier" in the *Rocky Mountain News* asked, "What in the name of all that is good is this country coming to? Can you tell? Are the red men to rule the country? Are peaceable citizens to submit to be butchered in their houses with a post in view of them filled with soldiers? What in the name of God do citizens pay taxes for if not to reap the benefits when overpowered by these red devils?" He recommended that citizens take matters into their own hands.[11]

In August, after a raid at Plum Creek in central Nebraska, the *News* printed a correspondent's account dripping with sarcasm: "Andrew Vail received the comforting intelligence that train No. 1, freight, was captured by the Spotted Tail friendlies and all the men killed, except the conductor, who with some that were wiped out on a handcar, makes, near as heard from, nine killed.

"The Indian commission sat at St. Louis yesterday, and nothing could be more appropriate or expected than this raid, to commemorate and to show the utter fallacy of such commissions."[12]

Julesburg, founded as a stop for overland travelers in 1852, was attacked twice by Indians within two months in early 1865. Warehouses were looted of goods the first time, and the warehouses and town burned down during the second raid.

The few citizens of Julesburg were determined that their town would survive. In February 1866 they began work on Julesburg II, four miles east of Fort Sedgwick. They had big dreams. The town site was a mile long and a half mile wide and included a public square with a courthouse and a schoolhouse. The main thoroughfare was Sedgwick Avenue, ninety-nine feet wide and designed to bring the Overland Trail through downtown. Their big dreams came to naught in only eighteen months, however; the coming of the railroad in June 1867 spelled doom for Julesburg II. The tracks of the Union Pacific were laid on the north side of the Platte, and Julesburg II stood on the south side. Anticipating the rails' arrival, residents fled to the new and thriving Julesburg III.

On July 23, Major Parry remarked to his father on the anticipation among townspeople of the coming of the railroad: "The railway is now laid within a mile of this place, along the north border of the Platte. You can readily think how rejoiced we all were when we heard the shrill whistle of the engine, and saw in the dim distance its dark form come puffing toward us. Every cloud of its white smoke seemed to bring with it peace and civilization over the plains of the far West."[13]

With the coming of the railroad, Julesburg's prospects soared. The tracks reached North Platte, Nebraska, in November 1866, when construction was halted for the winter. It was obvious that when spring arrived and construction resumed it wouldn't be long before the fast-moving tracklayers covered the eighty-six miles between North Platte and Julesburg III. The railroad, which needed every dollar it could raise, made no secret that Julesburg was to be the next "permanent" town along the right-of-way. The UP's Grenville Dodge, in a process that would be repeated many times, began placing newspaper advertisements to sell lots in the infant town for $50 to $150.

The first train pulled into Julesburg III on June 25, 1867. The cast of low-life characters—pimps, gamblers, pickpockets, thieves, shills, and "women, not the marrying kind," all of whom had abandoned North Platte—roared into town with their canvas saloons and brothels and false-front stores. Nine hundred of the estimated twelve hundred structures thrown up in a week purveyed some sort of vice.[14] Likely a bit of a hyperbole, but others observed that two-thirds of the town's structures were devoted to debauchery.

To be sure, there were religionists in the form of evangelists, but vice was a lot more attractive to the incoming hoards. Dubbed the "Wickedest City in America," Julesburg in three months mushroomed from forty men and one woman to an estimated seven thousand souls.

Strategically located on the Platte Valley route almost on the Colorado-Wyoming border and, later, as a stop on the transcontinental, Julesburg had high hopes. But when construction moved to Cheyenne, the town's chances as a rail center withered.

On July 30, 1867, the railroad's engineer of construction, Samuel B. Reed, described the town in a letter to his wife, Jennie. After reassuring her that he was only an observer, not a participant, Reed wrote:

> Julesburg continues to grow with magic rapidity, vice and crime stalk unabashedly in the midday sun. You know that I never keep from you any mean thing I do and now I am ready to confess to you what I have done since my return from Chicago; and let me say by way of apology, that it is the first offence of the kind I have knowingly committed. Fearing that you have already judged and condemned unheard, I will hasten with my confession. General Auger and staff returned here last Friday evening and nothing would do but they must see the town by gaslight. I sent for Dan Casement to pilot us. (I knew he could show us the sights.) The first place we visited was a dance house, where a fresh importation of strumpets had been received. The hall was crowded with bad men and lewd women. Such profanity, vulgarity and indecency as was heard and seen there would disgust a more hardened person than I. The next place visited was a gambling hell where all games of chance were being played. Men excited with drink and play were recklessly staking their last dollar on the turn of a card or the throw of a dice. Women were cajoling and coaxing the tipsy men to stake their money on various games; and pockets were shrewdly picked by the fallen women of the more sober of the crowd. We soon tired of this place and started forth for new dens of vice and crime and visited several similar to those already described. At last about 10 PM we visited the theater and were asked behind the curtain to see the girls. From here I left the party and retired to my tent fully satisfied with my first visit to such places.[15]

If Julesburg weren't the wickedest town in America it was certainly one of the most violent. The *Frontier Index* newspaper, which moved along with the advancing railroad at each end-of-track town, wrote with tongue in cheek, "There were only sixty-three loud quarrels on Front Street this week" and "There was a whaling good row last night in which eighty-seven participated, fourteen were wounded, six missing, and the killed not counted."[16]

Within weeks the town had one hundred twenty liquor dispensaries in addition to numerous gambling halls and whorehouses, wrote the *Omaha World-Herald*. "The principal amusements are getting tight, fighting, and occasionally shooting each other down for pastime."[17] One day later, the *Herald* wrote, "Seven Mexicans, five soldiers, eight bullwhackers, four loafers and two half breeds got into a big bone-and-sinew muss evening before last off Pacific Street. They fought well and hard for about an hour and then quit almost even, upon condition that the worst whipped should treat the crowd."[18]

Henry Stanley was astonished by what he saw when he passed through in August. Armed with a keen eye and a clever way with words, he wrote:

> As might be expected, gambling was carried on extensively, and the saloons were full. I walked on until I came to a dance house bearing the euphonious title of "King of the Hills," gorgeously decorated and brilliantly lighted. Coming suddenly from the dimly lighted street to the kerosene-lighted restaurant, I was almost blinded by the glare and stunned by the clatter. The ground floor was a crowded as it could well be, and all were talking loud and fast, and mostly every one seemed bent on debauchery and dissipation. The women appeared to be the most reckless, and the men seemed nothing loth to enter a whirlpool of sin.[19]

Resident W. S. Coburn described an alarming incident that took place during the height of the town's prominence, in the summer of 1867:

> The marshal had six prisoners in the log jail on all kinds of charges from stealing to murder. The jail was located on the next lot from where I was stopping.
>
> While the guests were eating dinner one day the prisoners were making a great noise, singing and hallooing, and some of the guests at the table made the remark that the prisoners must feel very happy. All this noise was for a purpose, however; some of their friends had furnished the prisoners with a saw and revolvers and they were making this noise to drown the noise of the saw while sawing a log out of the side of the jail so they might escape.
>
> When dinner was over I walked out to the front porch and as I was lighting a cigar, the six prisoners came around the corner of the hotel, each with two revolvers, yelling and shooting as they came. They soon found the marshal and disarmed him and compelled him to accompany them to all of the saloons and dance halls and drink with them. Thus they held the town for three hours, when they scattered and took to the sand hills.[20]

Eventually, law and order in its fashion arrived in Julesburg III, but because there were, for a time, rival city governments, enforcing laws was difficult, abetted by the fact that there was uncertainty whether the town was in Nebraska or Colorado. On the town's founding, citizens formed a government and passed an ordinance requiring businesses to take out a license. Unhappy with what amounted to a tax, businessmen called for election of a new city government. Leaders of the old government ruled an election illegal and subject to a fine of $50 for "opposing the authority of the city government."[21] An election was held, pitting the Law and Order Ticket against the People's Ticket. The businessmen's People's Ticket was declared the winner in an election that appeared to have many more votes than voters. Once the railroad moved on, who ran the town became irrelevant.

An additional problem was that some of the town's saloon and gambling parlor operators squatted on lands that the railroad claimed it owned, and the entrepreneurs refused to pay for their lots. This did not amuse Grenville Dodge, who was always looking for extra dollars to finance construction. He ordered the railroad's Jack Casement to round up some of his rugged tracklayers and chase out the deadbeats. Accompanied by two hundred men, Casement marched on the town and ordered his men to open fire, "not caring whom they hit." When Dodge later visited Julesburg, he asked Casement what had happened. Casement walked Dodge to the local cemetery and told him, "They all died, but bought peace."[22]

When the Union Pacific and its crews moved on for Cheyenne, 139 miles to the northwest, in the fall of 1867, Julesburg withered from a boom town to a small town, and by 1879 the population had dwindled to only fifteen. The final blow for Julesburg III came in 1882 when the Colorado Central Julesburg Branch was completed to Denver Junction, four miles east, and Julesburg moved with it. The town became incorporated in 1886 as Julesburg IV, which exists as a small farming community today.

When Stanley returned to Julesburg III in September on his summerlong tour of the West, he was ready to write it off: "Julesburg is now an overdone town, a played-out place. It was built in a single month. It is now about to be abandoned by the transient sojourners, and many of them are shifting their portable shanties to some prospective city west—Cheyenne or some 'prairie-dog town,' where cash can be made without work and by any means that will not subject the operator to an indictment before a Grand Jury for obtaining money under false pretenses."[23]

Julesburg III's role in the settlement of the West cannot be diminished. When the transcontinental reached there in the summer of 1867, a *Rocky Mountain News* reporter proclaimed proudly:

The completion of the Pacific Railroad to the mouth of [Lodgepole] Creek has completely changed the business of this whole country. The long lines of prairie schooners, with their clouds of white dust, loud whoa-haws and merry night camps, and the historic ranches on the south side of the Platte to Fort Kearney, have passed away.

A day or two since I saw a passenger only 50 hours from Philadelphia. Two days ago he saw the white crested waves of the Atlantic, now he is in sight of the everlasting snowcapped Rocky Mountains. A year ago you left Atchison by coach, and lumbered on day and night, weary miles, after having traveled crowded, cramped, jumped and jolted long days and endless nights, taking two days to make this point. Now you leave Omaha at night in a magnificent sleeping palace and reach here the next day at noon, fresh as when you started.

Was there ever before or will there ever be again anything like this great, striding race of railroads?[24]

Chapter Eleven

MILEPOST 516.4: CHEYENNE

It was no secret six months before the tracklayers arrived in November 1867 that the Union Pacific would make Cheyenne a major stopover on the transcontinental, a place where it would build a roundhouse, hotel, repair shops, and offices. It also was calculated that the grading and track-laying crews would have to pause here to wait out a typically ferocious Wyoming winter, meaning the hordes of workers and those who preyed on them would be marooned at least until the following spring. Grenville Dodge was in Cheyenne in July to help set up land sales as part of his job to locate and establish town sites and to authorize sales to the rapidly growing numbers of settlers already flooding the West.

It was no easy task. The first wave of new settlers were right on Dodge's heels. On July 9, six men and three women arrived to a new town laid out four miles square, complete with blocks, lots, streets, and alleys. Three days later, James R. Whitehead opened an office for the sale of Union Pacific lots, the first one going for $150. One month later, there were an estimated five hundred to six hundred people "living mostly under wagons or in tents."[1]

In August there were two thousand inhabitants and those same lots were bringing $2,000. The early inhabitants who occupied the town before the railroad steamed in settled into a shabby collection of shanties, lean-tos, and tents on land the Union Pacific said it owned. The squatters argued that the railroad could rightfully claim land only for the right-of-way, depot grounds, switches, and sidetracks. They refused to vacate.

But the reach of the Union Pacific was long. Dodge called for help from his friend General Christopher Columbus Augur, a Civil War commander who had been detailed to investigate the Lincoln assassination

Savvy businessmen, alerted to Cheyenne becoming a major point
on the railroad, threw up a village of tents even before the Union
Pacific arrived in November 1867. The price of lots skyrocketed
from $150 to $2,000 in a matter of weeks.

conspiracy. Augur was the commander at Fort D. A. Russell, built four miles outside of Cheyenne to protect the town and railroad workers from Indian attack. With the military's help, the Union Pacific would have its way. He had no official power to do so, but Augur organized his troops, marched them into Cheyenne, knocked down all the shacks, and herded the squatters to the south side of town to lecture them on ownership.

Land and its ownership was a constant battle for Dodge. Under the Pacific Railway Act of 1862, the railroad received 13.8 million acres of land west of the Missouri in a corridor twenty (later forty) miles wide, land the federal government declared was "lying vacant" or "occupied by savages."[2] Sales of these lands were critical to the financial health of the railroad. Early in 1867, Thomas Durant warned his executive committee, "The Company is greatly embarrassed in its operations and cannot sustain its credit much longer unless some means are adopted at once to raise money for its present necessities and the prosecution of work for the ensuing year will have to be abandoned."[3] Over two years, the Union Pacific sold 480,000 acres, including those $150 lots in Cheyenne, to put some $2 million onto its books.

Distinguishing railroad land from public lands could be difficult; surveys were slow, settlers in a hurry. In Cheyenne, squatters took advantage of the situation while legitimate purchasers were reluctant to buy land with no clear title.

Despite the legal difficulties, Cheyenne's explosive growth came out of nowhere, earning it the name "Magic City of the Plains." The railroad was the big draw. Just as North Platte, Nebraska, and Julesburg, Colorado, had blossomed, Cheyenne became the new epicenter for the unwashed and undisciplined. Right behind the first train into town came the remnants of Julesburg, 140 miles to the east. "Behind the locomotive," wrote David Haward Bain in *Empire Express*, his wonderfully detailed history of the building of the transcontinental, "stretched a long series of flatcars, upon which were stacked the broken-down shacks and dismantled frame buildings, tents, whiskey crates, brass beds, mattresses, looking glasses, barstools, and gaming tables of what was now a dusty desolate ghost town in the northeastern corner of Colorado. 'Gentlemen,' called a guard as he swung down off the train into an expectant platform crowd, 'here's Julesburg.'"[4]

By November the population had swelled to as many as six thousand. Some enthusiasts thought that at its early-day zenith Cheyenne was home to ten thousand souls, but that count was inflated by the several thousand workers employed by the Union Pacific. When the graders, tracklayers, and others moved on in the spring of 1868, the town's population withered to about thirty-five hundred.

> That Cheyenne was a rough place there is no doubt. The streets were awash in a cacophony of tongues, thanks to "a motley crew, every class from every land, a mixture of people second to none this side of Galata Bridge across the Golden Horn. Hunter and trapper, Sioux and Snake, Pawnee and Piegan, Kanaka and Chinamen, cowboy and railroad man, laborer and capitalist, engineer and sightseer, artist and lawyer, thief and highwayman, all sorts and conditions of men, rich and poor, big and little, some there for health, some to escape jail, some to have a good time, but most of us for a chance to win an honest living a little more easily than we could back in the old home."[5]

James Chisholm, a correspondent for the *Chicago Tribune*, told his readers, "The wildest roughs from all parts of the country are congregated here. Men who carry on the trade of robbery openly ... would not scruple to kill a man for $10. This class is decidedly in the majority."[6] It was rare to find a man using his real name; nicknames such as "Wild Bill," "Tex," and "Handsome Harry" were in vogue, and "any physical deformity was excuse for a name descriptive of the victim, so 'Peg Leg' limped along on a stump, while 'Flat Wheels' sported a limb drawn up by an accident."[7] Money was plentiful, thanks to the rapid sales of lots. Meanwhile, the railroad was piling up supplies for the resumption of work in the spring and paying outlandish prices for ties and other materials. The workers were idle and had plenty of time to spend their nights (and days) gambling and drinking.

The Reverend Joseph W. Cook, dispatched to the West as a missionary to save souls and who founded Saint Mark's Episcopal Church, the town's first, arrived in 1868. It was no place for a devout man of the cloth, though this was where his calling was most needed: "The wickedness is unimaginable and appalling. This is a great center for gamblers of all shades, and roughs and troops of lewd women, and bullwhackers. Almost every other house is a drinking saloon, gambling house, restaurant, or bawdy."[8] He wasn't far off; there were an estimated seventy saloons to tempt the thirsty, where "whiskey and poisonous compounds were retailed at fabulous prices."[9]

Bar owner James McDaniels, a promoter of the first order, kept the mobs entertained with a free museum, a zoo (including porcupines, apes, and snakes), and a theater. The watering holes ran the gamut from tiny holes-in-the-wall to the Old Greenback Rooms, a tent 100 by 112 feet billed as "the largest saloon in the western country." It was rivaled in raucous behavior and size by the Head Quarters Saloon, the successor to the famed Big Tent that had decorated previous Hell on Wheels towns. It was one hundred feet deep and thirty-six feet wide and feature billiard rooms, a well-appointed saloon, and rooms for private assignations. Even after the railroad and its thousands of workers moved on, gambling continued to be pervasive. In 1877, *Leslie's Illustrated Weekly* reported, "Gambling in Cheyenne, far from being merely an amusement or recreation, rises to the dignity of a legitimate occupation—the pursuit of nine-tenths of the population, both permanent and transient. There are twenty gambling saloons in the diminutive town."[10]

Liquor continued to vex the railroad. "Whiskey ranches," little more than small collections of shanties that served the workers along the route, were operated, said the railroad, by "miserable leeches." Samuel Reed, in charge of construction, complained to Henry C. Crane, Durant's attorney, that the ranches were causing frequent "sick days" and slowing down construction. He regretted, "exceedingly," that "nothing can be done to suppress the whiskey traffic along the line. A few nights since two men in Carmichael's Camp were shot (badly wounded). One man was shot dead through a window at Creighton's Camp. If these depredations are to be continued, it will soon be worth a man's life to go over the work. Let us have martial law if necessary to keep off the whiskey."[11]

Even before the railroad's arrival, the *Cheyenne Leader* was busy reporting almost-daily crimes: stealing of revolvers and blankets, a street fight, one hundred men gathered in the street to bet on a dogfight, a man mauled by an inebriated "friend," a gang that created a "muss" at a house of ill fame, and "a man fined for drawing a gun on a newsman."[12] The paper conveniently kept its readers up to date with a daily feature headlined "Last Night's Shootings."

Garroting seemed to be a favorite pastime, and daylight murders were not unheard of. Visitor Robert Lardin Fulton recalled, "One ruffian stabbed a companion within a few feet of the spot where a friend and I were passing. We rushed up to stop the assault but too late. As he was seized the murderer whined, 'I was forced to do it, gentlemen. He called me a vile name.' Human life was held as cheaply as on a battlefield, with tragedy so common that death seemed almost a matter of course."[13]

Some crimes were just too awful to tolerate. The *Leader*, reporting on the proceedings of the city commissioners, noted, "On motion, the bagpipe which is played each night on the corner of Eddy and Seventeenth streets was declared a nuisance and the chief of police was directed to prevent the playing of the same on the streets in the future."[14]

By the time the tracklayers hit town on the afternoon of November 13, 1867, Cheyenne was thriving. Brick and frame buildings replaced tents and dugouts. The *Leader* gushed, "This long anticipated event has transpired, and filled our city with rejoicing and enthusiasm. Our citizens swarmed along the grade and watched, with most intense delight and enthusiasm, the magic work of track laying." Curiously, there were no bands, no parades, no speeches, likely because the townspeople long knew it was coming. "There was no shouting and cheering but one full tide of joy that sprung from the deep and heart-felt appreciation of the grandeur of the occasion and the enterprise."[15] Where only a year before attacks and murders by Indians were frequent, there was a new city, and said the *Leader*, "the treacherous tomahawk shall henceforth be harmlessly shelved in the alcoves of the museum."[16]

Unlike many of the other overnight Hell on Wheels towns, Cheyenne had a strong contingent of upright citizens, some of whom arrived before the railroad, determined to make the city livable for families and businesses. They soon grew tired of the bummers and criminal element infesting their city, and it didn't take long for a vigilante committee to take over where weak local law enforcement failed. The city government was attacked for dead animals left lying in the streets for days, police brutality, muddy and filthy streets. The city, under the jurisdiction of far-off Bismarck in the Dakota Territory until the Wyoming Territory took effect in April 1869, was strapped for cash; the city commissioners rented out the first floor of the courthouse to a clothing store.

Reed commented in a letter to his wife, Jennie, on the moral sewer when he moved his offices to Cheyenne in November 1867:

> Vigilance Committee were busy last night. When I went from office to breakfast there had been brot in three dead men taken from the place where the vig. comt. had hung them during the night. Three men are reported hung outside of the town not yet brot in. One of the parties hung was tried yesterday for murder and acquitted by the jury. Gamblers thieves & robbers do not make good jurymen, so think the vig. committee judging from the acts. Last night's work may have a good influence on the morals of Cheyenne for a few days at least. Love to all. Kiss the children for me.[17]

The following January, three men accused of theft were found tied together on the street with a sign that read "$900 stole ... $500 recovered

Cheyenne's growth was so explosive it was dubbed the "Magic City of the Plains," as if it appeared out of nowhere. The streets, properly laid out but not paved—or even level—supported thriving businesses, including a dentist and a beauty shop.

COURTESY WYOMING STATE MUSEUM

... Next case goes up a tree. Beware of Vigilance Committee."[18]

They weren't kidding. The next month, masked men lynched Charles Martin and Charles Morgan. A despicable character, Martin nevertheless had been let off on a charge of murdering his partner several weeks earlier, and Morgan was arrested for stealing mules.

The day after his acquittal, Martin toured his favorite watering holes, making it a point to visit the Keystone dance hall and his many friends. Waiting outside for him were fifteen men in black masks who dragged him away as he shouted, "My God, men, what are you going to do with me?" A rude gallows was built on the east end of town, and Charley met his end with a piece of bed cord around his neck.

Chisholm reported in the *Tribune*, "It is a sign of good times when people begin to do a little hanging. The spectacle of a human being suspended in the air, with blue, swollen features, tongue and eyes protruding in a horrible manner, and fists clinched in the last convulsive struggle, is not a pleasing object to encounter in your morning ramble."[19] Especially not for lawbreakers. It was estimated that vigilantes dispatched at least twelve outlaws in one year.

The New York Times correspondent who took a ride on one of the railroad's many excursions in the summer of 1868 couldn't make up his mind about the place:

> Here we first saw the peculiarities of frontier life in all their phases. Gambling and every species of iniquity were openly carried on, and in this respect alone it differed, probably, from cities, which pretend to a higher degree of civilization. Certainly there are among the population as enterprising a class of people as ever founded a town. The hotels are good, the daily newspapers anything but fossilized and the evidences of business foresight and pluck numerous. Large amounts of capital are invested in merchandise, and the expectations of the inhabitants are raised and all their energies bent upon building up a substantial and permanent growth.[20]

Law enforcement could be free ranging. Colonel Luke Murrin, the town's magistrate and first mayor, decreed that every man who took part in gunplay would be fined $10, whether his aim was successful or not. One miscreant was told his fine was $10 "plus two bits." "Yes, your honor, but what's the two bits for?" "To buy your honorable judge a drink in the morning."[21]

When the scum of bawdy houses and saloons moved on with the

railroad, Cheyenne became a more settled, more civilized town. The first school was dedicated for the town's two hundred school-aged children on January 5, 1868, a day on which the temperature stood at a chilly twenty-three degrees below zero. Not long after, the first church was put up for the Episcopalians, and in October the Catholic congregation threw a bazaar and raised more than $1,400 through suppers and a raffle. Even before the first church building went up, the Reverend W. W. Baldwin preached to a congregation of seventy in City Hall on September 29, 1867, probably the second such religious gathering in the newborn city.

And yet, in 1868, Cheyenne suffered the same fate as its predecessors. After the construction crews' departure for Laramie and beyond, the citizens of Cheyenne were left to wonder what was to become of their jilted town. In a page-one editorial titled "The Hour of Trial," the *Leader* lamented, "At no time since the founding of Cheyenne has there been more universal gloom and doubt pervading the minds of our citizens than at the present hour. Cheyenne is a creation of the Union Pacific Railroad, and by the acts of that corporation does she stand or fall. The Union Pacific Railroad Company ... have encouraged the belief that this point was to be made the most important one upon the whole line. To disappoint the expectations and hopes of the adventurous population ... would be an act of such flagrant injustice as to forever condemn the men who caused it."[22]

The utopian promises of the railroad's arrival never panned out, and citizens complained that the railroad charged exorbitant freight and passengers rates, didn't pay its share of local taxes, and paid its remaining workers low wages. In other words, it was "a curse to the community," said the *Leader*.[23]

Work sped forward toward the eventual connection with the Central Pacific Railroad in Utah, and residents began packing up in February and heading to the next end-of-track metropolis, Laramie, fifty-seven rail miles to the west, which the line reached in May 1868. Construction was moving ahead at such a rapid pace that no other town along the route would rise to Cheyenne's prominence; Cheyenne, unlike many of the Hell on Wheels towns, survived.

It was serendipitous that Dodge put Cheyenne where he did. It was located just off the Lodgepole Trail, which provided access to the interior of the Wyoming Territory. At 6,041 feet its weather was pleasant if subject to high winds. It became the center of a thriving cattle industry, and, in 1870, the completion of the Denver Pacific Railroad meant freight and passengers from the East headed south to Denver would change trains in town.

Though its population dwindled from a high of six thousand in 1868, Cheyenne could boast a first-class hotel, Rollins House. Located on Sixteenth Street between Pioneer and Carey Avenues, it housed the Wyoming Territorial Legislative Assembly in 1871.

Civic leaders in Cheyenne were not thrilled with plans to build a branch line of the Union Pacific to Denver. Their worst fears were realized when the Wyoming town's dreams of becoming the capital of the Rocky Mountain region came crashing down after the Denver Pacific was completed. In a few short years, it was Denver that was the region's financial and business capital, and Cheyenne had to settle for being the capital of Wyoming.

Before construction of the UP had begun, Denver's boosters were confident that Colorado offered the best route for the transcontinental. Governor William Gilpin, a man known for hyperbole, promised the Colorado Territorial Legislature in 1861, "Our territory will be bisected, East and West, by the grandest work of all time, constructed to ... draw, to and fro, through the heart of the American Union, the travel and commerce of all nations and all continents of the world."[24]

Coloradans were crushed when UP surveyors decided in late 1866 to run the transcontinental route across Wyoming rather than through Denver and Colorado because building across Colorado would have meant surmounting one of the many high passes through the Rockies. Merchants fled Denver, at the time declared "too dead to bury," and moved to Cheyenne, 106 miles north. The snub did not dissuade Denver's backers, including heavyweights John Evans, Walter Cheesman, and William Byers, who worked tirelessly to get the UP to change its mind. Denver's population was stagnant—4,749 in 1860 and only ten more in 1870—and supporters believed that only the railroad could save the isolated town.

The Denver–Cheyenne line was projected to cost $2 million, an optimistic figure that eventually topped out at $6.2 million. Strapped for financing, directors of the Denver Pacific struck a deal with the UP: the DP would construct the roadbed, install bridges, and lay the ties while the UP would supply the rails and track gangs. As part of the deal, the UP demanded that the capitalization be increased from $2 million to $4 million, with the UP receiving $3.5 million of this stock. And when it was built, the DP would be leased to the Kansas Pacific. Eventually, both the DP and KP became part of the UP system.

The Denver Pacific broke ground north of downtown Denver at midday on May 18, 1868, when one thousand citizens, about one-fourth of the city's population, gathered for the gala ceremonies. The *Rocky Mountain News*, whose editor was Byers, a prime mover behind the DP, reported on May 7, "Mr. Roberts, contractor on the Denver Pacific, is to begin work next week. We suggest that we have a little celebration over the affair. It will be worthy of it. No one should get drunk, however; that should be deferred until the road is complete."

And celebrate they did. There were bands, playing "The Saint Louis Quickstep," "Philadelphia Grand March," and, most appropriately, "The Railroad Gallop." A keg of lager, courtesy of Billy Marchant, one of three contractors for the line, was tapped and quickly drained. Ex-governor Gilpin, a man known for his long-winded oration, spoke at length. John W. Smith, president of the Board of Trade, turned the first spade of dirt, and two women, Nettie Clark and Mrs. F. G. Stanton, were given the honor of steering the first plows.

By the end of the day, volunteers toiling across almost level ground had managed to grade a mile of right-of-way. By June, the first forty-six miles of the line were built, and grading started south from Cheyenne on September 8.

Construction proceeded at a slow rate, caused in part by the Union Pacific running out of available rail, but the long-awaited connection to the transcontinental reached the outskirts of Denver on June 22, 1870, setting off a wild celebration. For days, businessmen had been excitedly watching from the tops of buildings for the railroad's approach north of town.

The official last-spike ceremony took place at noon on June 24. A train pulled by the locomotive D. H. Moffat was the first into town. A parade marched from the Masonic Hall at Fifteenth and Larimer Streets to the railroad grounds at Nineteenth and Wazee Streets, where Evans was to drive the last spike. But there was no spike. Historian Kenneth Jessen recounted the awkward moment in *Railroads of Northern Colorado*:

> Billy Barton, proprietor of the Barton House in Georgetown, and the mines in the area had previously sent word to DP officials that they would be glad to furnish a spike of pure silver for the ceremony. When the day arrived for Barton and his compatriots to bring the spike down to Denver, they got drunk, pawned the spike for more booze, and then slept it off, missing the ceremony entirely.[25]

A plain steel spike, wrapped in white paper, was quickly substituted and the day was saved, except the ceremony dragged on for so long that attendees had to walk back to town in the dark.

Cheyenne's loss was Denver's boon. Denver had achieved its long-sought connection with the outside world. The *News* declared proudly on June 22, 1870, "We are now brought into close connection with the valley of the Mississippi and the Atlantic and Pacific sections, and a new era of progress and prosperity opens before us."

Chapter Twelve

MILEPOST 572.8: LARAMIE

When winter—a long, brutal one punctuated by heavy snows and bitter cold—ended in the spring of 1868, the Union Pacific builders set off ever westward, now at an accelerated pace. Exhorted by Thomas Durant and other rail officials, who were beginning to cast worried glances at the oncoming Central Pacific and its rapid advance eastward once it cleared the Sierra Nevada, the rush was on to cover as much ground as quickly as possible. Oakes Ames, an investor, urged Durant "to build three miles a day until next Dec. or Jany and get to Salt Lake before the Central."[1] Money and success depended upon it.

The route from Omaha to Cheyenne, 516 miles, was a relatively level one with few obstacles other than the lack of trees for ties, supply shortages, and the constant harassment of hostile tribes. Now the real work began.

Lying between Cheyenne and Laramie, the next projected end of track, were two barriers: Sherman Summit and Dale Creek. Officials also were looking askance at the oncoming winter, sure to stop construction and, as it turned out, one of the snowiest springs in Wyoming history. By November 1867, tracks reached seven miles west of Cheyenne. Just beyond that was Granite Canyon, where work halted for the winter.

The following March, surveyor Samuel Chittenden, working far out front of the graders and tracklayers, wrote to his mother from Fort Sanders near Laramie, "The roads have been blocked by snow for a week."[2]

In late March, a sudden and ferocious snowstorm stopped work again. Winter did not, however, halt work on one of the line's engineering wonders, the Dale Creek trestle. To get to the bridge required a long slog up Sherman Hill. A gradual slope led to its summit at 8,247 feet, the highest point along the Union Pacific and named for General William T.

Sherman, supporter of the transcontinental and friend of chief engineer Grenville Dodge.

Variously reported to be 130 or 135 or 138 feet high and 650 or 700 feet long, the spidery Dale Creek pine trestle spanned a very narrow stream—a man could step over it, one observer scoffed—but it lay in a wide, deep depression on the plains. It was built using thirteen spans, each forty feet long and anchored to granite footings. Crossing it by rail terrified even the most seasoned traveler.

As wondrous as it was as an engineering feat and as spectacular as it appeared in postcard views, the bridge caused problems for the railroad. With steam locomotives spewing hot cinders, fire was always a danger. When the original wood structure was replaced in 1876 with an equally shaky-looking steel version, high winds caused the bridge to sway, sometimes so much so that traffic had to be stopped; gusty winds threatened to lift empty freight cars off the tracks. A watchman was assigned to keep an eye on things, and signs on the bridge's approaches warned engineers "SLOW TRAINS/To 4 Miles Per Hour/CROSSING BRIDGE."

When carpenters, two of whom tumbled to their deaths during construction, finished their labors on the bridge on April 16, right behind them came the tracklayers, who "barely missed a beat, on April 21 swarming across what was then the highest railroad bridge in the world."[3] The first train crossed on April 23 and the pace of work increased. Samuel Reed, the project's head of construction, bragged in a letter home, "We are now *sailing* & mean to lay over three miles every day."[4]

A celebration was in order. Railroad executives on a tour of the end of track that spring gathered atop the windswept summit on April 16 to celebrate with speeches and the inevitable champagne toasts. Durant and Dodge led a brief celebration before a small crowd of laborers, soldiers, and invited guests, finishing with a ceremonial spike, a precursor to the ceremony when the UP and CP would meet in Utah a year later. A telegrapher nearby relayed an in-your-face message from Durant to Leland Stanford of the Central Pacific that read, "We send you greetings from the highest summit our line crosses between the Atlantic and Pacific oceans. Eight thousand two hundred feet above tide water. Have commenced laying the iron on the down grade westward."[5]

To which Stanford responded almost immediately, "We return your greeting with pleasure. Though you may approach the union of the two roads faster than ourselves, you cannot exceed us in earnestness of desire for that great event. We cheerfully yield you the palm of superior elevation."[6] The somewhat cordial exchange did nothing to lessen the

An engineering wonder, the Dale Creek Bridge between Cheyenne and Laramie nevertheless was a traveler's nightmare, swaying in high winds. Here, the first locomotive crosses the spindly wooden bridge on April 23, 1868.

rivalry between the two men, the two railroads, or the construction crews bent on outdoing each other.

Some eight years later, directors of the Union Pacific voted to erect on the summit an impressive stone monument to the Ames brothers, Oakes and Oliver, two of the first believers in the transcontinental and important to its financing. The pyramid-shaped monument stands sixty feet tall and is faced with individual bas-relief medallions of the Ames boys by Augustus Saint-Gaudens, regarded by many as the greatest American sculptor of all time. When it was completed in 1882, the monument stood beside the main line and passenger trains paused to let travelers detrain and walk around it, but in 1901 the line was rerouted and shortened, in part to eliminate having to cross Dale Creek on that rickety and breathtaking trestle, leaving the monument alone in its solitude. The bridge was demolished.

From Sherman Summit to Laramie was only thirteen miles in a straight line, but the steep downgrade made that impossible; the line zigged and zagged for twenty-three miles on a grade ninety feet to the mile before reaching level ground again. Setting brakes for the long downhill run was, at best, dangerous work, given that men had to scramble over the tops of freight cars to hand-crank brakes down. It was made worse by the fact that brakemen often worked with their backs to the front of the train, making them vulnerable to low-hanging objects, like snowsheds.

Before the railroad arrived, prospective residents eager to cash in on the real-estate booms that followed the railroad began trickling into the town site on the east bank of the Big Laramie River at the center of the Laramie Plains in April, throwing up tents and temporary lean-tos. Four hundred lots were sold in the first week at prices of $25 to $260, selling so fast that UP officials in charge of sales could barely keep up with demand.

The citizens of Cheyenne, who had been led by the UP to believe that their town was to have the biggest shops on the line, were not happy with the announcement the previous February that Laramie was to be home to the next end-of-track shop. Thousands of railroad workers and speculators who had missed out on the real-estate boom in Cheyenne took off for the west. Reflecting its town's feeling of betrayal, Cheyenne's leading newspaper, which at first ignored Laramie, couldn't resist poking fun, labeling it "the Puff Ball City," meaning it was only a shell of a real town. In covering the arrival of the first train in Laramie, the *Cheyenne Leader* reported sarcastically, "The Laramieites were happy and every man had his hand on his neighbor's purse and his mind on jumping his neighbor's lot. Real estate went up as the fluid extract of corn went down ... Oh, beloved Larry-mie so bright a star so soon extinguished by a snowstorm."[7] Even before the town was born, the *Leader* jeered, "Vive le Laramie City! Vive le humbug!"[8]

Joseph Barker, a minister from Omaha, visited Laramie with a contingent of businessmen and political leaders from Saint Louis in the fall of 1868. He found it quite charming. "The town stands on a level plain with the Laramie River in front at a distance of half a mile & the level prairie stretching off for five or six miles beyond to the south. This is the most beautiful place on the whole region. Here they have a fine large hotel & boarding house with a handsome lofty well-aired dining room."[9]

Laramie's first provisional government was elected on May 12 and former Cheyenne attorney M. C. Brown was voted in as mayor. It was a short-lived reign. After only three weeks in office, Brown resigned in a letter to the transient *Frontier Index* newspaper, "In consideration of the fact of the incompetency of many of the officers elected ... in conjunction with myself, and the incapacity and laxity of said officers in discharge of their duties, I find it impossible for me to administer the city government in accordance with my views of the necessities of the case."[10]

A series of weak territorial governments, hampered by imperfect law enforcement, followed. Like other Hell on Wheels towns, Laramie had its problems with a lawless element, which brought with it saloons, dance halls, and gambling hells. Violence was rampant shortly after the founding; men came to town from the railroad and tie camps to spend some time and money and simply disappeared.

Historian J. H. Triggs characterized Laramie and other end-of-track towns:

> Much has been said and much written about the peculiarities of a large majority of the people settling these termini towns along the Union Pacific Railroad. The worst that has ever been said of any of them does not, nor cannot, approach the real truth nor depict the heinousness of the offenses committed by many of these people. What has or can be said of any of the towns on the road can with equal truth be said of Laramie City. In about three months the population aggregated about 5,000 souls. Of these were probably about 1,000 strong, earnest, daring men, ready to face any danger, or ready to undertake any perilous task, if they could, in any honorable way, better their fortunes. One thousand more that were ready

Freund & Bro. followed the railroad's construction progress, selling rifles, pistols, and sporting articles. Men—and one dead antelope—pose outside the store in Laramie in 1868. Freund sold a Winchester carbine for $40 and a Winchester rifle for $50.

COURTESY UNION PACIFIC MUSEUM

to adopt any policy honorable or otherwise, so that they got money, and ran no great risk. The balance ... were made up of gamblers, thieves, highwaymen, robbers, cutthroats, garrotters, prostitutes ... who made their living by preying upon the poor laborers.[11]

The New York Times man arrived in town in June and took a skeptical view of the new town's chances of survival:

What can be said of Laramie? It is a "city" of six week's existence. It is a type of the towns springing up on the far front of civilization, probably surpassing in its features of rudeness the wild frontierism of times past. Its inhabitants are about 2,000 in number. They are composed of the class of men who, in the past few years have been driven from their occupations as trappers, hunters and border men across the Alleghenies, out of Ohio, Illinois, Indiana and Iowa, beyond the Mississippi, westward of the Missouri—drifted on with the speed of the Pacific Road.

Here at Laramie they have come from all parts of the West. Their houses being knocked up in a night are torn down in a day, to be carried off to the next point, which, in a week will be just as full of friskiness and influences of the hour.

I doubt whether it will ever be a place of great importance.[12]

He dismissed it as just another of many "fungus cities" along the route of the transcontinental.

It was another rough-and-tumble gathering, filled with the least of the riffraff who stalked the path of the railroad across Nebraska and Wyoming. Besides the usual pastimes of drinking, gambling, and fighting, street fights were a popular entertainment. The *Frontier Index* reported:

Afternoon before last, a sportsman turned a badger loose in the streets and put a dozen dogs after it to have a little fun. Somebody hollowed fight! And such a rush for the scene as you never before witnessed. There must have been 1,000 men and boys around the badger and the dogs. The badger was too much for the canine species; it would run a few steps and then stop and go for the dogs. The crowd would scatter pell mell whenever Mr. Badger would make a break; old men would fall down and roll over and squeal for dear life, expecting to be chawed up "intirely" by the little fighter. The fight lasted about an hour but to no use, the badger come out victorious. We laughed enough at that scrimmage to last us a lifetime. The badger will give the yelpers another round this evening.[13]

Not everyone was so amused. What Laramie lacked in leadership, it made up for in vigilantes. At first, it was a few men, about twenty, but their numbers soon swelled, to perhaps as many as five hundred. They meant business. Early on the morning of October 18, 1868, vigilantes gathered at the notorious Belle of the West saloon, intent on rounding up the worst of the worst. After a fifteen-minute gun battle, they nabbed Asa "Ace" Moore, his half-brother Con Weiger, and "Big Ned" or "Big Ed" Bernard. Charles Barton, a cornet player in the house band, and William Willie, a fireman on the railroad, were killed during the heated exchange of gunfire.

Ace, Con, and Big Ned were self-appointed town marshals suspected of murdering a number of those whom they arrested, perhaps thirteen or more men. All three were taken to a cabin under construction behind the Frontier Hotel and hanged together. Before they were strung up, Big Ned asked if he could remove his boots because he didn't want to die with them on, and Moore was so shot full of holes they weren't sure whether he was more dead or alive when they hanged him.

A fourth desperado, "Big Steve" Young, was "tried" by the vigilantes, but evidence against him was so lacking that they decided to run him out of town instead of hanging him. Young rode the train only as far as Fort Sanders, a few miles from town, hopped off, and walked back to Laramie, where he discovered his three stiffened companions still hanging where the vigilantes had left them. Outraged, he vowed revenge. The vigilantes were having none of that and immediately seized him, forcing him to climb a ladder leaning against a telegraph pole, where he met the same fate as his friends. All four were buried in a common grave less than a mile east of town.

A. P. Wood, a civil engineer with the Union Pacific, was having a late breakfast at the hotel that morning when the waiter exclaimed, "Come out on the porch, Mr. Wood, they're going to hang Big Steve!" In a 1925 reminiscence, Wood recalled,

> I went out at once and there at the south end of the hotel and in front of the freight depot there was gathered a crowd of a hundred or more people. A few of the active vigilance men had Big Steve, marching him up a ladder against a telegraph pole, to which was attached a hangman's rope, which was placed around Steve's neck.

Where lawlessness and violence thrived, vigilantes were sure to follow. Vigilantes, who numbered as many as five hundred in Laramie, hanged bad men "Ace" Moore, Con Weiger, and "Big Ned" Bernard on a makeshift gallows on October 18, 1868.

The ladder was knocked out and Big Steve was launched into eternity. I turned away and went back to the dining room. I found my appetite for breakfast had left me.[14]

The hangings of the foursome, and the subsequent departure for new territory by other toughs who got the vigilantes' message, instantly transformed Laramie into a more moral town that became known as the "Gem City." The first public school opened in February 1869, and five churches (Episcopalian, Methodist, Catholic, Baptist, and Presbyterian) opened their doors to parishioners. In addition, Triggs noted in his 1875 history of the town, "We have a large number of good citizens who are Free Thinkers, but without any organization, who are ever ready to unite with good people of all creeds and beliefs in every project calculated to benefit mankind."[15]

If Laramie was bad, Benton, at milepost 696 from Omaha and 123 miles west of Laramie, was worse. Named after Senator Thomas Hart Benton of Missouri, one of the first to back the building of a railroad across the continent, Benton was an important freighting stop for supplies to the mining camps of Utah, Montana, and Idaho.

Dodge envisioned the yet-to-be-built town as a terminal division for the road, and the UP laid out streets and sold lots to those who shared his vision. Within weeks, three thousand newcomers, with the usual assortment of Hell on Wheels bottom-feeders, landed in town. Charles Edgar Ames, a descendant of the Ames brothers, wrote, "For ten hours day, the streets were thronged with motley crowds, railroad men, and soldiers, merchants and miners; saloonkeepers and mule whackers. Among them, of course, was the usual quota of parasitic adventurers, men and women."[16] There were, he said, twenty-three saloons and five dance halls. Even the fabled four-thousand-square-foot Big Tent, first put up in North Platte, Nebraska, made its appearance in all its fancied splendor.

Railroad carpenter H. Clark Brown detrained there in the fall of 1868 and found a perfect hell. Years later he recalled, "There was an officer with a man by his side that had been arrested. They were about ten feet in front of us when the man with the officer said he wanted to go in to wash and he started for the door. The officer told him to come with him. He did not do so and the officer drew his revolver and shot him."[17]

Unfortunately for Benton and its supporters, good and bad, the town could not have been more poorly located. Perched on the eastern edge of the arid Red Desert in south central Wyoming, water was almost nonexistent without extensive drilling, and what was there was brackish. Drinkable water had to be hauled in from the North Platte River three miles away, and a bucket of it sold for ten cents. The ground was so alkaline nothing grew. "Far as [we] could see around the town, not a green tree, shrub, or spear of grass was to be seen," John Davis wrote in his journal. "The red hills, scorched and bare as if blasted by the lightnings of an angry God. All seemed sacred to the genius of drouth and desolation."[18]

Visiting correspondent Samuel Bowles called it "by day disgusting, by night dangerous, almost everybody dirty, many filthy and with the marks of the lowest vice; over a murder a day, gambling, hurdy-gurdy dancing, and the vilest of sexual commerce." He labeled it "a congregation of scum."[19]

Only three months later, the town vanished, its inhabitants off to find potable water and the next end-of-track town, leaving behind the refuse of humanity and a few crumbling chimneys.

Work now was progressing at such a rapid pace that the crews of graders and tracklayers were leapfrogging each other. Towns seem, to pop up randomly and disappear just as quickly; the end-of-track flotsam could barely keep up. On August 10, the *Cheyenne Leader* correspondent, who cleverly signed his report "S.P. IKE DRIVER," was in Benton and wrote,

> The track is making tracks across the trackless waste towards Green River at a rapid rate. Moonlight nights and Sundays are drafted into service for extra hours. From Big Laramie to Little Laramie; from Little Laramie to Rock Creek; from Rock Creek to Carbon; from Carbon to Benton; from Benton to [Rawlins] Springs, where more shops are built; from there to Green River, and from Green River to Ham's Fork, Echo Canyon, Weber, Salt Lake—anywhere at all so as to be going somewhere and taking one jump farther than the town was last in the lead. So we go, "Westward ever Westward," until— aha! What's this we meet? The Central Pacific, hurrying Eastward ever Eastward with Imperial wealth of Asiatic empires.[20]

Chapter Thirteen

MILEPOST 946.0: BEAR RIVER CITY

When Legh Freeman and his rig full of printing equipment rolled into Gilmer, Wyoming Territory, in October 1868, he was sure that the sparsely settled village was to be the next big thing along the transcontinental railroad.

Legh Freeman was always a booster. For more than two years, Legh, his older brother, Frederick, and their vagabond newspaper, the *Frontier Index*, rolled westward from Fort Kearny, Nebraska, set up shop in successive towns along the route of the Pacific Railroad, and extolled the virtues of each burg they published in, including North Platte, Nebraska; Julesburg, Colorado; Cheyenne, Fort Sanders, Laramie, and Green River in Wyoming; and Bear River City.

Legh Freeman assumed ownership of his first newspaper, the *Kearney (Nebraska) Herald*, at age twenty-three and summoned his older brother to join him in the publishing business, which promised financial return once the transcontinental began its westward push. Like Legh, Frederick served in the Southern army during the Civil War. The two men were markedly unalike in personality. Legh was fiery and headstrong; Frederick was even tempered and likeable.

Beginning at North Platte in May 1866, the brothers published the *Frontier Index* together or separately until its untimely demise in Bear River City, Wyoming, in November 1868. Not only did they publish their newspaper at North Platte, but they were making hefty profits doing job printing, charging $10 to $20 for one hundred words on small circulars. They also charged twenty-five cents a line for advertisements in the *Index*. It wasn't just the saloons and gambling parlors that advertised; their advertisers included restaurants, bakeries, breweries, ice cream parlors, banks, and hotels.

Legh's wanderlust—he loved roaming the West and eventually wound up spending a great deal of time in New Mexico—often left Frederick to handle production alone. Legh's fascination with the West began early. Left with a slight limp from a childhood accident, he created a fictional character for himself, Horatio Vattel, "Lightning Scout of the Mountains." This boyhood doppelganger resurfaced in the *Frontier Index* with a Horatio Vattel byline.

"Though he could be as sarcastic as anybody, Frederick's jibes at competitors were generally light-hearted. Legh's writing was heavy-handed by comparison," wrote one observer. "Legh's editorials slipped into the gutter at the slightest provocation."[1]

Frederick dropped out of the family business after its stint in Laramie, Wyoming, but Legh continued to trek forward with the railroad, promoting and talking up the next town on the line and calling out the criminal element.

He was particularly effusive in his praise of Bear River City, also known as Beartown to its inhabitants. Shortly after he arrived, he gushed, "This place is already outfitting the whole country westward to Humboldt Wells. Five thousand persons already obtain their mails at this post office. The town is the greatest success of any founded on the line of the Great National Highway."[2] He even used the oncoming winter to encourage settlement in his new favorite stop. "It is the very height of folly for any person engaged in commercial pursuits to think of moving west of this point until spring. It is already too late to begin a new town. A heavy snowstorm is liable to occur any moment at this season of the year."[3]

When Freeman moved there, there was disagreement over whether this center of a logging and coal district was in Utah or Wyoming. Located on Sulphur Creek, two miles east of the Bear River, it wasn't much to look at: the most common vegetation was blue-gray sagebrush. It was known as Gilmer when Freeman arrived, but he felt that a name that described its physical location would be more fitting. He applied to postal officials in Utah Territory for a name change and, after some disagreement (there was already a Bear River City in Utah), was granted the new name and became the town's postmaster.

Freeman fell in love with Bear River City, but he wasn't blind to its faults. Committed to whichever town he was in at the time, he and his newspaper campaigned against the "garroters," the criminal element, who infested the overnight towns. Bear River gave him plenty of opportunity to campaign.

Legh Freeman, fiery advocate of law and order and an outspoken racist, used his *Frontier Index* newspaper to inflame the Bear River Riot on November 20, 1868. He galloped out of town as the rioters closed in to torch his print shop.

Bear River City, close to Sulphur Creek and surrounded by sage-brush in western Wyoming, wasn't much to look at, but Legh Freeman and others had high hopes for it. The railroad bypassed the town, which quickly and entirely disappeared.

By November 1868, graders and tracklayers ballooned Bear River's population to two thousand, crowded into more than one hundred tents, shacks, and log cabins. And there were saloons, plenty of saloons. The railroad work gangs hit town, drank a lot, fought, and terrified the "good" citizens. Freeman wasn't about to let the roughs ruin his new base; he had seen enough of what the criminal element had wrought in towns where he'd set up his printing business.

There was Benton, windy, laced with alkali, and brimming with bad characters. There was Bryan, which disappeared in a few weeks and was described as "one of the bad places of the system. More murders were committed there on less provocation than at any place of the same size."[4]

And there was Green River, which Freeman did not have fond memories of. He repeatedly referred to it as "Bilkville" because, he wrote,

> A few men were bribed at Green River, with a town lot at Bryan. Others followed to what they supposed would be the winter R.R. terminus, believing that they were dealing with railroad officials, when in reality they were being humbugged by a set of swindling speculators who never did and never will belong to the Union Pacific Railroad. Again we warn the people already here, and those coming, not to be humbugged by these flying rumors thrown out by adventurers who take your money, from $250 to $500 per lot, with compunctions of a road agent or garroter.[5]

It was here that Freeman first tangled with lawman Tom Smith, who later played an important part in what lives on as the Bear River Riot.

Smith was a cop in New York City in the 1850s and moved to Utah and Nevada in 1860. When the Union Pacific launched the transcontinental in Omaha, he joined up as a troubleshooter for the company and as a foreman for Chesbrough and McGee, grading contractors for the UP. Along the way, he became the respected marshal at Green River.

When the end of track reached Bear River, Freeman, Smith, and hundreds of others followed. Freeman, who disagreed with Smith politically, was quick to accuse him in print of protecting "professional robbers" in Green River and held Smith responsible for a $70 debt owed to the *Frontier Index* by the town of Green River.

Freeman was not a man to forgive and forget. He railed in print against advertisers who failed to pay their bills. "Pay up," he wrote, "or pay the penalty of being advertised, and thus sink into an ignominious existence, and die the death of thieves, stealers from the men who first

As the leader of an outraged mob of railroad graders, "Bear River" Tom Smith did much to precipitate a running shootout that left at least eleven men dead. He later became sheriff in Abilene, Kansas, to be murdered and beheaded at age thirty.

aided you and your business community."[6] He followed through on his threat. Two weeks later, he named J. W. Bothwell "the red-haired, thin-visaged sneak" who hadn't paid his bill.

Born in Culpeper, Virginia, Freeman served in the Southern army, was captured, and became a "galvanized Yankee," serving in a company of former Confederates. He never quit being a Rebel. Freeman was prolific in his use of strong language about those who offended him. In an era when "personal journalism" reigned and there were no lawyers with libel suits in hand, newspaper editors frequently broiled their opponents in print. The *Frontier Index*, of which only forty-five editions are known to exist, was a blowtorch for Freeman's enemies. He called a Denver editor "that pimp [Ovando J.] Hollister" and the rival *Salt Lake Reporter* "that puked up sheet."

He was shocked when Ulysses S. Grant, who had successfully defeated Robert E. Lee and his troops to end the Civil War and was a Republican, became president. Freeman, a die-hard Democrat, excoriated Grant in his paper, calling him "a whisky bloated, squaw ravishing adulterer, monkey ridden, nigger worshipping mogul, a hell-born satrap, tanbark, stinking aristocrat, double-dealing hypocrite, libertine seducer, and polygamic squaw keeper, leather headed howling debaucher" and, for good measure, a "California barroom bummer."[7]

If Freeman weren't directly responsible for the outrage expressed in the Bear River Riot by the track workers, most of whom fought on the Northern side in the Civil War, he certainly inflamed them with an anti-Grant editorial in his newspaper on November 13:

> The road to the White House which Grant has traveled over during our last campaign is paved with the skeletons of many thousand soldiers whom he slaughtered uselessly during his western and southern military career. Eastern mothers must tremble for the safety of their daughters' virtue, knowing that the gaudy military uniform of their President and rule covers the filthy, lecherous carcass of a libertine, a seducer, and polygamic squaw keeper.[8]

Freeman made no secret of his rampant racism, which grew stronger as he moved west. The masthead of his newspaper carried the motto "Only WHITE MEN to be naturalized in the United States. The RACES and SEXES in their respective spheres as God Almighty originally created them." No one escaped his wrath: he was anti-black, anti-Chinese, anti-Indian, and anti-Mormon.

When he was publishing at Benton in August, Freeman praised local businessmen, most of whom advertised in his paper. But he singled out "a very prominent individual," a man, said Freeman, "who thought a negro was as good as a white man, and a darned sight better than some white men. We told him that we did not pretend to dispute with him as regards himself, for we thought a ring-tailed monkey was better than any white man who seeks to degrade Anglo-Saxons by comparison with any inferior race."[9]

He was determined to clean out the criminal element in Bear River City. In the November 3 issue of the *Frontier Index* he printed an editorial signed "All Good Citizens" that warned gamblers and their ilk to "vacate this city or hang within sixty hours of this noon." Conflict was inevitable. One week later, on November 10, vigilantes strung up three young ne'er-do-wells: Jimmy Powers, Jimmy Reed, and "Little Jack" O'Neil. The threesome would seem good candidates for hanging. Powers was caught committing a stickup. Reed assaulted and robbed a townsman. O'Neil allegedly knocked a man down in a saloon, beat him, and picked his pockets.

Alexander Toponce, who had a contract to supply beef to the rail workers, remembered, "I got up one morning at my camp near Bear Town and noticed something hanging near the railroad track and I walked down to see what it was. It was those three fellows whom I knew had been banished from Montana in 1864. A tag was pinned to their coats, "Warning to the Road Agents."[10]

Based on his rabid campaign against bummers in town, many assumed that Freeman, rumored to be a member of the vigilante committee, was behind the hangings. He took to print to deny it, but added darkly, "It is well known that wherever we have sojourned in the Territories, we have opposed violence in any form, and given the common law priority, but when very fiends assume to run our place of publication there are plenty of men who rather delight in doing dirty work, hanging without us, as was evidenced [on November 10] and as will be witnessed again if the ring leaders are found in town by midnight of this Friday, November 13."[11]

The stage was set for one of the most extraordinary events in the building of the transcontinental. The graders who were friends with at least one of the young men hanged by vigilantes thought Freeman's diatribes about the criminal element were aimed at them (they did enjoy hitting the saloons, fighting, and raising hell). In addition, many of them were former Union soldiers and resented Freeman's rants against Grant.

On November 19, several of the railroad boys, whooping it up in Bear River, were locked up in the town's brand-new jail for their excessive celebrations. That was the last straw for the graders, most of whom worked for subcontractor Chesbrough and McGee.

At 8:00 AM on Friday, November 20, a mob variously estimated at between two hundred and three hundred men armed with guns, shovels, and pickaxes marched on the town with the intention of freeing their comrades, giving Beartown's citizens a good thrashing, and, mainly, lynching Freeman. They busted into the newly built jail, let their friends loose, and tried to burn the jail down, but because it was built of green logs, it wouldn't burn.

They turned their attention to the heart of their wrath: Freeman and his *Frontier Index* newspaper tent. Toponce wrote that he hurried to the newspaper and alerted Freeman, who promptly mounted a mule and galloped out of town. In his version of the story Freeman claimed he gallantly rode "a white steed" to nearby Fort Bridger to summon help. Others said he was so happy to escape with his life that he just kept riding right out of town. The rioters destroyed his press, scattered type on the ground, and burned the tent to cinders.

Two eyewitness accounts, with some variation, give a good picture of what happened that morning, which followed by a day another Freeman screed about the "rowdies" in town. Toponce, the witness to the aftermath of the hanging of the three young men, wrote,

> I saw about fifty of the [Chesbrough] and McGee outfit coming along the track. They had read the paper. The leaders had ropes in their hands and they called out as they passed me that they were going to hang the editor.
>
> There was a mule standing ready saddled at the door of my tent and I jumped on him and raced down to the editor's tent. The crowd got to the front door as I got to the back of the tent. I cut a long slit in the back of the tent with my knife and got him out on the mule and he escaped.
>
> They simply ruined the printing office. The businessmen locked their stores and about a dozen got together in Nukles [S. F. Nuckolls & Co.] store with rifles to defend themselves.
>
> The leader of the mob was a man named Tom Smith. They tried to burn the jail but the logs were too green.
>
> The mob run the town from 8 o'clock [AM] to four in the afternoon, getting drunker and more dangerous all the time. About 4,

Smith knocked on the door of the [Nuckolls] store and when the proprietor opened the door a little and advised them to get out of town Smith shot him in the leg.

Then the shooting became general. It was a regular battle. The men with rifles barricaded in the store opened up and swept the streets. Seventeen men were killed in the mob and as many more were wounded, some of who died.[12]

Theodore Haswell, a grader himself, had a slightly different recollection:

They succeeded in burning the [*Frontier Index*] printing office and set fire to other buildings. Twenty-four of us gathered in a storeroom for defense and were quickly surrounded by the mob.

One of our group, who was acquainted with the most of the men in the mob, went out and attempted to reason with them, but returned shortly, convinced that it would be impossible to accomplish anything this way. Just as he returned, a shot was fired from the mob and he fell dead. Then the mob opened fire upon our group. [Tom] Smith, the leader of the mob, with a revolver in each hand, ran up to the front of the storeroom we were in, and emptied both guns at us.

Then we opened fire. Smith was severely wounded and five of the mob fell dead, and others were wounded. Almost immediately, the mob withdrew. The man who was killed [a citizen man named Stephen Stokes] was the only casualty in our group. With nearly every window of the building shot out and the woodwork torn with bullets, it seemed an act of Providence that we were not all killed.[13]

Many bystanders pinpointed Smith as one of the leaders of the mob, saying he had fueled their anger with liquor and encouraged their participation. Haswell, among the citizens defending their town, said that after a brief parlay on the street between Smith and Stokes, the mob chased Stokes back to Nuckolls's store, where he was shot dead. Historian Gary L. Roberts wrote that the "encounter between Stokes and Smith clearly precipitated the fight. Who opened fire first is unclear but by the time they neared the store, Smith was blazing away and the men inside the store were returning fire."[14]

The battle lasted only about ten minutes, though sporadic firing continued until late afternoon, with members of the mob drinking and terrorizing the town. Finally, the graders withdrew into the hills to tend to their wounded, but townspeople stayed watchful in case they returned during the night. A second attack never came. The next morning, troops from Fort Bridger arrived and martial law was declared. The Bear River Riot was over.

Accounts of the fracas were wildly exaggerated. First reports said that twenty-three of the mob were killed and another thirty or more wounded. Another witness claimed that bodies littered the street. Freeman himself told the *Salt Lake Telegraph* that forty were dead. The generally agreed-upon figures are eleven killed and three wounded.

Smith, who maintained that he was acting in the best interests of the townspeople and that he prevented further bloodshed, moved on to became marshal in Wahsatch, Utah, then traveled eastward to Kansas, where he became noteworthy for cleaning up the cow town of Abilene. Proud of the fact that he kept law and order there by using his fists instead of firearms, Smith was killed and beheaded in November 1870 at age thirty by a farmer he was trying to arrest for murder.

Freeman's newspaper career didn't go up in flames in Bear River City. He moved on to produce newspapers in Montana and Washington and, in 1875, was publishing his paper under the name *Ogden (Utah) Freeman*. He died in obscurity in Yakima, Washington, in 1915.

And what about Bear River City, whose bright future was predicted by Legh Freeman? After order was restored, the railroad and its workers were moving westward at increasing speed. Union Pacific officials, perhaps looking askance at the activities there, decided to build around Bear River City and make Evanston, ten miles to the northwest, a division town. There was not even a siding at Beartown, and nothing of the town remains.

Chapter Fourteen

MILEPOST 1056.6: CORINNE

When the Union Pacific work crews exited western Wyoming late in December 1868, the railroad once again faced its three ongoing nemeses: weather, shortage of funds, and the onrushing Central Pacific Railroad.

Construction had passed over the easiest part of the route, covering 955 track miles from Omaha to Evanston in three years. Now came the hard part. While graders and tracklayers were working furiously to beat the coming winter snow and cold, the UP's surveyors were already laying out line one hundred miles or more ahead of construction. They were rushing to reach Humboldt Wells in eastern Nevada, where officials hoped to hook up with the Central Pacific Railroad and take away the Utah market from the CP.

First, the UP had to conquer Echo Canyon and Weber Canyon, the quickest and easiest route through the Wasatch Range to Ogden, Utah, and farther west, although it wouldn't be all that easy. The steep and narrow Echo Canyon meandered thirty miles through the Wasatch and presented challenges the railroad hadn't encountered on such a scale. Towering red cliffs loomed over the canyon, promising landslides, rock cuts, and costly fills—not to overlook the digging of one or more tunnels. To speed the work, the railroad built temporary track and flimsy trestles, intending to return later and shore up their hasty workmanship.

Another persistent obstacle was the weather; it was a severe winter. It began to snow in late December 1868 and continued almost without pause until April. After a January snowstorm in Wyoming, howling winds buried the tracks under drifts. Then came a bitter cold wave when the temperature stayed below zero for days and at one point dipped to minus twenty. The storm halted travel between Rawlins and Laramie for three weeks. In February, a locomotive straining to break through massive snowdrifts exploded, killing its engineer, fireman, and conductor. A three-day blizzard swept across the region in March 1869, burying the line, bringing freight traffic to a halt, and delaying the delivery of vital supplies to the graders and tracklayers in Utah.

A warning of what lay ahead came from a young UP surveyor the previous summer. Samuel Chittenden wrote to his mother from the Bear River, "I do not believe it will be possible to run a railroad here in the winter. Half the time the snow falls and then drifts into all the hollows, filling them all up level, so I think you may expect me home around Christmas."[1]

The small railroad way station of Wahsatch perched at seven thousand feet in its namesake mountain range became the winter terminus. It was cold; for one week in January, the temperature never rose above minus three. Newspaper reporter and travel writer J. H. Beadle reported breakfasting there one morning while snow drifted through cracks an inch wide in the café's walls and his coffee froze. Graders were forced to work in cumbersome overcoats, further hampering their labors.

The combination of brutal winter weather—frozen ground had to be broken up with black powder explosions—and the Union Pacific's haste to cover as much territory as it could to keep the Central Pacific at bay produced some of the poorest track on the more than one thousand miles the UP laid. A correspondent for the *Rocky Mountain News* took a ride on the line in April 1869 and said of the track from Wahsatch to Corinne, "A worst piece of work cannot be imagined. The grade, having been laid in the winter on frozen ground, which is now beginning to thaw, is one pile of mud, fit for anything but what it is being used for. The rails rise and fall as the train passes over them; the track is full of curves and even at the rate the trains go—four or five miles an hour—is dangerous and unsafe. The temporary bridges now in use are nothing more or less than man traps, and it will be a miracle if some of them do not go down before the permanent ones are finished."[2]

Tunneling became a major impediment. Terrain dictated the building of three tunnels, the longest 772 feet, in Echo and Weber Canyons. Unhappy with the progress his crews were making, the UP's Thomas Durant struck a deal with Mormon leader Brigham Young to bring on several thousand of his followers to speed things up. Volunteers from around the region showed up to shovel and grade, but tunnels were beyond their skills. The tunnels were carved out mostly by hand with the liberal use of black powder and the much more volatile and more powerful nitroglycerin. Some workers walked off the job rather than work with nitro. After weeks of painfully slow progress, the UP brought in its mostly Irish crews from Wyoming to finish the job, but they too made only a few feet a day and the Mormons were put back to work. It took ten months to complete the tunnel, causing further anxiety about the Central Pacific, now working its way across Nevada and into Utah.

So that work farther down the line could continue, it was necessary for trackage to bypass the tunneling. An eight-mile-long rickety series of switchbacks, known as the Zig-Zag, was constructed as a temporary solution, tracks inching up "a perpendicular wall of rock," said one terrified passenger.

Still, he allowed that "we ran off the track only twice" and even looked with humor on their leaving the track in Weber Canyon:

> On the left, just below us, the Weber River was roaring and foaming, and on the right but a few feet from the track was a perpendicular wall of rock. It was a fearful place for an accident to happen, and the passengers were conversing about it when one of them, who was looking out of the window on the right-hand side, suddenly discovered a car off of the track and bouncing along over the ties. With one shout he disappeared through the window and tumbled out headlong on the ground.
>
> Everyone comprehended the situation in a second and the next second was going through door or window. When the train stopped there was scarcely one left in the car. The speedy exit which everyone made caused a general laugh, but above all the merriment there was a feeling of thankfulness that matters were no worse.[3]

They reached Ogden without further incident later that day.

As was frequently the case, the UP was facing severe money troubles. Workers, some of whom hadn't been paid for weeks, went on strike for $3.50 a day and double pay on Sundays. Faced with the loss of its most skilled on-the-ground workers, the railroad agreed to the demands. The company was $10 million in debt and had no hope of paying off its long-term obligations. This at a time when the Crédit Mobilier was paying stockholders $12.8 million in cash and another $4 million in UP stock.[4]

Young agreed to a deal that would pay him (and his church) $2.125 million for grading, tunneling, and bridge masonry between the head of Echo Canyon and Salt Lake. Under the arrangement, the railroad would transport Young's men and supply powder, steel, and tools for the work if the Mormons, working far in front of the railroad's tracklaying crews still laboring through Wyoming, finished by November 1, 1868.

Both sides benefited. The railroad, faced with the Central Pacific coming on at four miles a day, its eyes set on meeting the Union Pacific at Ogden, was desperate to speed construction. Jack Casement, the man in charge of construction, was working his crews day and night. Young, his followers faced with a third straight year of crops devastated by swarms of grasshoppers, saw an opportunity to supply jobs to his people. Plus, if Mormons built the line it would also help keep the boisterous UP crews and their bad habits at arm's length.

Unfortunately for the Mormons, the railroad was woefully lax in making payment, not only to the Saints but also to other contractors and subcontractors. Young was forced to wire Durant repeatedly, asking when he and his men would get paid; he would get no response or receive only part of what he asked for. He even dipped into his own pocket to make payroll. When the job was done, the Union Pacific still owed $1.41 million to the Mormons for their work. More than a year later, the Union Pacific paid Young less than half of what it owed him. The rest, they promised, would be negotiated.

The life saver for both the Union Pacific and Central Pacific was the government's loan of bonds for miles graded and track laid. It was another reason the railroads were locked in a frantic race to a still-undetermined meeting point: more miles meant more money. Because of the flat terrain it crossed in Nebraska and Wyoming, the UP received $16,000 in bonds for each mile it covered, but now that they were in mountainous terrain the payback rose to $48,000 a mile. Every little bit helped.

Both roads were prepared to do whatever was necessary to keep the government loans rolling in. The Pacific Railway Act of 1862 let the railroads grade three hundred miles in advance of continuous track and thus collect bonds for each forty—later twenty—miles graded. But vice president Collis P. Huntington and his CP had a glaring gap in its track at Donner Lake in the Sierra Nevada, far short of Humboldt Wells, the point at which his railroad could legitimately begin grading farther east. Huntington simply took the easiest tack—he lied. He drew a line on a map allegedly showing track where none existed. Washington bureaucrats, largely ignorant about western geography, bought it.

Once clear of the Wasatch Range, the Union Pacific's construction resumed a frantic pace, quickly leaving Ogden and Brigham City in its wake. In early April, tracklayers reached Corinne, the last of the full-blown Hell on Wheels towns. It was another invention of the railroad, but it had one distinction the other railroad towns did not: it was

Corinne, Utah, an island of gentiles in a sea of Mormons, thrived in the 1860s as a freighting center, sending dry goods and mining equipment to Montana and Idaho, but when the Union Pacific moved on to Promontory Summit, the town faded.

Supporters proclaimed Corinne would be "the Chicago of the Rocky Mountains" and these businessmen—a watchmaker, a barber, a hardware dealer, and a painter—did their best to make it happen. There were also nineteen saloons in town.

the only non-Mormon town in Utah, which would prove to be both an advantage and, ultimately, help lead to its demise.

Located on the broad, arid plains thirty-one miles west of Ogden and twenty-eight miles east of Promontory Summit, Corinne went up for sale in March 1869 when the UP platted lots and began selling them. Business was brisk. Entrepreneurs crowded onto narrow "downtown" lots on Montana and South and North Front Streets. More than three hundred lots ranging in price from $5 to $1,000 sold on the first day of the sale, their buyers convinced that Corinne, already an important jumping-off place for freighters headed to the mines in Idaho and Montana, would become a major metropolis, "the Chicago of the Rocky Mountains."

They were open for business when the tracks of the Union Pacific crossed the Bear River just east of town and rolled into Corinne on April 7, leading the *Salt Lake Telegraph* to enthuse, "The utmost excitement prevails on the subject of Corinne and hundreds are still flocking there. From two hundred fifty to three hundred tents, shanties and buildings have been erected, and each day sees their number increased."[5]

The majority of the incoming businesses catered to the rest and recreation of railroad workers. There were nineteen saloons, two dance halls, and eighty "syrens," or girls. Sundays most of the male citizen went hunting or fishing and the girls had a dance or got drunk. As open-air entertainment there were dogfights.[6]

A reporter who surveyed the town's commerce when he passed through in April counted "one house, or tent, of feminine frailty, one bar room and chop house, one grocery, one saloon with 'convenient apartments' ... one punk roost, one keg saloon, two mercantile adventures ... one town liquor store, one billiard hall, one washing, ironing, and plain sewing erection, several promiscuous ladies in eight-by-ten duck domiciles ... one or two wholesale and retail liquor establishments."[7]

As late as January 1869, four months before the historic meeting of the Union Pacific and Central Pacific a few miles away, the *Corinne Daily Journal* reported that Al Stubblefield's saloon offered bread, meat, coffee, and "sagebrush whiskey." Beadle, later editor for a brief time of the town's newspaper, noted that only two years earlier, "There is no newsstand, post office or barber shop." He commented that a stagecoach ran to Promontory as a "try-weekly, that is it goes out one week and *tries* to get back the next."[8]

Because Corinne was a cornerstone for freighters there were also hotels, boardinghouses, and a number of restaurants. Montana House advertised "meals 50 cents." There were blacksmiths, stock dealers, and wagon sellers. Forwarding and commission houses did a thriving business shipping dry goods and mining equipment north to Idaho and Montana by long wagon trains. After the railroad's freight trains began arriving from the East, the freighters would prosper by forwarding the goods. Or so the thinking went.

The town was named (probably) after the daughter of founder General J. A. Williamson, but some say its namesake was a well-known actress of the time, Corinne LaVaunt. It is pronounced "COR-inn" not "Co-REEN." The surrounding country was bleak, flat, dry, and, except for tufts of sagebrush, almost totally lacking in verdure. It was, noted one visitor, "like a head without hair, like a face without eyelashes."[9]

Everyone complained about the dust. "Teamsters and herders were in the habit of driving their large herds of cattle and horses directly through town to take them to water at Bear River," wrote historian Brigham D. Madsen. "As a result ... housewives could not hang out their clothes to dry and painters could not work on houses because clouds of alkali dust poured in through doors and windows, making the home almost uninhabitable."[10] The *Corinne Reporter* printed a rebuttal from a stockman who grew tired of the criticism: "If any person don't like the dust he ought to move to where it rains all the time."[11]

Those living in Corinne didn't think of it as just another hellhole on the transcontinental. During the first weeks of the town's existence, the mayor and the town council passed a bushel of regulations—to license dogs, to prevent pigs from running through the streets, to prohibit boys under twenty-one from drinking liquor, playing billiards, cards, or dice—and vainly tried to limit "gaming and houses of ill fame." The well-traveled Baron de Hübner summed up the populace:

> The streets of Corinne are full of white men armed to the teeth, miserable-looking Indians dressed in the ragged shirts and trousers furnished by the Central Government, and yellow Chinese with a business-like air and hard intelligent faces. No town in the Far West gave me so good an idea as this little place of what is meant by border life; i.e., the struggle between civilization and savage men and things.[12]

Corinne was determined to be a gentile island in a sea of Mormonism, and churches, hoping to hold back the ill-behaved railroaders, flocked in. The Presbyterians arrived first. The Methodist Episcopal Church, opened in September 1870, now houses the Corinne History

Museum and proclaims itself to be the oldest existing Protestant church building in Utah. It was a struggle for God-fearing men confronted with a mostly male population that had little time for religion. Corinne was built not on a community interest but on financial interests. It was money that made Corinne grow.

There were some ills even ministers couldn't cure. One man who had been to the mines in Montana warned a friend about Corinne: "Ah yes—one little item I forgot to mention—Bed Bugs—Town full of them—stay here—Metropolitan Hotel full of them—everybody gets lots of them and some to spare—I got some—stop when you come through and get some—Dont cost a cent."[13]

The coming of the railroad was a boon to the town financially, but Mormons, particularly their leader Brigham Young, cast a worried eye on the influx of what they called "gentiles," or non-Mormons. Young, who, paradoxically, would help build part of the transcontinental and saw the value in it to Mormons, warned his followers in a speech in 1866 about the influx of gentiles, citing ways to lessen their impact:

> To contract to build the railroads through Utah to keep out as many of the hell-on-wheels construction camps as possible; to establish a church-wide wholesale establishment under the name of Zions Cooperative Mercantile Institution that would move all imports; to organize cooperative retail outlets in each local church ward to eliminate non-Mormon stores; to support only local producers and manufacturers, and to boycott all gentile merchants and bankers.[14]

He painted a grim picture of life with gentiles. "What do they mean by civilization? Why, they mean by that, to establish gambling holes—they are called gambling hells—grog shops and houses of ill fame on every corner of every block in the city."[15]

In response, the gentile press, particularly aroused by the Mormons' claiming tithes in Corinne, which critics called taxes, and the church's approval of polygamy, accused the Mormons of being hypocrites and of attempting to strangle Corinne in its crib. The *Corinne Reporter*, frequently at odds with the church, declared in an editorial that the only difference between polygamy and prostitution was that the former involved multiple women and the latter multiple men, and that both constituted the same crime of "plural cohabitation."[16]

There was in the West a general distrust of the Mormons who, having been driven out of their eastern settlements decades earlier, were

The last of the full-blown hell-raising towns along the transcontinental, Corinne was the familiar collection of saloons and brothels after construction gangs arrived in the spring of 1869. "Sagebrush whiskey" was a favorite refreshment.

COURTESY CORINNE, UTAH, HISTORY MUSEUM

clannish and suspicious of outsiders. They were also industrious, self-sustaining, and protective of their families. Chittenden spoke for many of his fellow workers when he wrote home from Echo Canyon to his mother in May 1868, "All the people here are Mormons and some of the ranches here have two or three wives apiece. It is astonishing how they keep up the thing. I saw a family of nine on foot working their way back, carting their grub on their back and with only two blankets to sleep in. They said they carried about $2,000 when they joined the Mormons and now they leave in this style."[17]

Living largely isolated from the rest of the country, Mormons nevertheless were shrewd businessmen. "They consider it no sin to cheat a gentile and every Mormon we have bought anything of has tried to cheat our eye teeth out. We say nothing but keep an account."[18]

The Mormons who helped the Union Pacific finish its tracks to Promontory Summit also used railroads to bring down Corinne and its population of nonbelievers. Using secondhand equipment obtained from the UP as part payment for his workers, still unpaid despite their yeoman work in the winter of 1868 and spring of 1869, Young built the Utah Central, a standard-gauge line from mines in southern Utah to Ogden. The final blow to Corinne as a freighting center came in 1872, when the narrow-gauge Utah Northern, also built with Mormon backing, inaugurated service to Soda Springs, Idaho. Both lines crossed the Union Pacific/Central Pacific main line at Ogden, effectively crushing Corinne's commercial appeal.

By 1877, Corinne was no longer a gentile outpost. A ward, complete with a bishop, was designated by the church there. A man walking cross-country asked a local woman for permission to sleep in her barn and asked, "Are there many Mormons in Corinne?" She replied, "We are all Mormons here."[19]

Chapter Fifteen

MILEPOST 1084.4: PROMONTORY

The final stop on the great undertaking of the nineteenth century, one that would change the face of America, was Promontory Summit, where the lines of the Central Pacific and the Union Pacific joined in a haphazard and quickly arranged ceremony on May 10, 1869.

For months, the Central Pacific had been bent on reaching all the way to Green River, Wyoming, while the Union Pacific was aiming for however far it could get to the west. Neither management would back down, leading to the absurd situation of crews from both companies grading side-by-side for miles, sometimes crossing each other's paths. At one point, they crossed the same ravine, one with a bridge and the other with a fill. Because they depended on government bonds for financial support, neither side would yield.

Finally, the new administration of President Ulysses Grant warned that if the two sides couldn't reach agreement on a meeting point, the government would do it for them. Grenville Dodge of the Union Pacific and Collis Huntington of the Central Pacific met at a hotel in Washington in early April and made a deal. According to historian Maury Klein, "Both would build to Promontory and the Central Pacific would pay the Union Pacific for construction between the terminus [Ogden] and Monument [Point on the north end of Great Salt Lake, twenty-seven miles east of Promontory]."[1] The CP paid $2.84 million to the UP, more than $58,000 a mile, far less than what Dodge thought the line was worth, and took possession of the line east to Ogden. In addition, the CP got the government bonds for work west of the terminus.

The two railroads had another reason for settling: both were in desperate need of cash. With an agreement in place, the government would release the bond money both of them sought. Management at both roads thought they could create a new town five miles west of Ogden that would bring them more money in real-estate sales. It never became a reality because the site was without water or wood and promised no return in mineral wealth. Plus, it was obvious that the Mormons (specifically Brigham Young) would never permit the building of a new terminus so close to Ogden.

Promontory City, the town that sprouted on the broad, flat plain prior to the May 10 celebration, was a less raucous version of the succession of Hell on Wheels towns that the UP spawned on its trek across Nebraska, Wyoming, and Utah. The "town" consisted of one row of tents—never more than thirty—lining the north side of the tracks. There were, to be sure, the usual furbelows that provided entertainment for railroad workers, but there also were businesses that were more strikingly practical, including a dry goods store, a Chinese laundry, a bakery, and a cigar shop. The Union Pacific had by this time let go of most of its graders and tracklayers to save money, so there wasn't the audience for wild entertainments that there had been.

A report from the Railroad Commission, which kept an eye on construction for the federal government, predicted "Promontory City, as it is called, is not likely to become a commercial emporium, while it will have some fame and romantic interest attached to it as the place where the Atlantic and Pacific first embraced."[2]

The ceremony marking the connection of the two railroads—1,086 miles west of Omaha and 960 miles east of Sacramento—was scheduled to take place on May 8, a Saturday. Leland Stanford, one of the CP's Big Four and president of the company, and his entourage, including railroad commissioners J. W. Haines, F. A. Trittle, and William Sherman; S. W. Sanderson, chief justice of California; and A. P. K. Safford, the new territorial governor of Arizona, arrived a day early aboard Stanford's special train. They brought with them the "necessaries," three spikes that were to be driven at the ceremony: a gold spike engraved with the names of CP's directors and marked "The Last Spike"; a silver spike contributed by Nevada; and one of iron, gold, and silver from Arizona.

The jovial contingent was crestfallen when it was announced by Union Pacific that Thomas C. Durant and vice president Sidney Dillon and their party, riding their own private train from the East, would be unable to get to the site until May 10. The official reason was construction delays in Weber Canyon, but the real, unspoken reason was that the railroad's workers, angry that they hadn't been paid, had taken Durant's car off the train at a small station seventeen and a half miles east of

Evanston called Piedmont and chained it to the rails until they got their back pay. Durant wired headquarters for $80,000, and he and his private car were released.

Faced with the unhappy prospect of being idled in isolated country while waiting for the UP contingent, Stanford and his entourage were rescued by the UP's Jack Casement, who sent an excursion train, "stocked with a bountiful collation and ocean of champagne," said historian Robert Utley.[3] They weren't roughing it. The *San Francisco Daily Morning Chronicle* noted, "The most cordial harmony and good feeling marked their entertainment and all the toasts were drank with loud applause."[4] Grateful for the champagne-fueled diversion, the party spent the night in Ogden before returning to Promontory.

Despite two days of rain, May 10 greeted two trains from the East and West laden with officials, guests, and spectators with a dry day and temperatures in the upper sixties. The celebration was witnessed by remarkably few onlookers—estimates ranged from five hundred to six hundred eyewitnesses, nowhere near the ten thousand predicted—but the occasion has become familiar to students of western history. "The scene was so remote," UP vice president Sidney Dillon wrote later, "and we who were on the ground had been so much occupied with pushing construction and overcoming the pecuniary embarrassments and other complications with which we were beset, that there was no opportunity to make arrangements. But our feeling was that, however simple the ceremony might be, the people of the whole country, who had kept in such close touch with us and had given us such sympathy and encouragement from the beginning, should be with us in spirit at the culminating moment and participate in the joy of the occasion."[5]

Among those gathered at trackside were Central Pacific officials Stanford, James Strobridge, George Gray, and others; the Union Pacific sent Dillon, Thomas Durant, John Duff, Grenville Dodge, Samuel Reed, Jack and Dan Casement, and dozens of others. Conspicuous in their absence were Huntington; Charles Crocker, CP's general superintendent; CP treasurer Mark Hopkins; Oliver and Oakes Ames of the Union Pacific; and Mormon leader Brigham Young.[6] There were bands, a small contingent of military, Mormon Bishop John Sharp, and dozens of railroad workers who had stayed behind even though the work was finished.

Almost immediately, officials from the two railroads got into a disagreement over how the ceremony would play out. Stanford had brought his own spikes, and the Union Pacific wanted to have its own, separate celebration. Then came a somewhat heated discussion over which order

Celebrants gathered beside the Union Pacific and Central Pacific locomotives after the two met on the flat plains of Promontory Summit on May 10, 1869. Many workers went home after their labors were done, so the crowd was relatively small.

the two top officials would strike the spikes. Finally, five minutes before the noon ceremony was to begin the two sides reached agreement.

As the big moment arrived, the crowd grew restive, and loud. J. H. Beadle, writing for the *Utah Daily Reporter*, complained, "It is to be regretted that no arrangements were made for surrounding the work with a line of some sort in which all might have witnessed the work without difficulty. As it was, the crowd pushed upon the workmen so closely that less than twenty persons saw the affair entirely, while none of the reporters were able to hear all that was said."[7]

Reporters from twenty or more newspapers were there. The crush of the crowd around the two locomotives prevented their hearing precisely what was said by the speakers, leading to a lot of misinformation later. Reports of the number of women at the ceremony vary wildly, from one to twenty. J. N. Bowman, whose account of the day is generally regarded as the most accurate, wrote, "From the lists of the reporters, twenty-one [women] can be identified by name. The [official] photograph shows only two, perhaps three. Most of the women were the wives of officers or visitors, a few were unmarried, and four were young girls."[8] Another photograph, taken shortly before the ceremony began, shows a small boy standing on the tracks.

Twenty minutes after the beginning of the festivities, Strobridge and Reed dropped a special polished laurel tie from California into its place. The Reverend Dr. John Todd of Massachusetts gave a two-minute prayer that said, in part, "We have assembled here ... to do homage to Thy wonderful name, in that Thou hast brought this mighty enterprise, combining the commerce of the east with the gold of the west to so glorious a completion."[9]

A trackside telegrapher seated at a small table poised over his key to send the word that the great feat had been accomplished. W. N. Shilling tapped out this message at 12:40 PM: "We have got done praying. The spike is about to be presented."

Durant dropped two gold spikes into their predrilled holes but, apparently hung over from a party the night before, was unable to deliver his prepared speech; Dodge subbed for him. It was left to Stanford to tap the spikes into place, and then came the moment for driving "the last spike" (there were actually several ceremonial spikes). Stanford and Durant, standing on opposite sides of the newly laid track, each swung a silver maul—and missed, to the great delight of the gathered workers, who had driven thousands of spikes in their day. Some accounts make no mention of the "swing-and-miss" moment.

At 12:47 PM the telegrapher tapped out the momentous news: "Done!" The opposing locomotives, the Union Pacific's Number 119 and the Central Pacific's Jupiter, moved ahead slowly to the point where the rails were joined. At this moment, photographer Charles R. Savage snapped the famous picture—workmen offering bottles of champagne to each other from the pilots of the locomotives—that captures forever the jubilation (and, probably, relief) that went with the completion. Thanks to the news being sent almost instantaneously by telegraph, wild celebrations, complete with the ringing of bells and the booming of cannon, broke out in San Francisco, Chicago, New York City, and Washington, DC. The Pacific Railroad had become a reality. There were cheers galore at Promontory. "Cheers were given for the officers of the Central, followed by cheers for the officers of the Union Pacific; cheers for the 'Star Spangled Banner,' for the President of the United States, for the engineers and contractors, and for the laborers who have done the work."[10]

Souvenir hunters immediately went to work. There are rings and watch fobs allegedly made from the last spike, a claim debunked by those who say Stanford took the spike back to his private car. One is on display today at Stanford University. The confusion may be attributed to the fact that there were two gold spikes. After the laurel tie was removed and replaced with an ordinary one, spectators fell on it to grab a piece of history. Alexander Toponce, who was there, harrumphed, "There are enough splinters of the last tie in museums to make a good bonfire."[11]

For a time, the terminus of the two railroads, where passengers changed from UP to CP trains, remained at Corinne, twenty-eight miles to the east. Six months later, thanks to an agreement between the UP and CP, Ogden became the terminus. Promontory's days were numbered.

Less than one week after the festivities at Promontory, regularly scheduled trains were running east and west. There continued to be special excursions and luxury trains carrying rail officials. In June 1869, for example, Stanford and his entourage of twenty-five or so rode from Sacramento to Washington, DC. David Lemon, who served as fireman aboard the UP locomotive at Promontory, recalled in 1924, "I fired the engine that pulled the train from Promontory to Wahsatch. I saved a serious delay by successfully plugging a bad leak which the engine had developed. For this act President Stanford presented me with a whopping big orange."[12]

One of the most notable excursions was in 1870, when George Pullman organized a trip from Boston to San Francisco to demonstrate his new, luxurious eight-car train. Its upholstered and lavishly decorated

One of the most iconic photographs of American history froze in time the completion of the transcontinental railroad. Chief engineers Samuel Montague of the Central Pacific, left, and Grenville Dodge of the Union Pacific shook hands.

James L. Ehernberger collection

A photographer atop Union Pacific locomotive 119 captured celebrants, including companies of the 21st US infantry, lined up at right. "The succeeding moments ... were vigorously applied to refreshment, hilarity, and social pastimes," said one witness.

Courtesy Stanford University Libraries, Alfred Hart Collection, PC0002 cars included a smoking car, a wine room, and a barbershop. There was a baggage car that was used to keep an ample supply of wines cooled, a dining car, and two hotel cars (sleepers) so the trainload of important Boston nabobs were assured of their every need being met. By 1876, the same year the Centennial International Exhibition celebrating the nation's one hundredth anniversary opened in Philadelphia and the Battle of Little Bighorn took place in Montana, Pullman's lavish hotels on wheels were a regular feature on the western route.

After the celebrations and toasts of May 10, officials from both companies took their separate trains home and Promontory became an isolated way station on the transcontinental. A government-run visitors' center marks the spot, and the importance of the completion of the massive project is driven home to visitors. Even in 1869, the changes the railroad brought were not lost on the public.

J. W. Malloy, who was there that day, recalled in 1926:

> Do I remember that day? I'll say I do … How the crowd cheered, for practically all residents of the little town were there. We stood with mouths agape as we realized that the much-talked-of line was completed. Here indeed was the completion of a solid line of steel from Omaha to Sacramento—Nebraska and California joined. It was almost unbelievable. Truly, it was an occasion, for I think practically everyone there realized what a wonderful project had been completed—and completed it was, even to the bottle of champagne that was broken over the front of each engine.[13]

Endless congressional hearings and arguments and accusations over fraud and unpaid bills would continue for years, and the Union Pacific would suffer severe financial and managerial setbacks before the century rolled into 1900. But there is no doubt that it was a work for the ages.

Chapter Sixteen

TRAVEL BY TRAIN

Singing through the forests,
Rattling over ridges,
Shooting under arches,
Rumbling over bridges,
Whizzing through mountains,
Buzzing o'er the vale—
Bless me! This is pleasant,
Riding on the rail!

— John Godfrey Saxe, "Rhyme of the Rail"

Finally "done" in May 1869, the transcontinental was an immediate success, and one of the most dangerous conveyances available to the American public. It brought untold convenience for travel between the two halves of the country and made transfer of goods easier, but it was nevertheless an arduous journey fraught with accidents, rough traveling companions, and numerous uncertainties.

The government's financial support of construction was a two-edged sword. On the one hand, it made possible a massive project that no private investors would take on alone, and on the other, it created an environment where speed took precedence over permanence. A former Union Pacific superintendent recalled in 1923, "The track first laid was upon a very scrimpy subgrade with light rail, the ends joined in cast iron chairs [fasteners]."[1]

Under loans granted to the Union Pacific and Central Pacific for construction of the transcontinental, each would be paid for every mile constructed. Because both companies were frequently in need of cash, the government checks became vital and the roads' managements demanded that their crews lay track with ever-increasing speed. A mile a day became two miles, which became four, and, in one spectacular incident, ten miles.

Getting it done was more important than getting it done right. Speed led to shoddy work: uneven grades, sharp curves, ties put down without ballast, and wavy rails. Isaac Morris, one of those assigned by the government to examine the finished work, found poor workmanship, including unsafe bridges, too-narrow tunnels, and misaligned rails and wrote in one of his reports:

> [Ties] appear indeed to have been pitched on, and the rails spiked to them wherever they fell … No attention appears to have been paid to regularity of distance between the ties, they varying from 15 to 26 inches, the distance of the ends being rarely uniform. The material objection is, however, to the ties themselves. They are of soft white pine on the road I examined, as well as on the Central Pacific, the first being obtained from the neighboring mountains, the latter from the Sierra Nevada.[2]

In Morris's judgment, the pine ties would soon rot, and he offered the opinion that the transcontinental railroad was only about two-thirds complete when the rails of the CP and UP were joined at Promontory Summit in Utah in 1869. "There is a vast difference between getting rails down so that cars can pass over them and finishing a road."[3]

Riders noticed. One disgruntled passenger complained that while riding on the Union Pacific "the cars were rocking and bounding in a very unsatisfactory manner. We thought there was danger to be apprehended from so great a speed on such a rough road but the conductor said he had never run off the track yet."[4]

A similar roller-coaster ride befell James Kyner, who traveled from Omaha to Columbus, Nebraska, in a well-worn day coach:

> The ride to Columbus was a constant teetering upon my seat, swaying from side to side and jolting back when the track was climbing one of those gentle prairie swells, jerking forward when the car, over the top, coasted and rattled down upon the car ahead. There may have been a comfortable seat in that car but I had not found it by the time we reached Columbus.[5]

Both men were luckier than the fellow who, while riding in Utah's Echo Canyon in 1869 shortly after the completion of the transcontinental, recalled his scare during a derailment: "On we bounded over the ties, the car wheels breaking many of them as though they were but pipe-stems. Every instant we expected to roll down the ravine. We ordered the ladies to cling to the sides of the seats and keep their feet clear of the floor. It seemed as if that train could never be stopped! But it was brought to a standstill upon the brink of an embankment. Had the cars gone a few rods further the reader would probably never have been troubled by these hastily written pages."[6]

Not all riders were so critical. *The New York Times* correspondent, making a return trip from California to Omaha in July 1869, two months after the momentous connection at Promontory, gave his readers a glowing report:

> I can unhesitatingly inform the tourist who contemplates this journey that he will have his entire experience of rough travel before he reaches its eastern terminus at Omaha. From that point westward he will find himself bowling along at the rate of five and twenty miles an hour over track on which the smooth-gliding train will disturb neither his slumbers on the palace sleeping cars nor his cup of coffee or glass of claret in the dining cars, which now attend him on his jaunt from ocean to ocean.[7]

Until the mid-nineteenth century, train travel in the eastern United States was relatively safe, thanks to slow speeds, few trains, and short distances traversed. As longer routes opened, however, the number of accidents increased. On the eastern railroads, 1853 was a watershed year for accidents that resulted in many deaths. Fueled by cheap construction, riding the rails became a death trap for unsuspecting travelers. Bumpy grades, wooden bridges, washouts, and sharp curves awaited trains that were becoming longer and faster.

Two accidents that occurred a few days apart that spring awakened the nation to the dangers of train travel. On April 25, a fast-moving express plowed into an emigrant train near Chicago, killing twenty-one. A few days later, on May 6, forty-six unfortunates drowned when their train ran through an open drawbridge and plunged into a river near Norwalk, Connecticut. One of the worst crashes took place on July 17, 1856, when a ten-car excursion carrying schoolchildren on a picnic outing from Saint Michael's Roman Catholic Church in Philadelphia was delayed and was crashed into by a second train, killing sixty and maiming many more.

Out west, there were gruesome tales of bridge collapses, rails buried in mud in the spring thaw, and inattentive crews failing to stop their trains in time to avert disaster. Cattle and bison wandered onto the tracks, causing stoppages and derailments. Drunken cowboys in the saloons that lined tracks in most towns loved to take potshots at the locomotives. Nor were accidents the only danger. Cardsharps plied the trains, becoming so prevalent—an estimated three hundred on the Union Pacific system alone—that a deck of cards became known as a "railroad bible."

Huge improvements were taking place too. Telegraph service, inadequate in many parts of the country, became more universal after the Civil War, improving communication between trains and stations. Railroads replaced unreliable iron rail with steel, and railroads (and the rest of the country) began using standard time zones, which eliminated a confusing web of times based on local sun time; before standardization, there were twenty-seven local times in Illinois alone.

Nevertheless, the increasing number of trains running when the war ended and the fact that they were becoming faster and heavier led to a rash of rear-end collisions in which faster trains plowed into the back of slower or standing ones. As the difference in speeds between slow- and fast-moving trains increased—some ran at fifteen to twenty miles an hour while others raced along at thirty-five to forty-five—so did the number of accidents.

Effective onboard air-conditioning would not be perfected until 1929, so the cars became stifling after a few hours in the sun—"the misery of summer railway travel, including the heat, the glare, the dust, the cinders, and the rattle, plus the flies."[8] Adding to the heat, cleanliness among passengers was not always a priority, causing riders to desperately seek fresh air, which meant opening the windows. Smoke and hot cinders from the steam locomotives poured in, made worse by dust kicked up from the right-of-way. Accidents involving arms and heads sticking outside the train became so common that the railroads instituted a prohibition on such behavior. People were known to fall out of the cars, too. In one case, a five-year-old boy tumbled out a window just after a train, traveling thirty miles an hour, departed Cheyenne. The train was stopped and crews hurried back down the line, expecting to find him dead. Instead, he was perfectly alive and sustained only a few bruises.

Newspapers were full of accounts of misfortune. A UP construction train backing down the track hit a cow, tossing the caboose off the

Traveling by train was dangerous business in the 1800s. Poor track and communications led to frequent derailments and collisions, inspiring a cartoonist to spoof passengers, whose luggage, pets, and wigs go flying.

DICK KRECK COLLECTION

track and killing five men and wounding twelve others. *The New York Times* reported in February 1868 on a train traveling near midnight from Omaha to Chicago when a broken rail caused three cars to be hurled down a steep embankment. Two of the cars caught fire, though the passengers escaped with minor injuries.

Burning cars created especially horrible wrecks, in part because cars of the era were made of wood and heated by coal stoves standing at one end. This was not only inconvenient for riders, some of whom froze while others were kept comfortable, but it meant that when the cars were upset in a wreck, hot coals spewed down the aisle, igniting interiors. Adding fuel to the fire was the lighting, provided by kerosene lanterns mounted on the walls. It wasn't until 1887 that steam heat provided by the locomotive replaced stoves.

As if derailments, uneven track, and uncomfortable cars weren't enough, weather played havoc with schedules and safety, particularly along the UP's route in Wyoming. Women's suffrage advocate Susan B. Anthony journeyed westward in January 1872 and had "a fearful ordeal" when her train was stopped by drifting snow on Sherman Hill between Cheyenne and Laramie. The crew, trying to protect their passengers, pulled into a snowshed near the Dale Creek Bridge and parked there. "Here we remained all night and, with rarified air and the smoke from the engine, were almost suffocated, while the wind blew so furiously we could not venture to open the doors."[9] They dined on dried fish and crackers and finally reached Cheyenne after a four-day journey from Laramie, a distance of fifty-seven miles.

None of this dissuaded travelers eager to get a look at the West, as exotic to most Americans as lands across the Pacific Ocean. They flocked to the new modern mode of travel. By the end of 1869, 17,605 passengers had passed through Promontory, where passengers changed railroads. Another 13,067 headed east. More impressive, an estimated 150,000 rode the transcontinental in the first year; ten years later that number had risen to almost a million. Some noted that the train's leisurely pace, about twenty-two miles an hour compared to ten miles an hour for a stagecoach, was preferable to those in the East, where some sped along at forty-five miles an hour, because slower speeds allowed riders to "pursue all the sedentary avocations and amusements of a parlor at home."

Almost all diarists commented on the wide-open spaces (and, sometimes, the repetitiveness) that they crossed. An author of one of the many travel guides about the new route rhapsodized,

Nowhere are broader and higher mountains; nowhere richer valleys; nowhere climates more propitious; nowhere broods and atmosphere so pure and exhilarating; nowhere more bountiful deposits of gold and silver, quicksilver, and copper, lead, and iron; nowhere denser forests, larger trees; nowhere so wide plains; nowhere such majestic rivers; yet nowhere so barren deserts, so arid steppes; nowhere else that nature has planted its growths so thickly and so variously, and feeds so many appetites so richly; yet nowhere that she withholds so completely, and pains the heart and parches the tongue of man so deeply by her poverty.[10]

A cross-country journey by train was a totally new experience for many. What to wear, what to pack, and how to behave were questions many didn't know how to answer. Numerous travelers' guides quickly became available to thousands of new train riders, dispensing advice and describing the wonders to be seen. One of the most popular was *The Pacific Tourist*, which happily gave tips on what to wear, who to take as your traveling companion, tipping, and, one of the most important subjects, dining en route. "To be well on the Pacific Railroad," warned the guide, "eat at regular hours and never miss a meal."

Women, a good number traveling alone for the first time, were schooled on how to dress, what to bring along, and how to avoid pesky traveling salesmen in the cars. George Sala, who made several rail trips cross-country, advised,

Frequently during our journey the water in the toilet rooms on board the car was frozen, and washing was impossibility. The outward application of Jean Marie Farina to your temples, your wrists, and behind your ears, is the sweetest of boons. We may be good and happy without washing—the saintly anchorites of the Thebaid taught us that long ago; but that was in the days before Brown Windsor Soap and Bully's Vinaigre de Toilette.[11]

Florence Hartley's *Ladies Book of Etiquette* warned that if a man "sits near you and seems disposed to be impertinent, lower your veil and turn away." And, perhaps the best advice: "As you have to pass through so many extremes of temperature, always wear your underclothing, day and night, through the overland trip."[12] Another warned, "It is not customary, it is not polite, it is not right or just for a lady to occupy one whole seat with her flounces and herself and another with her satchel, parasol, big box, little box, bandbox, or bundle."[13]

The mode of transportation was a vast time-saver over the covered wagon, but the trip took the better part of seven days coast to coast, if all went well. A typical eastbound trip on the transcontinental left Sacramento at 6:30 AM Monday on the Central Pacific and reached Promontory Summit at 9:55 PM Tuesday. There, passengers were required to change to cars on the Union Pacific that left Promontory at 10:30 PM and reached Omaha about 9:30 Thursday morning. Then it was on to Chicago and New York, arriving exactly seven days after leaving Sacramento.

Passengers found ways to amuse themselves on the long ride; there was only so much staring at prairie dogs a person could do. They played games, read, engaged strangers in conversation, and organized makeshift musicales. One happy traveler recalled, "We have a good, lively crowd in our car and last evening were right melodious, or 'hideous,' with such popular melodies as 'Bingo,' 'John Brown's Body,' and 'Mary Had a Little Lamb.' I think John Brown's body would have risen out of his grave to hear such music."[14] On Sundays, there were religious services in one of the cars. The onboard entertainments brought people closer together—sometimes *too* close—and helped pass the time as the train ground slowly toward its destination. It could be, reported *Frank Leslie's Illustrated*, a raucous scene:

> Here, at 9 PM, in the drawing room sleeper, we find a cheerful musical party howling, "Hold the Fort!!" around the parlor organ, which forms its central decoration; three strong, healthy children are running races up and down the aisle, and scourging each other with their parents' shawl straps; a consumptive invalid, bent double in a paroxysm of coughing; four parties, invisible, but palpable to the touch, wrestling in the agonies of toilet behind the closely buttoned curtains of their sections, and trampling on the toes of passers-by as they struggle with opposing draperies; a mother engaged in person combat (also behind curtains) with her child in the upper fetch, and two young lovers, dead to all the world, are exchanging public endearments in a remote corner.
>
> Who could bear these things with perfect equanimity? Who could accept with smiles the company of six adults at the coming and washing stages of one's toilet? Who could rise in the society, and under the close personal scrutiny of 29 fellow beings, jostle them in their seats all day, eat in their presence, take naps under their very eyes, lie down among, and sleep—or try to sleep—within

For those who could afford it, cross-country train travel was an exercise in luxury. Pullman parlor cars outfitted with comfortable chairs, plush carpeting, mirrors, and exotic woods included a library and an organ for sing-alongs.

acute and agonized hearing of their faintest snores, without being ready to charge one's soul with twenty-nine distinct homicides?[15]

Those who could afford it booked passage on the new Pullmans, built for luxury with comfortable parlor chairs and trappings that rivaled the best hotels. It was expensive—those without money need not apply. A first-class ticket from Chicago to Sacramento in 1870 was $100, plus a $10 extra charge for a sleeping berth.

Others had produced diners and sleepers before George Pullman (as many as eight railroads were using more primitive sleepers before 1850), but it was his name that became synonymous with the finest accommodations on rails.

Pullman's master craftsmen built cars that were the height of fashion. Eventually, Pullman produced several kinds of specialty cars: sleepers, drawing rooms, the "hotel car," and diners. There was even a smoking car, where gentlemen could enjoy cigars and cigarettes. A car reserved for women was nonsmoking.

The sleeper held twenty-eight berths (upper and lower); the drawing room was furnished with a sofa and two large easy chairs that converted to double and single berths at night and also contained three staterooms for extra privacy.

A sleeper was a luxury only the first-class passengers enjoyed. There they found steam-heated cars, ventilation, clean sheets changed nightly, and porters and conductors ready to serve any whim, "always on call." There was some resistance to the sleeping cars because some found the idea of men and women, strangers to each other, sleeping a few feet apart morally objectionable. Nor was it easy to dress and undress in the small spaces, separated from fellow travelers only by a curtain. The upper crust among the passengers found plenty to complain about. "I dislike the sleeping-car section more than I ever have anything in the world," sniped prominent writer Helen Hunt Jackson. She itemized the problem of trying to dress in a small space provided by a berth, losing her balance, and toppling through her curtain onto an unfortunate Englishman passing by.

Mornings on the sleepers could be uncomfortable, thanks to men and women mingling and queuing to freshen up from their overnight slumbers. Anxious passengers were forced to stand in line, "waiting their turn, watching how their neighbor washed his ears."

Another complained, "You see a lady with a sponge and a toothbrush and towel, edging her way along the narrow passage between the

For those riding coach on the weeklong cross-country trip, fold-down seats offered cramped, uncomfortable sleeping and little privacy. Discomfort didn't deter riders, more than seventeen thousand of whom rode the Pacific Railroad in its first year of operation.

curtains, to take her turn at the washstand, where she waits perhaps some minutes for the gentleman to finish who is already in possession. When gets her turn she is waited for by another gentleman."[16]

Others, though confined to small spaces for days on end, learned to tolerate their fellow travelers. "When night comes, we all seem much as one family, mutually sympathetic and generous. A woman may even crimp her hair before the bachelor without provoking a surly remark ... all is taken in good part, and there is peace and goodwill in the great family."[17]

Food was always on the minds of those slowly making their way across the continent. The first on-train Pullman diner was built in Quincy, Illinois, by the Pullman Palace Car Company. The initial $20,000 beauty, called Delmonico after the famed New York City eatery, was sixty feet long and ten feet wide, and could seat forty-eight diners at a time. An ingenious ventilation system rid the car of "all foul air, smoke, and dust."

Meals in the diner were the equal of any found in the finest restaurants. For $1, a meal might include steak, veal cutlets, chicken, broiled ham, lamb chops, and oysters. There were nine kinds of breads, eggs offered eight ways, and even breakfast wines and champagnes, available for an extra fifteen cents. On special occasions, the Pullman chefs could put together a twelve-course dinner that might include blue-winged teal, antelope steaks, roast beef, boiled ham, broiled chicken, fresh fruit, and cornbread.

All of this, served amid opulent carpets, first-rate china and silver, damask curtains, crisp linen, and exotic highly polished woods, did not come cheap for the railroads. In fact, Pullmans were a money-losing amenity. The cars were expensive to build and to operate, weighing eighty tons and costing $50,000. Just stocking them was a herculean task requiring one thousand pieces of crockery and glass, nine hundred tablecloths, seven hundred pieces of silverware, and food for four hundred customers. It took as many as sixteen chefs and waiters to staff them.

The Central Pacific tried to emulate Pullman's beauties with its version, called Silver Palace Cars (they were painted silver on the exterior), to avoid paying royalties to Pullman, but they never lived up to the comfort and luxury of the originals.

As riding the train became more popular among the middle class, who could afford only the cheaper day coaches, demand for the Pullmans and their high-ticket prices waned. By 1871, Pullman was out of the car-building business, except for private palaces for the wealthy, and instead concentrated on renting and operating its cars on long-distance trains. The Union Pacific, facing another of its many financial crises, opted to drop dining cars until competition forced the company to put them back on in the late 1880s.

Those who chose not to pay to eat in the diner had other possibilities. One was the "butcher boy," or newsboy, who roamed the train selling books, papers, fruit, candy, bacon, and coffee. If one hadn't brought his own food or needed more than bacon and coffee, there were eating houses located on the right-of-way. Towns became recognized for their specialties—Sidney for antelope, Laramie for steak, Green River for biscuits, and Ogden for service and tidiness.

Roadside dining was, at best, a hit-or-miss affair. Restaurants and their food and service were left to independent operators, and a gleaming dining room was no guarantee of good food. "They are in the main varnished mockeries," wrote one traveler, "which we beg to assure you (and all travelers will endorse our remarks) offer few substantial comforts to hungry nomads. The traveler enters with voracious appetite, and expectant of good things but departs unsatisfied and grumbling ... Very weak coffee, heavy firebrick biscuits, and an apology for beefsteak. It is useless attempting to masticate the leathery beef for we have only twenty minutes. Seventy-five cents for sitting down to the task of testing the strength of your teeth and being served by pretty girls in chignons!"[18]

Meals at the various stops, where travelers scrambled to exit the train, find a place to sit, order, and eat in only twenty minutes, were almost always the same: beefsteak, fried eggs, and fried potatoes. At Evanston, Wyoming, debarking passengers were promised mountain trout, with a small addendum, "That you may not be disappointed about trout, inquire at the office as you go in."[19] Mealtime might feature "bread almost as gritty as the mountain boulders."[20] It was, said a weary traveler, "necessary to look at one's watch to tell whether it was breakfast, dinner, or supper."[21] Things only got worse farther west, where the stations were "miserable shanties, with tables dirty, waiters not only dirty but saucy."[22]

It could be worse. A. K. McClure, who crossed the continent by train in 1869, complained:

> We took our last square breakfast at Pleasant Valley station [Nebraska], for which we each paid $2 ... The coffee was nothing but water made bitter by some nauseous ingredient, the fat bacon was stale, the eggs rather worse than stale, the butter worse than the eggs, the bread worse than the butter, and the potatoes were

fried in the fat of the bacon. It would have required a first-class quartz mill to masticate the bread; and nothing more dainty than a buzzard could have eaten the other articles. The cook was an Irishman, who was filthy enough himself to sell as real estate.[23]

An entrepreneur by the name of Frederick Henry Harvey came to travelers' rescue. Born in London, Harvey revolutionized railroad food. He traveled extensively as an agent for the Burlington Railroad and experienced many awful meals on the road. In 1876, he approached the Santa Fe Railway with a proposal to operate their trackside diners. His Fred Harvey restaurants, or Harvey Houses, became the industry standard, famed for their service, cleanliness, and reasonably priced good food—and, of course, the Harvey Girls, his waitresses recruited in the East, dressed in immaculate black-and-white outfits, and trained to his exacting standards.

Harvey frequently toured his restaurants and was very demanding of his managers. For example, the cup code: "a cup turned upside down meant hot tea; a cup right side up in the saucer meant coffee; upside down and tilted against the saucer, iced tea; upside down and away from the saucer, milk."[24]

His efficiencies soon convinced other railroads to improve their trackside eateries, much to the relief of passengers, who sometimes had to bolt for trains that often departed without announcement before the allotted twenty-minute stopover, leaving leftover food to be served to the next unlucky soul.

Those who had little money to spend at Harvey Houses or who preferred to eat at their seats could pack a basket of edibles. A foreign visitor crossing the country by rail suggested:

> A little lunch basket nicely stowed with sweet and substantial bits of food will often save you the pain of long rides before meals, when the empty stomach craves food, and failing to receive it, lays you up with the most dismal of sick headaches; it also serves you splendidly whenever the train is delayed.
>
> In packing your little lunch basket, do not forget lemons or limes. Canned meats and fruits are easily carried. Bread and milk are easily procured. Avoid all articles which have odor of any description.[25]

While swells rode in mobile luxury, eating in luxurious dining cars or enjoying a simple but satisfying meal at a Harvey House, those in the emigrant cars had no such pleasure. As a young man, novelist Robert Louis Stevenson, famed for *Treasure Island* and other works, took it upon himself to experience a cross-country trip on an emigrant train. He didn't paint a very rosy picture:

> It was about two in the afternoon of Friday that I found myself in front of the Emigrant House, with more than a hundred others, to be sorted and boxed for the journey. A white-haired official, with a stick under one arm and a list [in] the other hand, stood apart in front of us, and called name after name in the tone of a command. At each name, you would see a family gather up its brats and bundles and run for the hindmost of three cars that stood awaiting us; and I soon concluded that this was to be set apart for the women and children. The second or central car, it turned out, was devoted to men traveling alone, and the third to the Chinese. [The cars] are only remarkable for their extreme plainness, nothing but wood entering in any part. There is scarce elbowroom for two to sit. There will not be space enough for one to lie.[26]

Emigrant traffic, made up of those heading west to start new lives, was important for the railroad. Though they paid the lowest fare (about $50 from New York to San Francisco), their numbers were a rich source of revenue, so the Union Pacific took good care of them, to a point. They built Emigrant Houses near the stations to house and feed those who couldn't afford a first-rate hotel. Meals were sold for twenty-five cents.

Emigrants were viewed with curiosity by some of their fellow travelers. A British tourist riding in a Pullman who stepped onto the platform in Omaha was appalled by what she saw:

> The platform overflows with them, they are everywhere, all with a more or less travel-stained look. Having penned up so long in such close quarters they are glad to get out and stretch their legs and rinse the dust from their grimy faces. Swarthy men with bare arms are splashing about in buckets; some are performing their ablutions under the pump, or in anything that comes handy …
>
> The women as a rule looked faded, wan, and anxious; the men energetic and strong, confident and assured, with a bright, never-say-die look upon their faces … It is a strange gathering, that flock of varying nationalities, all bound on one adventurous errand—a wave of the Old World breaking on the shores of the New.[27]

As the lowest class among passengers, emigrants got the worst cars—called Zulus for reasons lost to time—the worst service, and the worst timetable. Their trains were often attached to freights that repeatedly gave way to high-speed expresses. Emigrant trains were shoved to sidings to wait, sometimes for hours, until they were cleared to retake the main line. A trip from Omaha to Sacramento that took a regularly scheduled train four and a half days might last ten days for emigrants.

Emigrant passengers were pretty much on their own. The cars' all-wood interiors were spartan and poorly lighted. Without fold-down bunks (added to the cars years later), emigrants were forced to get as comfortable as they could at night. They might rent a straw-filled mattress for $1.25 to $2.50 and stretch out on a wooden bench, if the car wasn't too crowded, or sack out on the floor. Another quaint sleeping arrangement was "chumming," where male passengers shared a board and three cushions spread across two benches. If two men were strangers both had to agree to the arrangement.

It made for uncomfortable slumber. "The sleepers lay in uneasy attitudes," wrote Stevenson. "Here two chums alongside, flat upon their backs like dead folk; there is a man sprawling on the floor, with his face upon his arm; there another half seated with his head and shoulders on the bench. Others stirred, turned, or stretched out their arms like children; it was surprising how many groaned and murmured in their sleep ... now a snore, now a gasp, now a half-formed word. I was obliged to open my window for the degradation of the air."[28]

The emigrants became ad hoc families because there was no privacy. They entertained one another other with dances and song, fought in front of each other, and cooked their meals over the coal stove that was their sole source of heat. Because many of them were from other countries and their knowledge of English was limited, they relied on the kindness of the conductors, who were not always that kind. Trains could run hours behind schedule, so stops at roadside eateries were sometimes accomplished only by bribing the conductor. At the conductor's whim, emigrants could be deposited at any station, even if it wasn't the one they wanted.

All the togetherness and a lack of adequate sanitation made for odiferous travel. Stevenson, in ill health and uncomfortable most of the way, noted when his train reached Ogden, "We changed cars from the Union Pacific to the Central Pacific line of railroad. The change was doubly welcome for first we had better cars on the new line; and second, those in which we had now been cooped for more than 90 hours had

Emigrants, the lowest class of passengers but an important source of revenue, got poor accommodations on wood benches and even worse treatment, often taking ten days to make the four-and-a-half-day journey to the West Coast.

begun to stink abominably ... Our nostrils were assailed by rancid air. I think we are human in virtue of open windows. The car of the Chinese was notably least offensive and that of the women and children by a good way the worst. A stroke of nature's satire."[29]

Though it was touted as offering the ability to travel from coast to coast, the transcontinental route was not truly uninterrupted until 1872, when the Union Pacific completed an iron bridge across the Missouri River. Before the bridge, westbound passengers were required to leave their train at Council Bluffs on the east side of the river, unload their luggage, and board a carriage that would be transported across the river by ferry to Omaha, where they could resume their train journey.

A temporary bridge laid over ice that coated the Missouri in winter was unreliable. When the ice melted, it was again necessary to ferry passengers and their luggage between Omaha and Council Bluffs. H. Clark Brown, who served on the UP construction crew, recalled working to build the ice bridge:

> The water was 22 feet deep and we had piling 45 feet long to handle. If you think it did not take some hard work to start a pile 4½ feet long in 22 feet of water, you'd be as surprised as I was when one day a 3,000-pound hammer with the top of the pile went clear down to the bottom of the river. The only thing to do was to go and get a new hammer at the foundry. We had three shifts of men, each outfit working eight hours. A few years after this bridge was made, there was an iron bridge put in.[30]

The iron bridge was finished at a cost of $2,869,892 on February 20, 1872, two and a half years after the CP and UP tracks met in Utah.

Within a remarkably short span, travel by train became an accepted part of the American landscape. Its expansion was astonishing. There were 39,712 miles of rail built in the 1870s, and by 1880 the total topped 93,000 miles. Ten years later, it rose to 167,000 miles. Once other transcontinental lines—Chicago Burlington & Quincy, Great Northern, Northern Pacific, and Santa Fe—were finished, a building frenzy connected hundreds of burgs, some of which had no need of a railroad but whose residents feared their towns wouldn't prosper without one. Many small roads were born, struggled, and died.

But there was no turning back. The transcontinental trains and the waves of passengers and settlers they brought with them changed the face of the West, which only a few years before had been an uncharted

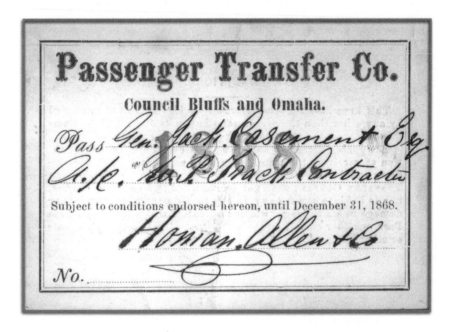

The transcontinental wasn't fully completed until 1872, when the Missouri River was bridged. Even Jack Casement, the genius behind the construction of the Union Pacific, had to change trains and go from Council Bluffs to Omaha by ferry.

wilderness. The transcontinental opened new lands for settlers, created new markets for businesses, and brought new jobs. For the first time, Americans were free to travel east and west in relative comfort and speed. "The railroad is not only a great business enterprise," *The New York Times* gushed before it was even completed, "but a great explorer and a great civilizer. To it we confidently look for aid in solving the Indian problems and the Mormon problem of the day."[31]

The builders overcame doubters and naysayers. "Probably no enterprise in the world has been so maligned, misrepresented and criticized as this," the UP's chief engineer Grenville Dodge recalled later. Writer Samuel Bowles looked forward, not back:

> Marked, indeed was the contrast between the stage ride of 1865 and the railroad ride of 1868 across the Plains. The then long-drawn, tedious endurance of six days and nights, running the gauntlet of hostile Indians, was now accomplished in a single 24 hours [between Omaha and end of track], safe in a swiftly moving train.
>
> The first results of the railroad are to kill what settlement and cultivation they had reached under the patronage of slow-moving emigration, stage travel, and prairie schooner freightage. The ranches which these supported are now deserted; the rails carry everybody and everything; the old roads are substantially abandoned. They are victims ... of a higher civilization; they drove out the Indian, the wolf, and the buffalo; the locomotive whistles their occupation away.[32]

EPILOGUE

The growth and spread of western railroads will forever be tied to the wanderlust of Americans. Whether for an adventure, a chance at a new life, or just plain old greed, those in the eastern half of the United States couldn't stay still.

It happened so fast.

While emigrants were trudging across the uncharted landscape west of the Missouri River in the 1850s, rail passengers were riding the cushioned seats of Pullman cars from the East into Chicago. Twenty years later, the completion of the transcontinental railroad with the driving of the last spike at Promontory, Utah, on May 10, 1869, obliterated the barriers of time and space.

"Of all the things done by the first transcontinental railroad, nothing exceeded the cuts in time and cost it made for people traveling across the continent," Stephen Ambrose wrote in *Nothing Like It in the World.* "Before the Mexican War, during the Gold Rush that started in 1848, through the 1850s, and until after the Civil War ended in 1865, it took a person months and might cost more than $1,000 to go from New York to San Francisco.

"But less than a week after the pounding of the Golden Spike, a man or woman could go from New York to San Francisco in seven days. That included stops. And the cost to go from New York to San Francisco, as listed in the summer of 1869, was $150 first class, $70 for emigrant."[1] Before the coming of the railroads, western cities like Denver or Helena, Montana, might get their mail from the East in months or even a year. After the arrival of the tracks, eastern newspapers arrived in as little as forty-eight hours. The western settlements thus moved closer to their counterparts in the East.

Then and now, there were naysayers. Historian Richard White reasoned in his 2011 book *Railroaded* that the transcontinental roads "should not have been built where and when they were. Given lower capital costs and improved technology as the nineteenth century wore on," he argued, "new railroads could have been built at far lower costs and with far less capital than had been required for the older railroads. Waiting instead of building would for the rest of the West have not necessarily been a bad thing."[2]

The same arguments were put forth in 1862. It wasn't practical, financially reasonable, or self-sustaining, went the arguments. But if not then, when? Ten years later? Fifty years later? And where else? The quickly rising West was where opportunity for investors lay, and it was where Americans of all classes were drawn. The idea was first proposed in 1845, and, after seventeen years, the public and, more important, manufacturers and other businesses were tired of the endless discussion.

The Pacific Railroad didn't turn on the emigrant spigot—that started with the covered wagon days in the 1840s—but it certainly released a torrent. The rising tide began as a trickle in the 1830s when hardy trappers were harvesting pelts on the plains and in the Rocky Mountains. Thousands of emigrants from the East followed, hauling their possessions and families in rugged covered wagons. They faced starvation, cholera, accidental death, and mayhem from Indian attack. They walked beside their overburdened wagons for a thousand miles, often making only twenty miles a day in dust storms or pounded by rain over unmapped, bumpy roads. They buried their children beside the trails. "It is," wrote one traveler, "a hardship without glory, to be sick without a home, to die and be buried like a dog."[3]

Often overlooked in the tide of western travel was the role of women. Sometimes pregnant when they left their homes in Ohio, Illinois, or Pennsylvania, they were expected to perform as equals with men, driving stock, handling the reins of oxen teams, and shooting with ease. They also performed the usual household chores: washing, cooking, taking care of the children, and ministering to those sick or just discouraged by the long journey, all of this complicated by being away from civilization, with fewer conveniences to make these tasks simpler. They had to deal with the separation from friends and families, most of whom they would never see again once they reached Oregon or California. Their diaries of their daily travails, collected in volumes like *Women's Diaries* by Lillian Schlissel, are heart wrenching.

Western travel evolved with astonishing speed. In a mere fifty years it went from covered wagons to stagecoaches to trains to automobiles, each form of transportation making its predecessor obsolete.

Wagon trains, which took months to cross the spacious prairies, were replaced by stagecoaches, rough, bumpy conveyances where as many as fourteen passengers were jammed into and on top of coaches rocking like ships on a prairie sea. Passengers thrown together endured weeks of cramped travel with all kinds of fellow human beings, not all of them to their liking. Meals, usually biscuits, bacon, and coffee, were taken at ramshackle stations. But it was faster than a covered wagon; coach passengers looked with pity on the wagon emigrants whom they passed on the road.

Then came the heroic task of building the railroad. The raucous and raunchy Hell on Wheels towns gave way to communities of more solid citizens. Omaha and North Platte, Nebraska; Cheyenne, Laramie, and Evanston, Wyoming; and Ogden, Utah, owe their births to the hard-working and hard-partying laborers who plotted the route, graded the right-of-way, and laid the rails.

Ultimately, the Union Pacific/Central Pacific iron highway, followed by the Kansas Pacific, Northern Pacific, Southern Pacific, Santa Fe, and Great Northern, stitched the West together, allowing settlers to populate farms and towns and access cities east and west with their products. Along with the telegraph, the railroad bound together what was once a country where people in New York had better access to London than they did to San Francisco.

Where mistakes made? Of course.

The obvious downside of the population explosion was the treatment of the Indians, who had been living on the land for thousands of years but became merely an impediment to whites flooding into their country. Extermination was the solution many sought. "Destiny is never unmixed," Don Rickey Jr. wrote in *Forty Miles a Day on Beans and Hay*, an excellent examination of the army's role in opening the West. "Indians ceased to be an obstacle to empire; they had become merely one of the colorful diversions," wrote historian Richard White.[4]

It was the adolescent days of giant corporations whose financial and influential tentacles reached into the highest levels of government. White acknowledged the majesty of the building of the transcontinental but also argued that "in terms of their politics, finances, labor relations, and environmental consequences, the transcontinental railroads were not only failures but near-disasters."[5] Much of the construction was shoddily done. The federal government paid the railroads by the mile of rail laid, so speed, not beauty, was the order of the day. The railroads spent years and tens of thousands of dollars rebuilding and relaying track to make it safer. Wrecks took the lives of many travelers and often made schedules an estimate rather than a rule. Native populations were brushed aside, driven off their ancestral lands. Bison were slaughtered by the millions without remorse.

Those behind the Union Pacific reaped fortunes from the Crédit Mobilier while the railroad struggled to pay its bills. Some roads were no more than stock frauds, and enthusiasts overbuilt lines to towns that had only false hopes of one day becoming cities.

The naysayers who argued that there was no need for such a railroad given that few whites lived on the Great Plains were proven wrong. As the editor of the *Leavenworth (Kansas) Daily Conservative* proclaimed, "The West! The West! Where is the West? Where is the West of today? Cities, towns, and farms are springing up and spreading forth. The Great American Desert is a myth. Can our statesmen of today look upon the horizon of the golden West and realize half its vastness?"[6]

Unlike what some historians and sociologists have written, the Pacific Railroad was not the end of the frontier. It was merely the first iron arrow shot through the future of the native inhabitants. Settlement would take years as settlers and speculators slowly ate into the vast acreage on either side of the railroad right-of-way and other transcontinental railroads joined the rush west. The Pacific Railroad merely established the process by which the ultimate end was achieved.

The builders and their financial backers were not visionaries; their interests were more financial. In 1892, a spokesman for the Southern Pacific Railroad, which, like the Central Pacific and Union Pacific decades earlier, bundled its railroad with land deals, said, "We want the country settled because it does not pay to run railroads to places where there are no people."[7] The railroad and telegraph turned America and the world of commerce in a whole new direction. In 1870, the first year of the transcontinental's operation and the year John D. Rockefeller founded Standard Oil, there were no telephones and no commercial electricity. The telephone was six years in the future, the Kodak camera ten years away. Until the arrival of the railroad, markets were bound by the inability to move goods speedily and safely. The line from Omaha to Sacramento carried 150,000 passengers in one year. Just over a decade later, that number jumped to almost a million. It became a conduit for emigrants from Europe and elsewhere to reach fertile land that promised a new life for those willing to labor.

Maury Klein summed it up in his three-volume history of the Union Pacific:

The impact of the railroad on American life can hardly be exaggerated. It rearranged the nation's economic geography, trained several generations of businessmen and financiers, and laid the foundation for many of the era's great fortunes. Everyone got a piece of the action. The railroad opened new land for settlers, new markets for merchants, new sources of profit for financiers, new resources for industrialists to exploit, new jobs for everyone from manager to itinerant laborer, and new enterprises for the ambitious.[8]

Once it was built, it became a part of the American landscape. Take a driving road trip, as my son, Kevin, and I did in 2009 across Wyoming and Nebraska on Highway 30, the old Lincoln Highway, and see the myriad towns, farms, and factories spawned by the railroad. Many of the towns that came into being then are shadows of their glory days, but the sweeping vistas of farmland, once thought of as a wasteland incapable of supporting either livestock or farming, a place that would go unsettled for "a million years," thrive more than one hundred years after emigrants swept across the territory. Speeding yellow locomotives of the Union Pacific, racing goods east and west, are modern-day evidence that while it may not have been "the grandest enterprise under God," as a founder of the Union Pacific trumpeted at the first track-laying ceremony in Omaha, it was close.

NOTES

Chapter One: Westward Ho!

1. George R. Stewart, "The Prairie Schooner Got Them There," *American Heritage*, February 1962, 7.
2. *Sangamon Journal*, March 18, 1846, in Ric Burns, "Never Take No Cutoffs: On the Oregon Trail," *American Heritage*, May/June 1993, 63.
3. Robert G. Athearn, *William Tecumseh Sherman and the Settlement of the West* (Norman: University of Oklahoma, 1956), 6.
4. Howard Stansbury, *Exploration and Survey of the Valley of the Great Salt Lake of Utah,* in Georgia Willis Read, "Women and Children on the Oregon-California Trail in the Gold Rush Years," *Missouri Historical Review* 39, no. 1 (October 1944): 10.
5. Burns, "Never Take No Cutoffs," 64.
6. Alonzo Delano diary, June 18, 1849, in *The Plains Across* by John D. Unruh Jr. (Urbana: University of Illinois Press, 1979), 133.
7. "Diary of the Overland Trail, 1849, and Letters 1848–50 of Captain David De Wolf," *Transactions of the Illinois State Historical Society* 32 (1925), in *History of Nebraska* by James C. Olson (Lincoln: University of Nebraska Press, 1966), 61.
8. Colonel George W. Stokes, "Echoes of the Old West," *The Union Pacific Magazine*, October 1923, 6.
9. William Smedley, "Across the Plains in Sixty-Two," *The Trail* 19, no. 10 (March 1927): 3.
10. Amanda Hardin Brown, "A Pioneer in Colorado and Wyoming," *The Colorado Magazine* 35, no. 3 (July 1958): 161–177.
11. Ralph K. Andrist, "Gold," *American Heritage*, December 1962, 11.
12. Francis Parkman, *The Oregon Trail: Sketches of Prairie and Rocky Mountain Life* (Boston: Little, Brown, 1892), 21.
13. Stansbury, in Unruh Jr., *The Plains Across,* 150.
14. Olson, *History of Nebraska*, 60.
15. Will Bagley, "Pioneers Not Exempt from Nature's Call," *The Salt Lake Tribune*, February 25, 2001, B1.
16. John Wood diary, in *The Wake of the Prairie Schooner*, by Irene D. Paden (New York: MacMillan, 1945), 117.
17. *Women's Diaries of the Westward Journey,* collected by Lillian Schlissel (New York: Schocken Books, 1982), 135.
18. Emmy E. Werner, *Pioneer Children on the Journey West* (Boulder, CO: Westview Press, 1995), 126.
19. J. Goldsborough Bruff, *Gold Rush: The Journals, Drawings, and Other Papers of J. Goldsborough Bruff* (New York: Columbia University Press, 1949), 291.
20. James A. Crutchfield, *The Way West* (New York: Forge, 2005), 152.

21. Unruh Jr., *The Plains Across,* 414.
22. J. S. Holliday, *The World Rushed In* (New York: Simon & Schuster, 1981), 288.
23. Joseph A. Stuart diary, October 19, 1849, in Holliday, *The World Rushed In*, 290.
24. Isaac J. Wistar diary, August 26, 1849, in Holliday, *The World Rushed In*, 290.
25. Werner, *Pioneer Children on the Journey West,* 158.

Chapter Two: A Woman's Place

1. Georgia Willis Read, "Women and Children on the Oregon-California Trail in the Gold Rush Years," *Missouri Historical Review* 39, no. 1 (October 1944): 12.
2. Keturah Belknap diary, in *Best of Covered Wagon Women*, ed. Kenneth L. Holmes (Norman: University of Oklahoma Press, 2008), 27.
3. Ibid., 28.
4. Ibid., 29.
5. Catherine Haun diary, in *Women's Diaries of the Westword Journey*, collected by Lillian Schlissel (New York: Schocken Books, 1982), 173.
6. Keturah Belknap diary, in *Best of Covered Wagon Women*, ed. Kenneth L. Holmes (Norman: University of Oklahoma Press, 2008), 27.
7. Pamelia Fergus to her husband, James, in *The Gold Rush Widows of Little Falls*, by Linda Peavy and Ursula Smith (Saint Paul: Minnesota Historical Society Press, 1990), 183.
8. Ellen Tootle diary, in *Best of Covered Wagon Women*, 234.
9. Mrs. John Berry letter, in *The Way West*, by James A. Crutchfield (New York: Forge, 2005), 157.
10. J. S. Holliday, *The World Rushed In* (New York: Simon & Schuster, 1981), 128.
11. Cecilia Adams and Parthenia Blank diary, in *Best of Covered Wagon Women*, 161.
12. Holliday, *The World Rushed In*, 151.
13. Miriam Davis diary, in *Women's Diaries*, 83.
14. J. S. Holliday, *The World Rushed In* (New York: Simon & Schuster, 1981), 128.
15. Emmy E. Werner, *Pioneer Children on the Journey West* (Boulder, CO: Westview Press, 1995), 115.
16. Amanda Hardin Brown, "A Pioneer in Colorado and Wyoming," *The Colorado Magazine* 35, no. 3 (July 1958): 164.
17. Mary Ellen Jones, *Daily Life on the Nineteenth Century American Frontier* (Westport, CT: Greenwood Press, 1998), 130.
18. Werner, *Pioneer Children on the Journey West*, 118.
19. Mrs. Isaac Moore diary, in *Pioneer Women: The Lives of Women on the Frontier*, by Linda Peavy and Ursula Smith (Norman: University of Oklahoma Press, 1996), 31.
20. Amelia Knight diary, in *Women's Diaries*, 205.
21. Fred Lockley, *Conversations with Pioneer Women* (Eugene, OR: Rainy Day Press, 1981), 111.
22. Charlotte Stearns Pengra diary, in *Women's Diaries*, 80.
23. Amelia Knight diary, in *Best of Covered Wagon Women*, 205.
24. Ibid.
25. John Mack Faragher, *Women and Men on the Overland Trail* (New Haven: Yale University Press, 1979), cited in *Women's Diaries of the Westward Journey*, collected by Lillian Schlissel (New York: Schocken Books, 1982), 160.
26. Ellen Tootle diary, in *Best of Covered Wagon Women*, 235.
27. Mary Ellen Jones, *Daily Life on the Nineteenth Century American Frontier* (Westport, CT: Greenwood Press, 1998), 130.
28. Ibid., 237.
29. Helen Carpenter diary, in *Pioneer Women*, 45.
30. Pamelia Fergus to her husband, James, in *Pioneer Women*, 27.
31. Ellen Tootle diary, in *Best of Covered Wagon Women*, 234.
32. Nell Brown Propst, "Willa Clanton: A Remarkable Link with Colorado's Past," *The Colorado Magazine* 56, no.1 (Winter/Spring 1979): 45.

33. David Roberts, *Devil's Gate: Brigham Young and the Great Mormon Handcart Tragedy* (New York: Simon & Schuster, 2008), 255.

34. Frances Fuller Victor, *Eleven Years in the Rocky Mountains* (Hartford, CT: Columbia Books, 1877), 87.

35. J. Goldsborough Bruff, *Gold Rush: The Journals, Drawings, and Other Papers of J. Goldsborough Bruff* (New York: Columbia University Press, 1949), 223.

36. Ibid., 226.

37. William Davenport to *Liberty (Missouri) Tribune*, August 1, 1864, in *Best of Covered Wagon Women*, 266.

38. Mary Ringo diary, in *Best of Covered Wagon Women*, 267.

39. Ibid.

40. Elizabeth Elliott diary, in *Best of Covered Wagon Women*, 261.

41. Ibid., 262.

42. Katherine Dunlap diary, in *Women's Diaries*, 135; Ada Millington diary, in *Women's Diaries*, 132; Amelia Knight diary, in *Best of Covered Wagon Women*, 216; Maria Elliott diary, in *Pioneer Children on the Journey West*, 126.

43. Catherine Haun diary, in *The Way West*, 154.

44. Amelia Knight diary, in *Women's Diaries*, 215.

45. Edith Lockhart diary, in *Pioneer Children on the Journey West*, 153.

46. Elizabeth Smith Geer diary, in *Women's Diaries*, 54.

47. Amelia Knight diary, in *Best of Covered Wagon Women*, 221.

48. Cecilia Adams and Parthenia Blank diary, in *Best of Covered Wagon Women*, 160.

49. Bruff, *Gold Rush*, 51.

50. Ibid., 223.

51. Keturah Belknap diary, in *Best of Covered Wagon Women*, 37.

52. Holliday, *The World Rushed In,* 146.

53. Juliet Brier diary, in *The Way West*, 155.

54. Mary Ringo diary, in *Best of Covered Wagon Women*, 275.

55. Sallie Hester diary, in *Pioneer Children on the Journey West*, 111.

56. Ada Millington diary, in *Pioneer Children on the Journey West*, 155.

57. Elizabeth Keegan diary, in *Pioneer Children on the Journey West*, 127.

58. Sarah Royce, *Across the Plains: Sarah Royce's Western Narrative* (Tucson: University of Arizona Press, 2009), 72.

Chapter Three: Bullwhackers

1. Theodore R. Davis, "A Stage Ride to Colorado," *Harper's New Monthly Magazine*, July 1867, 137.

2. Mark Twain, *Roughing It* (1872; repr., Berkeley: University of California Press, 1993), 20.

3. Ibid.

4. William Henry Jackson, *Time Exposure* (1940; repr., Albuquerque: University of New Mexico Press, 1986), 102.

5. Ibid., 112.

6. Robert W. Richmond and Robert W. Mardock, eds., *A Nation Moving West* (Lincoln: University of Nebraska Press, 1966), 216.

7. Davis, "A Stage Ride to Colorado," 138.

8. Frank A. Root and William E. Connelly, *The Overland Stage to California* (1901; repr., Glorieta, NM: Rio Grande Press, 1970), 338.

9. Demas Barnes, *From the Atlantic to the Pacific, Overland* (New York: D. Van Nostrand, 1866), 29.

10. Henry Milton Stanley, *My Early Travels and Adventures in America and Asia* (1895; repr., Lincoln: University of Nebraska Press, 1982), 169.

11. Ibid.

12. Barnes, *From the Atlantic to the Pacific, Overland*, 7.

13. Catharine Wever Collins, "An Army Wife Comes West" *The Colorado Magazine* 31, no. 4 (October 1954): 247.
14. George E. Vanderwalker, "The Bullwhacker or Prairie Sailor," *The Trail* 1, no. 9 (1909): 26.
15. Davis, "A Stage Ride to Colorado," 147.
16. W. J. Carney, "How the Julesburg Mail Was Lost," *The Railroad Man's Magazine*, December 1910, 493.
17. William F. Hooker, "The Bullwhacker," *Collections of Wyoming Historical Society*, in *Sons of the West* by Lorah B. Chaffin (Caldwell, ID: Caxton Printers, 1941), 129.
18. John A. Sells, *Stagecoaches: Across the American West 1850 to 1920* (Blaine, WA: Hancock House, 2008), 14.
19. Root and Connelly, *The Overland Stage to California*, 48.
20. Ibid.
21. Ibid., 49.
22. Ibid.
23. Henry P. Steele, "Coming West in '67," *Sons of Colorado* 2, no. 8 (January 1908): 9.
24. Twain, *Roughing It*, 7.
25. Bayard Taylor, *Colorado: A Summer Trip* (1867; repr., Niwot: University Press of Colorado, 1989), 168.
26. Ibid., 170.
27. A Lady Pioneer, "Crossing the Great American Desert in the 60s," *The Trail* 1, no. 5 (October 1908): 5.
28. Oscar Osburn Winther, *The Transportation Frontier: Trans-Mississippi West 1865–1890* (New York: Holt, 1964), 68.
29. Root and Connelly, *The Overland Stage to California*, 96.
30. Richard Erdoes, *Saloons of the Old West* (New York: Knopf, 1979), 112.
31. Ibid.
32. Ibid, 113.
33. Samuel Bowles, *Across the Continent: A Summer's Journey to the Rocky Mountains* (Springfield, MA: S. Bowles, 1866), 21.
34. A Lady Pioneer, "A Coach Trip in 1865," *The Trail* 1, no. 2 (March 1909): 5.
35. Vanderwalker, "The Bullwhacker or Prairie Sailor," 28.
36. Root and Connelly, *The Overland Stage to California*, 186.
37. Bowles, *Across the Continent*, 73.
38. *Leavenworth (Kansas) Daily Conservative*, February 17, 1864, in *A Nation Moving West*, 2.

Chapter Four: Indians!

1. John D. Unruh Jr., *The Plains Across* (Urbana: University of Illinois Press, 1979), 156.
2. Nancy Hunt diary, in *Women's Diaries of the Westward Journey* collected by Lillian Schlissel (New York: Schocken Books, 1982), 119.
3. Unruh, *The Plains Across*, 162.
4. Ibid., 175.
5. J. S. Holliday, *The World Rushed In* (New York: Simon & Schuster, 1981), 147.
6. Robert G. Athearn, *William Tecumseh Sherman and the Settlement of the West* (Norman: University of Oklahoma Press, 1956), 189.
7. Lieutenant General William T. Sherman to General John Rawlins, August 17, 1866, in *Protection Across the Continent*, House of Representatives, 39th Cong., 2d sess., 4.
8. General James Henry Carleton to Lieutenant General William T. Sherman, October 17, 1866, Headquarters of the Army, Records of the War Department, National Archives, in Athearn, *William Tecumseh Sherman and the Settlement of the West*, 91.
9. Henry Milton Stanley, *My Early Travels and Adventures in America and Asia* (1895; repr., Lincoln: University of Nebraska Press, 1982), 133.
10. David Haward Bain, *Empire Express: Building the First Transcontinental Railroad* (New York: Viking, 1999), 231.

11. Don Rickey Jr., *Forty Miles a Day on Beans and Hay* (Norman: University of Oklahoma Press, 1963), 72–73.

12. Bain, *Empire Express*, 7.

13. William T. Sherman, *Personal Memoirs of Gen. W. T. Sherman* (New York: Webster, 1890), 390.

14. Ibid., 391.

15. Ibid., 7.

16. Remi Nadeau, *Fort Laramie and the Sioux Indians* (Englewood Cliffs, NJ: Prentice Hall, 1967), 217.

17. Henry J. Williams, *The Pacific Tourist* (New York: H. J. Williams, 1877), 37.

18. David Fridtjof Halaas and Andrew E. Masich, *Halfbreed: The Remarkable True Story of George Bent* (Cambridge, MA: Da Capo Press, 2004), 218.

19. Ibid.

20. Unruh, *The Plains Across*, 185.

21. Frank A. Root and William E. Connelly, *The Overland Stage to California* (1901; repr., Glorieta, NM: Rio Grande Press, 1970), 379.

22. Nathaniel P. Hill to his wife, Alice, August 11, 1864, in "Nathaniel P. Hill Inspects Colorado," *The Colorado Magazine* 34, no. 1: 35.

23. *Montana Post*, January 26, 1867.

24. Horace Greeley, *An Overland Journey from New York to San Francisco in the Summer of 1859* (New York: Sexton, Barker, 1860), 119.

25. Stanley, *My Early Travels and Adventures in America and Asia*, xvi.

26. Athearn, *William Tecumseh Sherman and the Settlement of the West*, 14.

27. Captain Albert Barnitz to Jennie Barnitz, in *Life in Custer's Cavalry*, ed. Robert Utley (New Haven, CT: Yale University Press, 1977), 70.

28. Kansas State Historical Society, *Kansas State Historical Collections 1912* 12: 296.

29. George Bird Grinnell, *The Fighting Cheyennes* (Norman: Oklahoma University Press, 1956), 281.

30. Maury Klein, *Union Pacific: The Birth of a Railroad 1862–1893* (New York: Doubleday, 1987), 151.

31. Grinnell, *The Fighting Cheyennes*, 266.

32. Charles L. Convis, *Old West Railroaders* (Carson City, NV: Pioneer Press, 2001), 6.

33. George Bent to George Bird Grinnell, March 19, 1914, George Bird Grinnell Papers, MS.5, Folder 82, Gene Autry Museum (formerly Southwest Museum Collection).

34. John A. Sells, *Stagecoaches: Across the American West 1850 to 1920* (Blaine, WA: Hancock House, 2008), 257.

35. Annual report, 1865, *The Congressional Globe*, 39th Cong., 1st sess., in Bain, *Empire Express*, 244.

36. Glenda Riley, *Women and Indians on the Frontier 1825–1915* (Albuquerque: University of New Mexico Press, 1984), 226.

37. Stephen Ambrose, *Nothing Like It in the World* (New York: Simon & Schuster, 2000), 173.

38. Nadeau, *Fort Laramie and the Sioux Indians*, 133.

39. Bayard Taylor, *Colorado: A Summer Trip* (1867; repr., Niwot: University Press of Colorado, 1989), 184.

40. *Cheyenne Leader*, September 5, 1880.

Chapter Five: "A Great Purpose"

1. David Haward Bain, *Empire Express: Building the First Transcontinental Railroad* (New York: Viking, 1999), 17.

2. Horace Greeley, *An Overland Journey from New York to San Francisco in the Summer of 1859* (New York: Sexton, Barker, 1860), 312.

3. Fred W. Lander to Congressman Reuben Fenton, March 13, 1860, *The New York Times*, March 28, 1860.

4. Ibid.

5. Greeley, *An Overland Journey from New York to San Francisco*, 315.

6. *Rocky Mountain News*, November 24, 1859.

7. Ibid.

8. Greeley, *An Overland Journey from New York to San Francisco*, 319.

9. Maury Klein, *Union Pacific: The Birth of a Railroad 1862–1893* (New York: Doubleday, 1987), 18.

10. Ibid., 19.

11. Keith Wheeler, *The Railroaders* (New York: Time-Life Books, 1973), 43.

12. Ibid.

13. Samuel H. Chittenden to his mother, Mrs. L. C. Chittenden, May 31, 1868, Samuel H. Chittenden Collection, American Heritage Center, University of Wyoming, Laramie.

14. Grace Raymond Hebard, *The Pathbreakers from River to Ocean* (Chicago: Lakeside Press, 1912), 234.

15. Robert E. Riegel, *America Moves West* (New York: Holt, Rinehart and Winston, 1971), 470.

16. Ibid., 472.

17. Klein, *Union Pacific*, 42.

18. W. T. Sherman, *Memoirs, Volume 2* (New York: Webster, 1891), 411.

Chapter Six: "The Grandest Enterprise Under God"

1. Albert D. Richardson, *Beyond the Mississippi: From the Great Rim to the Great Ocean* (Hartford, CT: American Publishing Co., 1867), 565.

2. John Carson, *The Union Pacific: Hell on Wheels!* (Santa Fe, NM: Press of the Territorian, 1968), 11.

3. Archibald R. Adamson, *North Platte and Its Associations* (North Platte, NE: The Evening Telegram, 1910), 12.

4. George Francis Train, *My Life in Many States and in Foreign Lands* (New York: Appleton, 1902), xiv.

5. Ibid., 325.

6. Garry Hogg, *Union Pacific: The Building of the First Transcontinental Railroad* (New York: Walker, 1967), 106.

7. E. C. Lockwood, "With the Casement Brothers While Building the Union Pacific," *The Union Pacific Magazine*, February 1931, 4.

8. Oscar Osburn Winther, *The Transportation Frontier: Trans-Mississippi West 1865–1890* (New York: Holt, 1964), 111.

9. Robert W. Howard, *The Great Iron Trail* (New York: Putnam's, 1962), 201.

10. Lockwood, "With the Casement Brothers While Building the Union Pacific," 4.

11. W. L. Park, "Tales from Old-Timers, No. 3," *The Union Pacific Magazine*, May 1923.

12. Samuel Chittenden to his mother, March 2, 1868, Samuel H. Chittenden Collection, American Heritage Center, University of Wyoming, Laramie.

13. Samuel Chittenden to his mother, May 31, 1868, Samuel H. Chittenden Collection, American Heritage Center, University of Wyoming, Laramie.

14. Ibid.

15. Samuel Chittenden to his mother, June 17, 1868, Samuel H. Chittenden Collection, American Heritage Center, University of Wyoming, Laramie.

16. Major General Grenville M. Dodge, *How We Built the Union Pacific Railway* (1870; repr., Denver: Sage Books, 1965), 15.

17. David Haward Bain, *Empire Express: Building the First Transcontinental Railroad* (New York: Viking, 1999), 352.

18. C. H. Sharman, "Tales from Old-Timers, No. 24," *The Union Pacific Magazine*, October 1925, 6.

19. H. Clark Brown, "Tales from Old-Timers, No. 31," *The Union Pacific Magazine*, May 1926, 12.

20. Stephen E. Ambrose, *Nothing Like It in the World* (New York: Simon & Schuster, 2000), 223.
21. Arthur N. Ferguson diary, August 3, 1868, Manuscript Collection, Union Pacific Railroad Museum, Council Bluffs, IA.
22. *The New York Times*, June 17, 1867.
23. Maury Klein, *Union Pacific: The Birth of a Railroad 1862–1893* (New York: Doubleday, 1987), 168.
24. A. P. Wood, "Tales from Old-Timers, No. 19," *The Union Pacific Magazine*, January 1925, 36.
25. Robert Athearn, *William Tecumseh Sherman and the Settlement of the West* (Norman: University of Oklahoma, 1956), 19.
26. W. A. Bell, "Pacific Railroads," *Fortnightly Review*, May 1869, 572–573, in *Special Report on Promontory Summit* by Robert Utley (Santa Fe, NM: U.S. Department of the Interior, National Park Service, Region Three, 1960).
27. Klein, *Union Pacific*, 8.
28. *The New York Times*, December 4, 1867.
29. Dodge, *How We Built the Union Pacific Railway*, 49.
30. "Monthly Record of Current Events," *Harper's New Monthly*, July 1869, 294.
31. Levi O. Leonard and Jack T. Johnson, *A Railroad to the Sea* (Iowa City, IA: Midland House, 1939), 169.
32. *The New York Times*, October 8, 1868.

Chapter Seven: "Hell on Wheels"

1. Sarah H. Gordon, *Passage to Union: How the Railroads Transformed American Life, 1829–1929* (Chicago: Ivan R. Dee, 1996), 159.
2. John Richie Schultz, "Features of Colorado Life as Seen by Bayard Taylor in 1866," *The Colorado Magazine* 12, no. 5 (September 1935): 164.
3. Alice Polk Hill, *Tales of the Colorado Pioneers* (Denver: Pierson & Gardner, 1884), 138.
4. *Philadelphia Inquirer*, March 12, 1869.
5. Robert Lardin Fulton, *The Epic of the Overland* (San Francisco: A. M. Robertson, 1925), 70.
6. Thomas R. Buecker, ed. "Letters of Caroline Frey Winnie...." *Nebraska History* magazine, Volume 62, No. 1 (1981).
7. Stephen Ambrose, *Nothing Like It in the World* (New York: Simon and Schuster, 2000), 219.
8. John Debo Galloway, *The First Transcontinental Railroad* (New York: Simmons-Boardman, 1950), 297.
9. Mary Lou Pence and Lola M. Homsher, *The Ghost Towns of Wyoming* (New York: Hastings House, 1956), 54.
10. Levi O. Leonard and Jack T. Johnson, *A Railroad to the Sea* (Iowa City, IA: Midland House, 1939), 169.
11. Stephen E. Ambrose, *Nothing Like It in the World* (New York: Simon & Schuster, 2000), 355.
12. Mary Ellen Jones, *Daily Life on the Nineteenth-Century American Frontier* (Westport, CT: Greenwood Press, 1998), 207.
13. Henry Milton Stanley, *My Early Travels and Adventures in America and Asia* (1895; repr., Lincoln: University of Nebraska Press, 1982), 163.
14. *Pittsburgh Commercial Gazette*, in *A Railroad to the Sea*, 174.
15. Maury Klein, *Union Pacific: The Birth of a Railroad 1862–1893* (New York: Doubleday, 1987), 561.
16. George Kraus, *High Road to Promontory* (New York: Castle Books, 1969), 111.
17. Samuel Bowles, *Our New West: Records of Travel: A Full Description of the Pacific Railroad* (Hartford, CT: Hartford Publishing, 1869), 56.
18. Samuel Chittenden to his mother, October 22, 1868, Samuel H. Chittenden Collection, American Heritage Center, University of Wyoming, Laramie.

19. *The New York Times*, September 18, 1870.
20. Demas Barnes, *From the Atlantic to the Pacific, Overland* (New York: D. Van Nostrand, 1866), 101.

Chapter Eight: Milepost 0.0: Omaha

1. *The New York Times*, August 3, 1868.
2. Henry M. Stanley, *My Early Travels and Adventures in America and Asia* (1895; repr., Lincoln: University of Nebraska Press, 1982), 107.
3. A. K. McClure, *Three Thousand Miles through the Rocky Mountains* (Philadelphia: J. P. Lippincott, 1869), 45.
4. *The New York Times*, August 2, 1868.
5. Joseph Barker, "Omaha in 1868–1869: Selections from the Letters of Joseph Barker," *Nebraska History* 59, no. 4 (Winter 1978): 501.
6. Robert W. Richmond and Robert W. Mardock, eds., *A Nation Moving West* (Lincoln: University of Nebraska Press, 1966), 339.
7. Ibid., 340.
8. Howard P. Chudacoff, "Where Rolls the Dark Missouri Down," *Nebraska History* 52, no. 1 (1971): 1.
9. W. F. Rae, *Westward by Rail* (London: Longmans, Green, 1870), 71.
10. Barker, "Omaha in 1868–1869: Selections from the Letters of Joseph Barker," 513.
11. Anne M. Butler, *Daughters of Joy, Sisters of Misery* (Urbana: University of Illinois, 1987), xvii.
12. James Chisholm, *South Pass 1868: James Chisholm's Journal of the Wyoming Gold Rush*, ed. Lola M. Homsher (Lincoln: University of Nebraska Press, 1960), 100.
13. Josie Washburn, *The Underworld Sewer* (1909; repr., Lincoln: University of Nebraska Press, 1996), 70.
14. Bayard Taylor, *Colorado: A Summer Trip* (1867; repr., Niwot: University Press of Colorado, 1989), 178.
15. *The New York Times*, July 22, 1868.
16. *The New York Times*, July 6, 1871.
17. David Bristow, *A Dirty, Wicked Town: Tales of 19th Century Omaha* (Caldwell, ID: Caxton Press, 2000), 70.
18. Miriam Leslie, "Out West on the Overland Train," *Frank Leslie's Illustrated*, February 9, 1878, 29.
19. Barker, "Omaha in 1868–1869: Selections from the Letters of Joseph Barker," 516.
20. Rae, *Westward by Rail*, 70.
21. Albert D. Richardson, *Beyond the Mississippi: From the Great Rim to the Great Ocean* (Hartford, CT: American Publishing Co., 1867), 564.

Chapter Nine: Milepost 291.0: North Platte

1. Archibald R. Adamson, *North Platte and Its Associations* (North Platte, NE: The Evening Telegraph, 1910), 25.
2. Ibid.
3. Henry M. Stanley, *My Early Travels and Adventures in America and Asia* (1895; repr., Lincoln: University of Nebraska Press, 1982), 107.
4. Stanley, in *The Union Pacific: Hell on Wheels!* edited by John Carson (Santa Fe, NM: Press of the Territorian, 1968), 22.
5. Ibid.
6. Adamson, *North Platte and Its Associations*, 42.
7. Maury Klein, *Union Pacific: The Birth of a Railroad 1862–1893* (New York: Doubleday, 1987), 100.
8. Charles Edgar Ames, *Pioneering the Union Pacific* (New York: Meredith, 1969), 232.

9. *Rocky Mountain News*, June 16, 1870.

10. Nelson Trottman, *History of the Union Pacific* (New York: Ronald Press, 1923), 129.

11. Stanley, in *The Union Pacific: Hell on Wheels!*, 201.

12. H. W. Guy, "Tales from Old-Timers, No. 20," *The Union Pacific Magazine*, February 1925, 15.

Chapter Ten: Milepost 377.4: Julesburg

1. David Haward Bain, *Empire Express: Building the First Transcontinental Railroad* (New York: Viking, 1999), 380.

2. Irene D. Paden, *The Wake of the Prairie Schooner* (New York: MacMillan, 1945), 130.

3. Olga Curtis, "The Killing of Jules: A Deathless Legend," *Empire Magazine* (*The Denver Post*), August 12, 1979, 30.

4. Charles T. Linton, "My Early Western Experience," *Sons of Colorado* 1, no. 12 (May 1907): 6.

5. General William T. Sherman to General John A. Rawlins, December 27, 1866, in *Protection Across the Continent* (Washington, DC: Government Printing Office, 1867).

6. *Rocky Mountain News*, January 7, 1914.

7. David Fridtjof Halaas and Andrew E, Masich, *Halfbreed: The Remarkable True Story of George Bent* (Cambridge, MA: DeCapo Press, 2004), 169.

8. *Rocky Mountain News*, January 7, 1914.

9. Doris Monahan, *Destination: Denver City* (Athens: Ohio University Press, 1985), 221.

10. Henry C. Parry to his father, Judge Edward Owen Parry, June 10, 1867, "Letters from the Frontier, 1867," *Annals of Wyoming* 30, no. 2 (October 1958): 132.

11. *Rocky Mountain News*, June 14, 1867.

12. *Rocky Mountain News*, August 2, 1867.

13. Henry C. Parry to his father, July 23, 1867, "Letters from the Frontier, 1867," 133.

14. O. E. Davis, *The First Five Years of the Railroad Era in Colorado* (Denver: Sage Books, 1948), 11.

15. Samuel B. Reed to Jennie Reed, July 30, 1867, in *A Railroad to the Sea* by Levi O. Leonard and Jack T. Johnson (Iowa City, IA: Midland House, 1939), 172.

16. *Frontier Index*, July 19, 1867.

17. *Omaha World-Herald*, July 10, 1867.

18. *Omaha World-Herald*, July 11, 1867.

19. Henry M. Stanley, *My Early Travels and Adventures in America and Asia* (1895; repr., Lincoln: University of Nebraska Press, 1982), 165.

20. Luella Shaw, *True History of Some of the Pioneers of Colorado* (Hotchkiss, CO: W. S. Coburn, J. Patterson and A. K. Shaw, 1909), 242.

21. Monahan, *Destination: Denver City*, 172.

22. Stephen E. Ambrose, *Nothing Like It in the World* (New York: Simon & Schuster, 2000), 219.

23. Stanley, *My Early Travels and Adventures in America and Asia*, 191.

24. *Rocky Mountain News*, July 8, 1867.

Chapter Eleven: Milepost 516.4: Cheyenne

1. W. W. Corlett, *The Founding of Cheyenne 1885*, in *History of Wyoming* by T. A. Larson (Lincoln: University of Nebraska Press, 1965), 42.

2. Robert G. Athearn, *Union Pacific Country* (Chicago: Rand McNally, 1971), 148.

3. Ibid., 57.

4. David Haward Bain, *Empire Express: Building the First Transcontinental Railroad* (New York: Viking, 1999), 411.

5. Robert Lardin Fulton, *Epic of the Overland* (San Francisco: A. M. Robertson, 1925), 64.

6. James Chisholm, *Chicago Tribune*, March 21, 1868, in *South Pass 1868* by Lola Homsher (Lincoln: University of Nebraska Press, 1960), 17.

7. Fulton, *Epic of the Overland*, 67.

8. Wyoming Tales and Trails website, "Hell on Wheels," www.wyomingtalesandtrails.com.

9. David Dary, *Seeking Pleasure in the Old West* (New York: Knopf, 1995), 226.

10. Richard Erdoes, *Saloons of the Old West* (New York: Knopf, 1979), 145.

11. Samuel Reed to Henry C. Crane, March 13, 1868, Nebraska State Historical Society Collection, Lincoln.

12. Larson, *History of Wyoming*, 45.

13. Fulton, *Epic of the Overland*, 70.

14. *Cheyenne Leader*, November 16, 1867.

15. *Cheyenne Leader*, November 14, 1867.

16. Ibid.

17. Samuel B. Reed to Jennie Reed, November 1867, Nebraska State Historical Society Collection, Lincoln.

18. Larson, *History of Wyoming*, 47.

19. James Chisholm, *Chicago Tribune*, March 21, 1868.

20. *The New York Times*, June 18, 1868.

21. Edwin L. Sabin, *Building the Pacific Railway* (Philadelphia: J. P. Lippincott, 1919), 261.

22. *Cheyenne Leader*, May 9, 1868.

23. Ibid.

24. "House Journal of the Legislative Assembly of the Territory of Colorado," September 9, 1861, 12.

25. Kenneth Jessen, *Railroads of Northern Colorado* (Boulder, CO: Pruett, 1982), 21.

Chapter Twelve: Milepost 572.8: Laramie

1. Maury Klein, *Union Pacific: The Birth of a Railroad 1862–1893* (New York: Doubleday, 1987), 150.

2. Samuel Chittenden to his mother, March 14, 1868, Samuel H. Chittenden Collection, American History Center, University of Wyoming, Laramie.

3. Ibid.

4. Klein, *Union Pacific*, 150.

5. Thomas Durant to Leland Stanford, April 16, 1868, reported in the *New York Tribune*, April 18, 1868.

6. Leland Stanford to Thomas Durant, April 17, 1868, Huntington Papers, Syracuse University Library, in *Empire Express: Building the First Transcontinental Railroad* by David Haward Bain (New York: Viking, 1999), 476.

7. *Cheyenne Leader*, May 5, 1868.

8. *Cheyenne Leader*, April 27, 1868.

9. Howard P. Chudacoff, "Where Rolls the Dark Missouri Down," *Nebraska History* 52, no. 1 (1971): 135.

10. *Frontier Index*, June 16, 1868.

11. J. H. Triggs, *History and Directory of Laramie City, Wyoming Territory* (Laramie City: Daily Sentinel Print, 1875), 5.

12. *The New York Times*, June 22, 1868.

13. *Frontier Index*, June 16, 1868.

14. A. P. Wood, "Tales from Old-Timers, No. 19," *The Union Pacific Magazine*, January 1925, 37.

15. Triggs, *History and Directory of Laramie City, Wyoming Territory*, 27.

16. Charles Edgar Ames, *Pioneering the Union Pacific* (New York: Meredith, 1969), 291.

17. H. Clark Brown, "Tales from Old-Timers, No. 31," *The Union Pacific Magazine*, May 1926, 12.

18. John P. Davis, *The Union Pacific Railway* (Chicago: S. C. Griggs and Company, 1894), 144.

19. Samuel Bowles, *Across the Continent: A Summer's Journey to the Rocky Mountains* (Springfield, MA: S. Bowles, 1866).

20. *Cheyenne Leader*, August 10, 1868.

Chapter Thirteen: Milepost 946.0: Bear River City

1. Scott B. Eckberg, "The Frontier Index: Chronicle of a World on Wheels," National Park Service, http://usparks.about.com/od/historicalparks/a/Golden-Spike-NHS.htm.
2. *Frontier Index*, October 30, 1868.
3. *Frontier Index*, November 6, 1868.
4. Robert Lardin Fulton, *The Epic of the Overland* (San Francisco: A. M. Robertson, 1925), 69.
5. *Frontier Index*, November 6, 1868.
6. *Frontier Index*, October 13, 1868.
7. *Frontier Index*, May 19, 1868.
8. *Frontier Index*, November 13, 1868.
9. *Frontier Index*, August 11, 1868.
10. Mrs. Barry O'Connor, "Story of the Union Pacific Railroad and Bear Town," (unpublished manuscript), Wyoming State Archives and Historical Department, Cheyenne.
11. *Frontier Index*, November 13, 1868.
12. Kate Toponce, *Reminiscences of Alexander Toponce, Pioneer* (Ogden, UT: Privately printed, 1923), 170–171.
13. Theodore Haswell, "Driving the Golden Spike, May 10, 1869," *The Union Pacific Magazine*, May 1925, 11.
14. Gary L. Roberts, "The Bear River Riot," (unpublished manuscript, copy in author's collection).

Chapter Fourteen: Milepost 1056.6: Corinne

1. Samuel Chittenden to his mother, August 20, 1868, Samuel H. Chittenden Collection, American History Center, University of Wyoming, Laramie.
2. *Rocky Mountain News*, April 29, 1869.
3. Ibid.
4. Stephen Ambrose, *Nothing Like It in the World* (New York: Simon & Schuster, 2000), 318.
5. *Salt Lake Telegraph*, April 9, 1869.
6. J. H. Beadle, *The Undeveloped West* (Philadelphia: National Publishing Company, 1873), 120.
7. *Salt Lake Telegraph*, April 13, 1869.
8. Brigham D. Madsen and Betty M. Madsen, "Corinne, the Fair: Gateway to Montana Mines," *Utah Historical Quarterly* 37, no. 1 (Winter 1969): 104.
9. *Ogden Junction*, May 24, 1871, in *Corinne: The Gentile Capital of Utah* by Brigham D. Madsen (Salt Lake City: Utah State Historical Society, 1980), 68.
10. Madsen, *Corinne: The Gentile Capital of Utah*, 58.
11. *Corinne Reporter*, July 13, 1878.
12. Madsen, *Corinne: The Gentile Capital of Utah*, 69.
13. Ibid., 118–120.
14. Ibid., 3.
15. Ibid.
16. Jeffrey D. Nichols, *Prostitution, Polygamy, and Power: Salt Lake City, 1847–1918* (Urbana: University of Illinois Press, 2002), 28.
17. Samuel Chittenden to his mother, May 31, 1868, Samuel H. Chittenden Collection, American History Center, University of Wyoming, Laramie.
18. Samuel Chittenden to his mother, June 21, 1868, Samuel H. Chittenden Collection, American History Center, University of Wyoming, Laramie.
19. Madsen, *Corinne: The Gentile Capital of Utah*, 123.

Chapter Fifteen: Milepost 1084.4: Promontory

1. Maury Klein, *Union Pacific: The Birth of a Railroad 1862–1893* (New York: Doubleday, 1987), 208.

2. Railroad Commission report, May 28, 1869, http://usparks.about.com/od/historicalparks/a/Golden-Spike-NHS.htm.

3. Robert Utley, "Special Report on Promontory Summit, Utah" (Santa Fe, NM: Department of the Interior, National Park Service, Region Three, 1960), 62.

4. *San Francisco Daily Morning Chronicle*, May 11, 1869.

5. Sidney Dillon, "Driving the Last Spike of the Union Pacific," *Scribner's*, August 1892, 257.

6. Bernice Gibbs Anderson, "The Driving of the Golden Spike," *Utah Historical Quarterly* 24, no. 2 (April 1956): 163.

7. *Utah Daily Reporter*, May 12, 1869, in "Special Report on Promontory Summit, Utah," 65.

8. J. N. Bowman, "Driving the Last Spike at Promontory," *Utah Historical Quarterly* 37, no. 1 (Winter 1969): 91.

9. Anderson, "The Driving of the Golden Spike," 153.

10. Ibid., 155.

11. Kate Toponce, *Reminiscences of Alexander Toponce, Pioneer* (Ogden, UT: Privately printed, 1923), 150.

12. "David Lemon—Old Timer," *The Union Pacific Magazine*, May 1924, 5.

13. J. W. Malloy, "Veteran Recalls Driving of Golden Spike," *The Union Pacific Magazine*, May 1926, 5.

Chapter Sixteen: Travel by Train

1. W. L. Park, "Tales from Old-Timers, No. 3," *The Union Pacific Magazine*, May 1923, 12.

2. Dee Alexander Brown, *Hear That Lonesome Whistle Blow* (New York: Holt, Rinehart and Winston, 1977), 184.

3. Ibid.

4. William Lawrence Humason, in *The Railroaders* by Keith Wheeler (New York: Time-Life Books, 1973), 155.

5. James H. Kyner, *End of Track* (Caldwell, ID: Caxton Printers, 1937), 82.

6. W. L. Humason, *From the Atlantic Surf to the Golden Gate* (Hartford, CT: W. C. Hutchings, 1869), 18.

7. *The New York Times*, August 7, 1869.

8. *Harper's Weekly*, November 16, 1867.

9. Susan B. Anthony, quoted in "Building the Union Pacific," www.wyomingtalesandtrails.com.

10. Samuel Bowles, *Our New West: Records of Travel: ... A Full Description of the Pacific Railroad* (Hartford, CT: Hartford Publishing, 1869), 45.

11. Ibid., 179.

12. Ibid., 8.

13. James McCague, *Moguls and Iron Men* (New York: Harper & Row, 1964), 338.

14. Giles Barton Lumbard, "By Train from Omaha to Sacramento One Hundred Years Ago," *The American West*, November 1975, 14.

15. *Frank Leslie's Illustrated*, February 9, 1878.

16. Liston Edgington Leyendecker, *Palace Car Prince* (Niwot: University Press of Colorado, 1992), 106.

17. A. K. McClure, *Three Thousand Miles through the Rocky Mountains* (Philadelphia: J. P. Lippincott, 1869), 24.

18. Henry Milton Stanley, *My Early Travels and Adventures in America and Asia* (1895; repr., Lincoln: University of Nebraska Press, 1982), 146.

19. George Augustus Sala, *America Revisited*, vol. 2 (London: Vizetelly & Co., 1882), 178.

20. Oscar Osburn Winther, *The Transportation Frontier: Trans-Mississippi West 1865–1890* (New York: Holt, 1964), 68.

21. Keith Wheeler, *The Railroaders* (New York: Time-Life Books, 1973), 139.

22. Brown, *Hear That Lonesome Whistle Blow*, 142.

23. McClure, *Three Thousand Miles through the Rocky Mountains*, 204.

24. Lesley Poling-Kempes, *The Harvey Girls* (New York: Paragon House, 1989) in *Rival Rails*:

The Race to Build America's Greatest Transcontinental Railroad by Walter R. Borneman (New York: Random House, 2010), 278.

25. Sala, *America Revisited,* vol. 2, 8.

26. Robert Louis Stevenson, *From Scotland to Silverado* (Cambridge, MA: Harvard University Press, 1966), 124.

27. Lady Duffus Hardy, *Through Cities and Prairie Lands: Sketches of an American Tour* (New York: Worthington, 1890), 84.

28. Stevenson, *From Scotland to Silverado,* 139.

29. Ibid., 142.

30. H. Clark Brown, "Tales from Old-Timers, No. 31," *The Union Pacific Magazine,* May 1926, 12.

31. *The New York Times,* January 26, 1869.

32. Bowles, *Our New West,* 45, 50.

Epilogue

1. Stephen Ambrose, *Nothing Like It in the World* (New York: Simon & Schuster, 2000), 369.

2. Richard White, *Railroaded: The Transcontinentals and the Making of Modern America* (New York: Norton, 2011), xxiv.

3. John D. Unruh Jr., *The Plains Across* (Urbana: University of Illinois Press, 1979), 350.

4. White, *Railroaded,* 46.

5. Ibid., 507.

6. *Leavenworth (Kansas) Daily Conservative,* February 17, 1864, in *A Nation Moving West* by Robert W. Richmond and Robert W. Mardock, eds., (Lincoln: University of Nebraska Press, 1966), 2.

7. Dennis Drabelle, *The Great American Railroad War* (New York: St. Martin's Press, 2012), 231.

8. Maury Klein, *Union Pacific: The Birth of a Railroad 1862–1893* (New York: Doubleday, 1987), xi.

BIBLIOGRAPHY

Books

Adamson, Archibald R. *North Platte and Its Associations*. North Platte, NE: The Evening Telegraph, 1910.

"Along the Line of the Kansas Pacific Railway in Western Kansas in 1870." In *A Business Directory Saint Louis to Denver, 1870*. Saint Louis: N. W. Josselyn & Co., 1870.

Ambrose, Stephen. *Nothing Like It in the World*. New York: Simon & Schuster, 2000.

American Social Science Association. *Handbook for Immigrants to the United States*. Cambridge, MA: Riverside Press, 1871.

Ames, Charles Edgar. *Pioneering the Union Pacific*. New York: Meredith, 1969.

Anderson, George L. *Kansas West*. San Marino, CA: Golden West Books, 1963.

Athearn, Robert. *In Search of Canaan*. Lawrence: Regents Press of Kansas, 1978.

———. *Union Pacific Country*. Chicago: Rand McNally, 1971.

———. *Westward the Briton*. New York: Scribner, 1953.

———. *William Tecumseh Sherman and the Settlement of the West*. Norman: University of Oklahoma, 1956.

Atwell, H. Wallace. *Great Transcontinental Railroad Guide*. Chicago: George A. Crofutt & Co., 1868.

Bain, David Haward. *Empire Express: Building the First Transcontinental Railroad*. New York: Viking, 1999.

Bare, Ira L., and Will H. McDonald, eds. *An Illustrated History of Lincoln County, Nebraska*, vol. 1. Chicago: The American Historical Society, 1920.

Barnes, Demas. *From the Atlantic to the Pacific, Overland*. New York: D. Van Nostrand, 1866.

Beadle, J. H. *The Undeveloped West*. Philadelphia: National Publishing Company, 1873.

Beebe, Lucius, and Charles Clegg. *Hear the Train Blow*. New York: Grosset & Dunlap, 1952.

Best, Gerald M. *Iron Horses to Promontory*. San Marino, CA: Golden West Books, 1969.

Borneman, Walter R. *Rival Rails: The Race to Build America's Greatest Transcontinental Railroad*. New York: Random House, 2010.

Bowles, Samuel. *Across the Continent: A Summer's Journey to the Rocky Mountains*. Springfield, MA: S. Bowles, 1866.

———. *Our New West: Records of Travel: ... A Full Description of the Pacific Railroad*. Hartford, CT: Hartford Publishing, 1869.

Bracken, Jeanne Minn, ed. *Iron Horses across America*. Carlisle, MA: Discovery Enterprises, 1955.

Bristow, David. *A Dirty, Wicked Town: Tales of 19th Century Omaha*. Caldwell, ID: Caxton Press, 2000.

Brown, Dee Alexander. *Hear That Lonesome Whistle Blow*. New York: Holt, Rinehart and Winston, 1977.

Bruff, J. Goldsborough. *Gold Rush: The Journals, Drawings, and Other Papers of J. Goldsborough Bruff.* New York: Columbia University Press, 1949.

Butler, Anne M. *Daughters of Joy, Sisters of Misery.* Urbana: University of Illinois, 1987.

Carson, John. *The Union Pacific: Hell on Wheels!* Santa Fe, NM: Press of the Territorian, 1968.

Chaffin, Lorah B. *Sons of the West.* Caldwell, ID: Caxton Printers, 1941.

Chisholm, James. *South Pass 1868: James Chisholm's Journal of the Wyoming Gold Rush.* Edited by Lola M. Homsher. Lincoln: University of Nebraska Press, 1960.

Convis, Charles L. *Old West Railroaders.* Carson City, NV: Pioneer Press, 2001.

Cook, Reverend Joseph W. *Diary and Letters of the Reverend Joseph W. Cook, Missionary to Cheyenne.* Laramie, WY: The Laramie Republican Co., 1919.

Crofutt, George A. *Crofutt's Trans-Continental Tourist's Guide.* New York: Crofutt, 1871.

Crutchfield, James A. *The Way West.* New York: Forge, 2005.

Cummings, Amos Jay. *A Remarkable Curiosity.* Boulder: University Press of Colorado, 2008.

Dary, David. *Red Blood & Black Ink: Journalism in the Old West.* New York: Knopf, 1998.

———. *Seeking Pleasure in the Old West.* New York: Knopf, 1995.

Davis, E. O. *The First Five Years of the Railroad Era in Colorado.* Denver: Sage Books, 1948.

Davis, John P. *The Union Pacific Railway.* Chicago: S. C. Griggs and Company, 1894.

Davis, Richard Harding. *The West from a Car Window.* New York: Harper, 1904.

Deverell, William. *Railroad Crossing: Californians and the Railroad 1850–1910.* Berkeley: University of California Press, 1994.

Dodge, Major General Grenville M. *How We Built the Union Pacific Railway.* 1876. Reprint, Denver: Sage Books, 1965.

Douglas, George H. *All Aboard: The Railroad in American Life.* New York: Paragon, 1992.

Drabelle, Dennis. *The Great American Railroad War.* New York: St. Martin's Press, 2012.

Driggs, Howard R. *Westward America.* New York: Putnam's, 1942.

Dykstra, Robert R. *The Cattle Towns.* New York: Knopf, 1968.

Ehernberger, James L., and Francis G. Gschwind. *Sherman Hill.* Callaway, NE: EG Publications, 1973.

Erdoes, Richard. *Saloons of the Old West.* New York: Knopf, 1979.

Faithfull, Emily. *Three Visits to America.* Edinburgh: David Douglas, 1884.

Forrest, Kenton, and Charles Albi. *Denver's Railroads.* Golden, CO: Colorado Railroad Museum, 1981.

Francaviglia, Richard V. *Over the Range.* Logan: Utah State University Press, 2008.

Freedman, Russell. *Children of the Wild West.* New York: Clarion, 1983.

Fried, Stephen. *Appetite for America.* New York: Bantam, 2010.

Fulton, Robert Lardin. *The Epic of the Overland.* San Francisco: A. M. Robertson, 1925.

Galloway, John Debo. *The First Transcontinental Railroad.* New York: Simmons-Boardman, 1950.

Goodstein, Phil. *Denver from the Bottom Up: Sand Creek to Ludlow.* Denver: New Social Publications, 2003.

Gordon, Sarah H. *Passage to Union: How the Railroads Transformed American Life, 1829–1929.* Chicago: Ivan R. Dee, 1996.

Greeley, Horace. *An Overland Journey from New York to San Francisco in the Summer of 1859.* New York: Sexton, Barker, 1860.

Grienberg, Alexandra. *A Half Year in the New World.* Newark: University of Delaware Press, 1954.

Grinnell, George Bird. *The Fighting Cheyennes.* Norman: University of Oklahoma Press, 1956.

Grinstead, Steve, and Ben Fogelberg, eds. *Western Voices.* Golden, CO: Fulcrum, 2004.

Griswold, Wesley. *A Work of Giants.* New York: McGraw-Hill, 1962.

Hafen, LeRoy R., ed. *Overland Routes to the Gold Fields, 1859.* Glendale, CA: Arthur H. Clark Co., 1942.

Halaas, David Fridtjof, and Andrew E. Masich. *Halfbreed: The Remarkable True Story of George Bent.* Cambridge, MA: Da Capo, 2004.

Hanks, Ted L. *Benton, Wyoming*. Salem, WA: T. L . Hanks, 2002.

Hardy, Lady Duffus. *Through Cities and Prairie Lands: Sketches of an American Tour*. New York: Worthington, 1890.

Hebard, Grace Raymond. *The Pathbreakers from River to Ocean*. Chicago: Lakeside Press, 1912.

Heuterman, Thomas H. *Movable Type*. Ames: Iowa State University Press, 1979.

Hill, Alice Polk. *Tales of the Colorado Pioneers*. Denver: Pierson & Gardner, 1884.

Hirshson, Stanley P. *Grenville M. Dodge: Soldier, Politician, Railroad Pioneer*. Bloomington: Indiana University Press, 1967.

History of the State of Nebraska. Chicago: Western Historical, 1882.

Hogg, Garry. *Union Pacific: The Building of the First Transcontinental Railroad*. New York: Walker, 1967.

Holliday, J. S. *The World Rushed In*. New York: Simon & Schuster, 1981.

Holmes, Kenneth L. *Best of Covered Wagon Women*. Norman: University of Oklahoma Press, 2008.

Homsher, Lola. *South Pass 1868*. Lincoln: University of Nebraska Press, 1960.

Horgan, Paul. *Josiah Gregg and His Vision of the Early West*. New York: Farrar, Straus and Giroux, 1941.

Howard, Robert W. *The Great Iron Trail*. New York: Putnam's, 1962.

Humason, W. L. *From the Atlantic Surf to the Golden Gate*. Hartford, CT: W. C. Hutchings, 1869.

Jackson, Helen Hunt. *Bits of Travel at Home*. Boston: Roberts Brothers, 1878.

Jackson, William Henry. *Time Exposure*. 1940. Reprint, Albuquerque: University of New Mexico Press, 1986.

Jensen, Oliver. *Railroads in America*. New York: American Heritage Publishing, 1975.

Jessen, Kenneth. *Railroads of Northern Colorado*. Boulder, CO: Pruett, 1982.

Johnson, Charles A. *Stagecoaches along Cherry Creek*. Denver: Golden Bell Press, 1980.

Jones, Mary Ellen. *Daily Life on the Nineteenth Century American Frontier*. Westport, CT: Greenwood Press, 1998.

Kennedy, William Sloane. *Wonders and Curiosities of the Railway*. Chicago: S. C. Griggs and Company, 1884.

Kipling, Rudyard. *From Sea to Sea*. New York: Doubleday, 1899.

Klein, Maury. *Union Pacific: The Birth of a Railroad 1862–1893*. New York: Doubleday, 1987.

———. *Union Pacific: The Rebirth 1894–1969*. New York: Doubleday, 1989.

Knight, Oliver. *Life and Manners in the Frontier Army*. Norman: University of Oklahoma Press, 1978.

Kraus, George. *High Road to Promontory*. New York: Castle Books, 1969.

Kyner, James H. *End of Track*. Caldwell, ID: Caxton Printers, 1937.

Langford, Nathaniel Pitt. *Vigilante Days and Ways*. 1890. Reprint, Missoula: Montana State Press, 1957.

Larson, T. A. *History of Wyoming*. Lincoln: University of Nebraska Press, 1965.

Leonard, Levi O., and Jack T. Johnson. *A Railroad to the Sea*. Iowa City, IA: Midland House, 1939.

Lester, John E. *The Atlantic to the Pacific, What to See and How to See It*. Boston: Shepard & Gill, 1873.

Leyendecker, Liston Edgington. *Palace Car Prince*. Niwot: University Press of Colorado, 1992.

Lockley, Fred. *Conversations with Pioneer Women*. Eugene, OR: Rainy Day Press, 1981.

Loveland, Jim A. *Dinner Is Served*. San Marino, CA: Golden West Books, 1996.

Mackell, Jan. *Red Light Women of the Rocky Mountains*. Albuquerque: University of New Mexico Press, 2009.

Madsen, Brigham D. *Corinne: The Gentile Capital of Utah*. Salt Lake City: Utah State Historical Society, 1980.

Marcy, Randolph Barnes. *The Prairie Traveler: A Handbook for Overland Travelers*. 1859. Reprint, Mineola, NY: Dover, 2006.

Mattes, Merrill J. *The Great Platte River Road*. Lincoln: Nebraska State Historical Society, 1969.

McCague, James. *Moguls and Iron Men*. New York: Harper & Row, 1964.

McClure, A. K. *Three Thousand Miles through the Rocky Mountains*. Philadelphia: J. P. Lippincott, 1869.

Michno, Gregory, and Susan Michno. *A Fate Worse Than Death*. Caldwell, ID: Caxton Press, 2007.

Miller, Nyle H., Edgar Langsdorf, and Robert W. Richard. *Kansas: A Pictorial History*. Topeka: Kansas Centennial Committee and the State Historical Society, 1961.

Monahan, Doris. *Destination: Denver City*. Athens: Ohio University Press, 1985.

———. *Julesburg and Fort Sedgwick: Wicked City—Scandalous Fort*. Sterling, CO: Doris Monahan, 2009.

Nadeau, Remi. *Fort Laramie and the Sioux Indians*. Englewood Cliffs, NJ: Prentice Hall, 1967.

Nichols, Jeffrey D. *Prostitution, Polygamy, and Power: Salt Lake City, 1847–1918*. Urbana: University of Illinois Press, 2002.

Olson, James C. *History of Nebraska*. Lincoln: University of Nebraska Press, 1966.

Ormes, Robert M. *Railroads and the Rockies*. Denver: Sage Books, 1963.

Otero, Miguel Antonio. *My Life on the Frontier 1864–1882*. New York: The Press of the Pioneers, 1935.

Paden, Irene D. *The Wake of the Prairie Schooner*. New York: MacMillan, 1945.

Parkman, Francis. *The Oregon Trail: Sketches of Prairie and Rocky Mountain Life*. Boston: Little, Brown, 1892.

Peavy, Linda, and Ursula Smith. *Pioneer Women: The Lives of Women on the Frontier*. Norman: University of Oklahoma Press, 1996.

———. *The Gold Rush Widows of Little Falls*. Saint Paul: Minnesota Historical Society Press, 1990.

Pence, Mary Lou, and Lola M. Homsher. *The Ghost Towns of Wyoming*. New York: Hastings House, 1956.

Perkin, Robert L. *The First Hundred Years*. Garden City, NY: Doubleday, 1959.

Pine, George W. *Beyond the West*. Utica, NY: T. J. Griffiths, Baker & Jones Co., 1870.

Pulcipher, Robert S. *George W. Kassler, Pioneer*. The Denver Westerners Brand Book, vol. 30. Boulder, CO: Johnson Publishing, 1977.

Quiett, Glenn Chesney. *They Built the West: An Epic of Rails and Cities*. New York: Appleton-Century, 1871.

Rae, W. F. *Westward by Rail*. London: Longmans, Green, 1870.

Ravage, John W. *Black Pioneers*. Salt Lake City: University of Utah Press, 1997.

Reed, Robert C. *Train Wrecks: A Pictorial History of Accidents on the Main Line*. New York: Bonanza Books, 1968.

Reinhardt, Richard. *Out West on the Overland Train*. Palo Alto, CA: American West Publishing, 1967.

Richardson, Albert D. *Beyond the Mississippi: From the Great Rim to the Great Ocean*. Hartford, CT: American Publishing Co., 1867.

Richmond, Robert W., and Robert W. Mardock, eds. *A Nation Moving West*. Lincoln: University of Nebraska Press, 1966.

Rickey, Don, Jr. *Forty Miles a Day on Beans and Hay*. Norman: University of Oklahoma Press, 1963.

Riegel, Robert E. *America Moves West*. New York: Holt, Rinehart and Winston, 1971.

Riley, Glenda. *Women and Indians on the Frontier, 1825–1915*. Albuquerque: University of New Mexico Press, 1984.

Roberts, David. *Devil's Gate: Brigham Young and the Great Mormon Handcart Tragedy*. New York: Simon & Schuster, 2008.

Robertson, William, and W. F. Robertson. *Our American Tour*. Edinburgh: W. Burness, 1871.

Robinson, Philip. *Sinners and Saints*. Boston: Roberts Brothers, 1883.

Root, Frank A., and William E. Connelly. *The Overland Stage to California*. 1901. Reprint, Glorieta, NM: Rio Grande Press, 1970.

Royce, Sarah. *Across the Plains: Sarah Royce's Western Narrative*. Edited by Jennifer Dawes Adkison. Tucson: University of Arizona Press, 2009.

Sabin, Edwin L. *Building the Pacific Railway*. Philadelphia: J. P. Lippincott, 1919.

Sala, George Augustus. *America Revisited*, vol. 2. London: Vizetelly & Co., 1882.

Secrest, Clark. *Hell's Belles: Denver's Brides of the Multitudes*. Aurora, CO: Hindsight Publications, 1996.

Sells, John A. *Stagecoaches: Across the American West 1850 to 1920*. Blaine, WA: Hancock House, 2008.

Seymour, Silas. *Incidents of a Trip through the Great Platte Valley*. New York: D. Van Nostrand, 1867.

Shaw, Luella. *True History of Some of the Pioneers of Colorado*. Hotchkiss, CO: W. S. Coburn, J. Patterson and A. K. Shaw, 1909.

Sherman, William T. *Personal Memoirs of Gen. W. T. Sherman*. New York: Webster, 1890.

———. *Personal Memoirs of Gen. W. T. Sherman*, Volume 2. New York: Webster, 1891.

Simonin, Louis L. *The Rocky Mountain West in 1867*. Lincoln: University of Nebraska Press, 1966.

Smiley, Jerome. *The History of Denver*. Denver: Sun-Times Publishing, 1901.

Smith, Page. *As a City Upon a Hill*. New York: Knopf, 1966.

Stanley, Henry Milton. *My Early Travels and Adventures in America and Asia*. 1895. Reprint, Lincoln: University of Nebraska Press, 1982.

Stevenson, Robert Louis. *From Scotland to Silverado*. Edited by James D. Hart. Cambridge, MA: Harvard University Press, 1966.

———. *From the Clyde to California: Robert Louis Stevenson's Emigrant Journey*. Edited by Andrew Noble. Aberdeen, Scotland: The University Press, 1985.

Stewart, John J. *The Iron Trail to the Golden Spike*. New York: Meadow Lark Press, 1994.

Taylor, Bayard. *Colorado: A Summer Trip*. 1867. Reprint, Niwot: University Press of Colorado, 1989.

Taylor, Joseph Henry. *Sketches of Frontier and Indian Life on the Upper Missouri and Great Plains*. Pottstown, PA: J. H. Taylor, 1889.

Thyne, Denise. *Gone but Not Forgotten*. Julesburg, CO: GAB Printing, 1996.

Tice, John H. *John H. Tice. Over the Plains, on the Mountains; or, Kansas, Colorado, and the Rocky Mountains*. Saint Louis: Industrial Age Printing Co., 1878.

Toponce, Kate. *Reminiscences of Alexander Toponce, Pioneer*. Ogden, Utah: Privately printed, 1923.

Townshend, R. B. *A Tenderfoot in Colorado*. 1923. Reprint, Boulder: University Press of Colorado, 2008.

Train, George Francis. *My Life in Many States and in Foreign Lands*. New York: Appleton, 1902.

Triggs, J. H. *History and Directory of Laramie City, Wyoming Territory*. Laramie City: Daily Sentinel Print, 1875.

Trottman, Nelson. *History of the Union Pacific*. New York: Ronald Press, 1923.

Twain, Mark. *Roughing It*. 1872. Reprint, Berkeley: University of California Press, 1993.

Unruh, John D., Jr. *The Plains Across*. Urbana: University of Illinois Press, 1979.

Utley, Robert, ed. *Life in Custer's Cavalry*. New Haven, CT: Yale University Press, 1977.

———. *Special Report on Promontory Summit, Utah*. Santa Fe, NM: Department of the Interior, National Park Service, Region Three, 1960.

Utley, Robert, and Francis Ketterson. *Golden Spike*. Washington, DC: National Park Service, 1969.

Vickers, William B. *History of the City of Denver*. Chicago: O. L. Baskin, 1880.

Victor, Frances Fuller. *Eleven Years in the Rocky Mountains*. Hartford, CT: Columbia Books, 1877.

Walton, George. *Sentinel of the Plains*. Englewood Cliffs, NJ: Prentice Hall, 1973.

Ward, Geoffrey C. *The West: An Illustrated History*. Boston: Little, Brown, 1996.

Washburn, Josie. *The Underworld Sewer*. 1909. Reprint, Lincoln: University of Nebraska Press, 1996.

Weidel, Nancy. *Cheyenne 1867–1917*. Mount Pleasant, SC: Arcadia Publishing, 2009.

Werner, Emmy E. *Pioneer Children on the Journey West*. Boulder, CO: Westview Press, 1995.

Wheeler, Keith. *The Railroaders*. New York: Time-Life Books, 1973.

White, Henry Kirke. *History of the Union Pacific Railway*. Chicago: University of Chicago Press, 1895.

White, John H., Jr. *The American Railroad Passenger Car*, part 1. Baltimore, MD: Johns Hopkins University Press, 1978.

White, Richard. *Railroaded: The Transcontinentals and the Making of Modern America*. New York: W. W. Norton, 2011.

Williams, Dallas. *Fort Sedgwick: Hell Hole on the Platte*. Julesburg, CO: Fort Sedgwick Historical Society, 1993.

Williams, Henry J. *The Pacific Tourist*. New York: H. J. Williams, 1877.

Williams, John Hoyt. *A Great and Shining Road*. New York: Times Books, 1988.

Winther, Oscar Osburn. *The Transportation Frontier: Trans-Mississippi West 1865–1890*. New York: Holt, 1964.

Women's Diaries of the Westward Journey. Collected by Schlissel, Lillian. New York: Schocken Books, 1982.

Zarnow, William Frank. *Kansas: A History of the Jayhawk State*. Norman: University of Oklahoma, 1957.

Articles, Brochures, Manuscripts, and Letters

Anderson, Bernice Gibbs. "The Driving of the Golden Spike." *Utah Historical Quarterly* 24, no. 2 (April 1956).

Andrews, Ralph L. "Golden Spike Mementos." *The Union Pacific Magazine*, May 1926.

Andrist, Ralph K. "Gold." *American Heritage*, December 1962.

Bagley, Will. "Pioneers Not Exempt from Nature's Call." *The Salt Lake Tribune*, February 25, 2001.

Barker, Joseph. "Omaha in 1868–1869: Selections from the Letters of Joseph Barker." Edited by Charles W. Martin. *Nebraska History* 59, no. 4 (Winter 1978).

Beebe, Lucius. "Pandemonium at Promontory." *American Heritage*, February 1958.

Beermann, R. J. "Historic Weapon Found after 50 Years." *The Union Pacific Magazine*, August 1927.

Bertenshaw, James. James Bertenshaw Family Letters, Collection 07269, Box 1, FF 6. American Heritage Center, University of Wyoming, Laramie.

Bowles, Samuel. "The Pacific Railroad—Open." *Atlantic Monthly*, April 1869.

Bowman, J. N. "Driving the Last Spike at Promontory 1869." *Utah Historical Quarterly* 37, no. 1 (Winter 1969).

Brown, Amanda Hardin. "A Pioneer in Colorado and Wyoming." *The Colorado Magazine* 35, no. 3 (July 1958).

Brown, H. Clark. "Tales from Old-Timers, No. 31." *The Union Pacific Magazine*, May 1926.

Brown, R. J. "The Frontier Index: The Case of the Vagabond Newspaper." http://www.historybuff.com/library/reffrontier.html.

Burns, Ric. "Never Take No Cutoffs: On the Oregon Trail." *American Heritage*, May/June 1993.

Byers, O. P. "When Railroading Outdid the Wild West Stories." *The Union Pacific Magazine*, October 1926.

Carney, W. J. "How the Julesburg Mail Was Lost." *The Railroad Man's Magazine*, December 1910.

Case, Frank M. "Experiences on the Platte River Route in the Sixties." *The Colorado Magazine* 5, no. 4 (August 1928).

Chittenden, Sam. Letters 1868, Chittenden Collection. American History Center,

University of Wyoming, Laramie.

Chudacoff, Howard P. "Where Rolls the Dark Missouri Down." *Nebraska History,* Vol. 52, no. 1 (1971), Nebraska State Historical Society.

Collins, Catharine Wever. "An Army Wife Comes West." *The Colorado Magazine* 31, no. 4 (October 1954).

Combs, Barry B. "The Union Pacific Railroad and the Early Settlement of Nebraska." *Nebraska History* 51, no. 1 (Spring 1969).

Coolidge, Susan. "A Few Hints on the California Journey." *Scribner's Monthly,* Vol. 6 (May 1873).

Cope, C. C. "Tales from Old-Timers, No. 11." *The Union Pacific Magazine,* February 1924.

Coutant, Charles Griffin. "Settlement of Larimer County." Unpublished manuscript, Collection 10610. American Heritage Center, University of Wyoming, Laramie.

Curtis, Olga. "The Killing of Jules: A Deathless Legend." *Empire Magazine (The Denver Post),* August 12, 1979.

Danker, Donald F. "The Influence of Transportation upon Nebraska Territory." *Nebraska History* 42, no. 2 (1966).

"David Lemon — Old Timer." *The Union Pacific Magazine,* May 1924.

Davis, Theodore. "A Stage Ride to Colorado." *Harper's New Monthly Magazine* 35, no. 206 (July 1867).

Dillon, Sidney. "Driving the Last Spike of the Union Pacific." *Scribner's,* August 1892.

Dodge, Major General Grenville M. "How We Built the Union Pacific Railway." *The Trail* 10, no. 12 (May 1918).

Dolbee, Cora. "The Second Book on Kansas." *Kansas Historical Quarterly* 4, no. 2 (May 1925).

Eckberg, Scott B. "The Frontier Index: Chronicle of a World on Wheels." http://usparks .about.com/od/historicalparks/a/Golden-Spike-NHS.htm.

Facts and Fantasy of Uinta County's Past. Evanston, WY: Uinta County Museum, 1991.

Farley, Alan W. "Samuel Hallett and the Union Pacific Railway Company in Kansas." *Kansas Historical Quarterly* 25, no. 1 (Spring 1959).

Ferguson, Arthur N. "Journal of Arthur N. Ferguson." Unpublished manuscript, Union Pacific Railroad Museum, Council Bluffs, Iowa.

"The Financing of Early Colorado Railroads." *The Colorado Magazine* 18, no. 6 (November 1941).

"First Railroad Excursion to Nebraska." *Nebraska History and Record of Pioneer Days* 1, no. 1 (1918).

Gibson, Etta. "Sketch of the Four Julesburgs." Unpublished manuscript, Julesburg (Colorado) Historical Society Museum.

Gill, Frank B. "Built to Preserve the Union." *The Union Pacific Magazine,* August 1922.

"Golden Spike and Last Tie." *The Union Pacific Magazine,* May 1925.

The Great Union Pacific Railroad Excursion to the Hundredth Meridian. Chicago: Republican Company, 1867.

Guy, H. W. "Tales from Old-Timers, No. 20." *The Union Pacific Magazine,* February 1925.

Haswell, Theodore. "Driving the Golden Spike, May 10, 1869." *The Union Pacific Magazine,* May 1925.

Henderson, Harold J. "The Building of the First Kansas Railroad South of the Kaw River." *Kansas Historical Quarterly* 15, no. 3 (August 1947).

Hurlbut, Walt H. "A Mother's Prayer." *The Trail* 6, no. 1 (June 1913).

Knox, Thomas W. "Across the Continent, Overland Scenes." *Frank Leslie's Weekly,* February 19, 1870.

Knudsen, Dean. "Sand Creek Avenged." *Wild West,* October 1991.

A Lady Pioneer. "A Coach Trip in 1865." *The Trail* 1, no. 2 (March 1909).

———. "Crossing the Great American Desert in the '60s." *The Trail* 1, no. 5 (October 1908).

Lane, C. J. "Driving the Last Spike." *The Union Pacific Magazine,* May 1922.

Lass, William E. "From the Missouri to the Great Salt Lake." *Nebraska History* 66 (1985).

Leonard, L. O. "At Promontory 60 Years Ago This Month." *The Union Pacific Magazine*, May 1929.

Leslie, Miriam. "Out West on the Overland Train." *Frank Leslie's Illustrated*, February 9, 1878.

Lester, Gurdon. "Enrout for Pikes Peak: The 1860 Travel Diary of Gurdon P. Lester." Edited by Virginia Foote Anderson and Richard E. Jensen. *Nebraska History* 81, no. 1 (Spring 2000).

Linton, Charles T. "My Early Western Experience." *Sons of Colorado* 1, no. 12 (May 1907).

Lockwood, E. C. "With the Casement Brothers While Building the Union Pacific." *The Union Pacific Magazine*, February 1931.

Loomis, N. H. "Union Pacific as a Factor in United States History." *The Union Pacific Magazine*, February 1924.

Lumbard, Giles Barton. "By Train from Omaha to Sacramento One Hundred Years Ago." *The American West*, November 1975.

Madsen, Brigham D., and Betty M. Madsen. "Corinne, the Fair: Gateway to Montana Mines." *Utah Historical Quarterly* 37, no. 1 (Winter 1969).

Malloy, J. W. "Veteran Recalls Driving of Golden Spike." *The Union Pacific Magazine*, May 1926.

"Man Who Gave Railroads to Colorado." *The Railroad Man's Magazine*, October 1906.

Martin, W. Charles, ed. "Joseph Barker and the 1868 Union Pacific Railroad Excursion from Omaha." *Nebraska History* 58, no. 2 (Summer 1977).

Mattes, Merrill J. "The South Platte Trail: Colorado Cutoff of the Oregon-Colorado Trail." *Overland Journal* 10, no. 3 (Fall 1992).

McCain, G. S. "A Trip from Atchison, Kansas, to Laurette, Colorado." *The Colorado Magazine* 27, no. 2 (April 1950).

McLear, Patrick E. "The Saint Louis Cholera Epidemic of 1849." *Missouri Historical Review* 63, no. 2.

Medberg, J. K. "Our Pacific Railroads." *Atlantic Monthly*, September 1867.

Miller, Nyle H., and Robert W. Richmond. "Sheridan, a Fabled End-of-Track Town on the Union Pacific Railroad, 1868–69." *Kansas Historical Quarterly* 34, no. 4 (Winter 1968).

Mock, S. D. "Colorado and the Surveys for the Pacific Railroad." *The Colorado Magazine* 17, no. 2 (March 1940).

Morris, Isaac. "Condition of the Union Pacific Railroad." Washington, DC: US Congress, House of Representatives Executive Document 180, 1876.

"Mrs. Matilda Peterson of Louisville Recounts Trip of Fifty Years Ago over Union Pacific" Tales from Old-Timers, No. 25. *The Union Pacific Magazine*, November 1925.

"Nathaniel P. Hill Inspects Colorado." *The Colorado Magazine* 34, no. 1 (January 1957).

Nelson, Christen. "Tales from Old-Timers, No. 12." *The Union Pacific Magazine*, March 1924.

Noel, Thomas J. "All Hail the Denver Pacific: Denver's First Railroad." *The Colorado Magazine* 50, no. 4 (Fall 1973).

Nordhoff, Charles. "California." *Harper's New Monthly Magazine*, May 1872.

O'Brien, Emily Boynton. "Army Life at Fort Sedgwick, Colorado." *The Colorado Magazine*, Vol. 6, No. 5 (September 1929).

O'Connor, Mrs. Harry. "Story of the Union Pacific Railroad and Bear Town." Unpublished manuscript, Wyoming State Archives, Cheyenne.

"Oldest Pensioner at Golden Spike Driving." *The Union Pacific Magazine*, May 1922.

"On the Plains." *Harper's Weekly*, April 21, 1866.

Our Railroad Heritage: The Union Pacific in Wyoming. Evanston, WY: Uinta County Museum Board, 1992.

Park, W. L. "Tales from Old-Timers, No. 3." *The Union Pacific Magazine*, May 1923.

Parker, Mrs. C. F. "A History of Julesburg and Surrounding Country." Unpublished manuscript, Julesburg (Colorado) Historical Society Museum.

———. "Old Julesburg and Fort Sedgwick." *The Colorado Magazine* 7, no. 4 (July 1939).

Parry, Henry C. "Letters from the Frontier—1867." *Annals of Wyoming* 30, no. 2 (October 1958).

Paul, R. Eli. "Battle of Ash Hollow." *Nebraska History* 62, no. 3 (1981).

Peterson, Matilde. "Tales from Old-Timers, No. 75. *The Union Pacific Magazine*, November 1925.

Priest, Joel, Jr. "A Museum of the Pony Express." *The Union Pacific Magazine*, June 1931.

Propst, Nell Brown. "Willa Clanton: A Remarkable Link with Colorado's Past." *The Colorado Magazine* 56, no. 1 (Winter/Spring 1979).

Putnam, John H. "A Trip to the End of the Union Pacific in 1868." *Kansas Historical Quarterly* 13, no. 3 (August 1944).

Read, Georgia Willis. "Women and Children on the Oregon-California Trail in the Gold Rush Years." *Missouri Historical Review* 39, no. 1 (October 1944).

"Report of Lieut. James H. Simpson." Washington, DC: Department of the Interior, Engineer Office, 1865.

Roenigk, A. "Railroad Grading among Indians." *Kansas Historical Collections* 8 (1904).

Ross, A. R. "A Hard Winter." *The Colorado Magazine* 36, no. 2 (April 1949).

Roth, Randolph, Michael D. Maltz, and Douglas L. Eckberg. "Homicide Rates in the Old West." *Western Historical Quarterly* 42, no. 2 (Summer 2011).

"Sade Smith's Escape." *Sons of Colorado* 1, no. 2 (June 1906).

Sageser, A. Bower. "Building the Main Line." *Kansas Historical Quarterly* 21, no. 1 (Spring 1955).

Schultz, John Richie. "Features of Colorado Life as Seen by Bayard Taylor in 1866." *The Colorado Magazine* 12, no. 5 (September 1935).

Sharman, C. H. "Tales from Old-Timers, No. 24." *The Union Pacific Magazine*, October 1925.

Shortbridge, James R. "The 'Missing' Railroad Towns along the Union Pacific and the Santa Fe Lines in Kansas." *Kansas History* 26, no. 23 (Autumn 2003).

Smedley, William. "Across the Plains in Sixty-Two." *The Trail* 19, no. 10 (March 1927).

Smoot, W. C. A. "Tales from Old-Timers, No. 9." *The Union Pacific Magazine*, December 1923.

Snell, Joseph W., and Robert W. Richmond. "When the Union and Kansas Pacific Built through Kansas, Part 1." *Kansas Historical Quarterly* 32, no. 2 (Summer 1966).

———. "When the Union and Kansas Pacific Built through Kansas, Conclusion." *Kansas Historical Quarterly* 32, no. 2 (Summer 1966).

Socolofsky, Homer E. "Kansas in 1876." *Kansas Historical Quarterly* 43, no. 1 (Spring 1977).

Sopris, S. T. "Denver's First Railroad." *The Trail* 1, no. 2 (July 1908).

Spring, Agnes Wright. "Rush to the Rockies, 1959." *The Colorado Magazine* 36, no. 2 (April 1959).

Stanton, Edwin M. "Protection across the Continent." House of Representatives, 39th Cong., 2d sess., 1866.

Steele, Henry P. "Coming West in '67." *Sons of Colorado* 2, no. 8 (January 1908).

Stewart, George R. "The Prairie Schooner Got Them There." *American Heritage*, February 1962.

Stokes, Colonel George W. "Echoes of the Old West." *The Union Pacific Magazine*, October 1923.

———. "Thomas Ewing Jr. and the Origins of the Kansas Pacific Railway Company." *Kansas Historical Quarterly* 42, no. 2 (Summer 1976).

"Tales from Old-Timers, No. 18." *The Union Pacific Magazine*, December 1924.

"Tales from Old-Timers, No. 25." *The Union Pacific Magazine*, November 1925.

Taylor, David G. "Boom Town Leavenworth." *Kansas Historical Quarterly* 38, no. 4 (Winter 1972).

Test, General Edward F. "History of Freight Claim Department." *The Union Pacific Magazine*, September 1924.

Thom, William B. "More of the 'Wild Western' Romance of the Kansas Pacific." *The Union Pacific Magazine*, March 1929.

Thompson, Major James B. "Crossing the Plains in '64." *Sons of Colorado* 2, no. 10 (March

1908).

"Touring Kansas and Colorado in 1871: The Journal of George C. Anderson, Part I." Transcribed by Barbara Hutchins and Lynn Nelson. *Kansas Historical Quarterly* 22, no. 3 (Autumn 1956).

Trautmann, Frederic. "Across Nebraska by Train in 1877: The Travels of Ernst von Hesse-Wartegg." *Nebraska History* 65, no. 3 (Summer 1984).

Vanderwalker, George E. "Indian Alarms." *Sons of Colorado* 1, no. 4 (September 1906).

———. "The Bullwhacker or Prairie Sailor." *The Trail,* Vol. 1, no. 9 (February 1909).

Vroom, Peter D. "George M. Pullman and the Colorado Tradition." *The Colorado Magazine* 37, no. 3 (May 1940).

Wann, Fred A. "Reminiscences." *The Union Pacific Magazine,* May 1922.

Watson, Edward. Edward Watson Diaries, 1867. American Heritage Center, University of Wyoming, Laramie.

Webster, Frank Lundy. "Tales from Old-Timers, No. 27." *The Union Pacific Magazine,* January 1926.

Wibberley, Leonard Patrick O'Connor. "The Coming of the Green." *American Heritage,* August 1958.

Williams, Albert. "More 'Wild West' Stories from Kansas Pacific History." *The Union Pacific Magazine,* March 1929.

Witter, Clara. "Pioneer Life." *The Colorado Magazine* 4, no. 4 (December 1927).

Wood, A. P. "Tales from Old-Timers, No. 19." *The Union Pacific Magazine,* January 1925.

Woodhouse, J. D. "Dodge, Fighting Railroad Builder." *The Railroad & Current Mechanics,* December 1913.

Wyoming Tales and Trails. "Building the Union Pacific." http://www.wyomingtales andtrails.com/sherman2.html.

Magazines and Newspapers

Akron (Colorado) Weekly Pioneer Press, American Heritage, Atlantic Monthly, Boulder (Colorado) Daily Camera, Cheyenne Leader, Chicago Tribune, The Colorado Magazine, Corinne (Utah) Reporter, Daily (Denver) Colorado Tribune, Daily Morning Chronicle, Denver Daily Tribune, The Denver Post, Fortnightly Review, Frank Leslie's Illustrated, Frontier Index, Harper's New Monthly Magazine, Harper's Weekly, Julesburg (Colorado) Grit-Advocate, Montana Post, The New York Times, New York Tribune, Omaha World-Herald, Philadelphia Inquirer, The Railroad Man's Magazine, Railway Pioneer, Rocky Mountain News, Salt Lake Telegraph, Scribner's, Sons of Colorado, Sterling (Colorado) Advocate, The Trail, The Union Pacific Magazine, Utah Historical Quarterly.

Libraries and Museums

American Heritage Center, University of Wyoming, Laramie, WY; Colorado Railroad Museum, Golden, CO; Corinne History Museum, Corinne, UT; Denver Public Library, Western History and Genealogy Department; Fort Sedgwick Historical Society, Julesburg, CO; Kansas State Historical Society, Topeka, KS; Lincoln County Historical Museum, North Platte, NE; Nebraska State Historical Society, Lincoln, NE; Uinta County History Museum, Evanston, WY; Union Pacific Railroad Museum, Council Bluffs, IA; Western Postal Museum, Tucson, AZ; Wyoming State Archives and Historical Department, Cheyenne, WY.

INDEX

ABOUT THE AUTHOR

Dick Kreck retired from *The Denver Post* after thirty-eight years as an editor and columnist. He previously worked at the *San Francisco Examiner* and the *Los Angeles Times*. He is the author of five other books, including *Murder at the Brown Palace: A True Story of Seduction and Betrayal* and *Smaldone: The Untold Story of an American Crime Family*. He lives in Denver, Colorado.

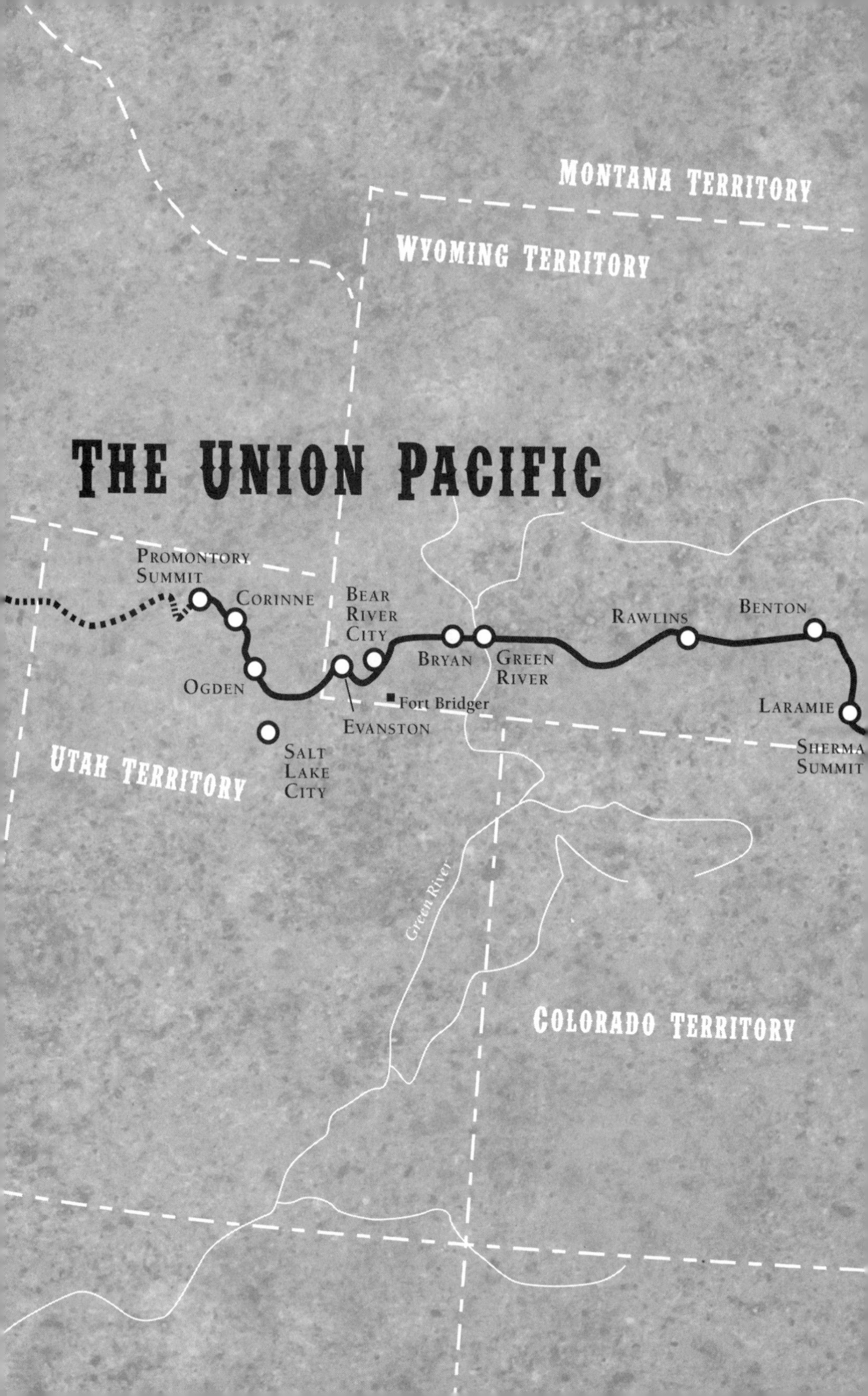

THE UNION PACIFIC

MONTANA TERRITORY

WYOMING TERRITORY

PROMONTORY
SUMMIT

CORINNE

BEAR
RIVER
CITY

BRYAN

GREEN
RIVER

RAWLINS

BENTON

OGDEN

EVANSTON

■ Fort Bridger

LARAMIE

SHERMAN
SUMMIT

SALT
LAKE
CITY

UTAH TERRITORY

Green River

COLORADO TERRITORY